The Invisible Industry

Larry Kulchawik

Bob McGlincy

ISBN: 9798330608331 (Digital)

ISBN: 9798330630752 (Paperback)

ISBN: 9798330630769 (Hardcover)

Library of Congress Control Number: 2024924853

Published by Books Writer USA

First Published, 2024

Books Writer USA

James.andrew@bookswriterusa.com

323-366-4568

Authors: Larry Kulchawik and Bob McGlincy

Book Cover Design- Sarah Miorelli
Student at FIT-NYC/Masters Degree in Exhibit Design

Printed in the United States of America

First Printing Edition 2024

Website: www.tradeshowstheinvisibleindustry.com

FORWARD

Don Svehla

"Engaging. Exciting. And informative."

These words popped into my mind as I read "The Invisible Industry," a new book by Larry Kulchawik and Bob McGlincy that discusses how trade shows and business events have evolved into a trillion-dollar industry—an industry that, despite its size, is unknown to most of the world. An "invisible" trillion-dollar industry—imagine that!

This book shares the amazing journey from street vendors in Persia to the Expositions and World's Fairs in Europe to trade show marketing and brand activations in the United States. The authors keep the history riveting by discussing the people and products that have changed the way we live, as well as telling the stories of the unsung heroes and behind-the-scenes players that have made it all happen.

My two old friends, Bob McGlincy and Larry Kulchawik, each have decades of experience in the industry. They contacted friends and acquaintances who were happy to share their experiences, stories and company histories from the days after World War II through the evolving changes of the past fifty years. The book unfolds the many changes in exhibiting methods over the decades, the birth of convention centers, the start of exhibit suppliers, the economic impact and why trade show/event marketing is often called an Invisible Industry.

I share their passion when it comes to the history of our industry and the challenges that the people in the trade show workforce were faced with to put on a show. It was with this in mind that I launched my magazine, Exhibit City News, 30 years ago.

I hope you enjoy reading this book and learning about this important and impactful industry. Maybe it won't stay invisible in the future.

"History never looks like history when you are living though it" …. John Gardner

Table of Contents

Forward   iii

Introduction   - 1 -

Part One: The First One Hundred Years

   Chapter One: Before The Beginning   - 9 -

   Chapter Two: The First Modern Trade Show 1851   - 18 -

   Chapter Three: New Horizons   - 63 -

   Chapter Four: Electrifying The World   - 89 -

   Chapter Five: The Start of Trade Shows in the United States   - 130 -

Part Two: World Fairs to US Trade Shows

   Chapter Six: The Regional Evolution of Exhibit Builders and Convention Centers in America   - 150 -

   Chapter Seven: Evolution of Exhibit Design & Methods at Trade Show   - 226 -

   Chapter Eight: The Birth of Exhibit Installation Companies in The USA   - 245 -

Part Three: Trade Shows- Yesterday, Today, and Tomorrow

   Chapter Nine: Change Makers- The People who Moved the Needle   - 271 -

   Chapter Ten: *Economic Impact *Sectors *Staying Power *Show Types *American Model of Organization   - 343 -

   Chapter Eleven: Into the Future- Where is the Industry Heading?   - 360 -

   Final Thoughts   - 390 -

Word from the Authors & Acknowledgements   - 395 -

INTRODUCTION

Trade Shows Mean Business.

The convention and business events industry is a powerful economic engine. According to a 2023 Events Industry Council report, titled "Global Economic Significance of Business Events," the industry:

- Drives millions of jobs.
- Delivers hundreds of billions of dollars in business sales.
- Propels the economy with a **trillion-dollar** contribution to the GDP.

The Center for Exhibition Industry Research released a 2024 study stating that, in 2023, business-to-business trade shows in the United States

- Supported 2.5 million jobs, and
- Contributed $161 billion in business sales.

While the two organizations review different data, the bottom line is the same: the economic significance of the convention and business events industry is huge! However, most people are unaware of this industry's size and its impact on everyday life. That's why it's often referred to as "the invisible industry."

What is a Trade Show?

Many reading this book may be from the industry and already know the answer. For others, here is one definition:

Trade shows are unique three-dimensional experiences where people mingle, share ideas, and display products that relate to a specific industry. These events combine elements of advertising, branding, architecture, education, networking, and sales.

Trade shows engage audiences, stimulate the senses, and energize the economy. They bring targeted buyers and sellers together in one place, at one time, and magically transform an empty convention center into a magnificent marketing extravaganza – a business carnival pulsating with energy and excitement. Trade shows showcase new technologies, establish brands, and change the world around us.

How do Trade Shows Work?

In its most basic form, a trade show is an industry-specific marketplace. The industry calls this gathering of people a "convention" and terms buyers "attendees" and sellers "exhibitors." Attendees walk the trade show floor; they can view exhibits; network; attend educational sessions; discuss new ideas; examine competing merchandise; and decide what and when to purchase. Exhibitors display their products and services in a branded environment, showcasing new ideas and technology—all in the hopes of creating new and repeat business. Sales may be immediate and closed on the show floor, or the decision to buy may be deferred and finalized after the show.

Trade shows provide a catalytic effect because of stimuli experienced at a business event. Catalysts come in the form of new, often unexpected, bits of information and ideas that cause a market to reevaluate a company's business prospects. The best new ideas in any industry are often first introduced at a trade show.

Trade shows are business malls for connecting people and selling products. They are mini universities for advanced educational opportunities and the cross-pollination of ideas.

Why is it Invisible?

When exhibit industry professionals attend a family gathering, a party, or even a dinner, the question often arises, *"So what do you do for a living?"* When the reply is, *"Trade Shows,"* the person asking usually responds with a puzzled look. *"You know, like the auto show or the boat show"*. *"Oh yeah,"* they say, *"now I understand!"* Only they don't; not really. Consumer shows are the visible tip of the iceberg, but there is much, much more that is not seen by most people.

Private trade shows are closed events. With these business-to-business shows, there is no public advertising, and most people have no idea that the event is taking place. Even B2B invited attendees might know only a few specific shows and not the totality of the industry. They might see some trees, but very few see the forest and many outside the industry are not even aware that the forest exists.

Trade Shows Attract People

There are approximately 10,000 B2B (Business to Business) conventions in the United States annually, with attendance ranging from two thousand to two hundred thousand—or more—at a single event.

Why is this Industry Important?

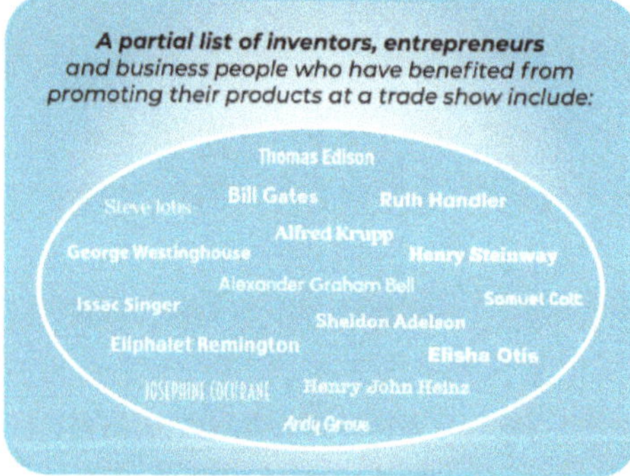

Forget, for the moment, the direct financial benefits (the jobs created, the sales made, the taxes generated). Trade shows impact the world in unseen ways with new inventions and individual business growth. Trade shows target an array of diverse industries and impact every segment of the economy. Business sectors include: technology; healthcare; food; manufacturing; government; defense; construction; sporting goods; financial services; and others. Wherever one looks, whatever industry or niche one can think of, there is a trade show for it—and the shows may be local, regional, national, or international in scope.

Trade shows are a great way to display an invention or product—first to individuals and then to the world.

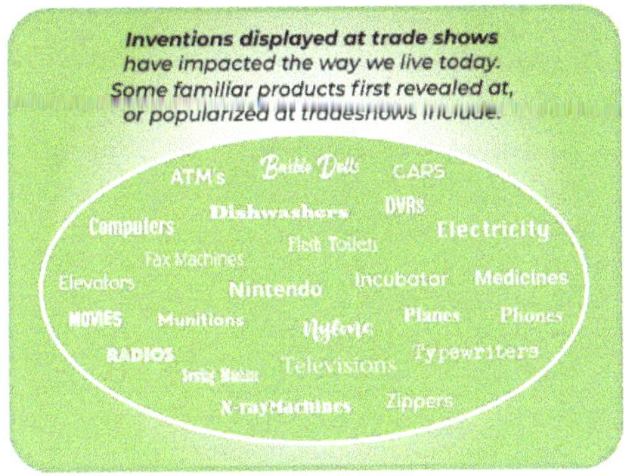

A great idea, or a new technology, is meaningless if no one knows about it. Businesses who exhibit at trade shows, introduce new ideas, and gain market share because of it. They run the alphabet from Apple, Bell, and Caterpillar all the way to Xerox, Yahoo, and Zeiss.

Trade shows work; they work incredibly well. The US and world economies have greatly benefited from the ideas and products that were initially displayed at expositions and conventions.

How did this happen?

This book is about a trillion-dollar "Invisible Industry". Reading it will transport you from the early World Fairs and Expositions, where the seeds of thought were planted, to the formation and

shape of the American model for organizing a trade show event. The chapters highlight the development of trade shows and how they have evolved in America to become a powerful marketing tool for companies to introduce their latest ideas and products. The power of face-to-face marketing within a predetermined space for a predetermined industry unleashes "emotion" between buyers and sellers. This emotion encourages the decision to buy and to accept a new idea. The trade show event allows for new ideas and quality products to be displayed and sold across all continents.

An Example of the Power of Trade Shows.

Apple Inc. became the world's first corporation with a market capitalization of one trillion dollars. That happened on August 2, 2018. But it didn't start that way.

Steve Jobs and Steve Wozniak drew up a partnership agreement on April 1, 1976. At the time, they were working out of the Jobs family garage in Los Altos, CA. On January 1, 1977, Apple Computer, Inc. was incorporated and valued at $5,309. On December 12, 1980, they took the company public. Nineteen days later, on December 31, the company was worth $1,790,000,000. (That is not a typo: that is $1.79 billion). How did this happen? It's simple: They went to trade shows and displayed their product.

Apple showcased their first "computer" on August 28, 1976, at the Personal Computer Festival in Atlantic City. They displayed a microprocessor system; it lacked an enclosure, keyboard and power source. Apple did not close a sale or write a single order at the show. Jobs walked the show floor and realized they would have to build a complete, ready-to-run machine.

The Apple II, with color graphics, debuted at the First West Coast Computer Faire in San Francisco on April 17, 1977. Understanding the importance of marketing and wanting "a big launch", Jobs secured a prime space at the front of the exhibit hall. The pipe and drape show had 175 booths and attracted 12,652 people over the two-day event.

Apple was the only company with a hard-wall exhibit. Despite having just three working computers, Apple wrote 300 sales orders and would sell 2,500 units in the next eight months. In 1977, Apple's revenue was $773,977. The company continued to exhibit at trade shows and promote their product; their revenue increased tenfold in 1978, improved to $47.9 million in '79, and was a staggering $117.9 million in 1980.

Apple helped launch the personal computer market, but they were not alone. Altair exhibited at the PC Festival in 1976. Commodore unveiled their PET at CES in 1977; Tandy displayed its TRS-80 that same year. IBM entered the PC market at Fall Comdex in 1981. The Commodore 64 debuted at CES in 1982. One thing these companies had in common was that *after displaying their products at tradeshows, each company's sales increased.*

Trade shows work. They display products and inventions. They establish brands and generate sales. They can even jump-start a business empire.

A Word On The Book:

This book is dedicated to sharing how trade shows and public business events in the USA got started and grew to become an invisible industry.
Authors Larry Kulchawik and Bob McGlincy have each spent 50 years in the industry serving exhibitors and working with exhibitors, suppliers, and industry associations. They each have interviewed industry associates who shared their experiences about the rich history of trade shows.

The book starts with the birth of trade in the Persian market places, and moves to the concepts of World Fairs, but will concentrate specifically on the evolution and development of the trade show industry in the United States.

As the authors, we fully realize how the modern trade shows of today have the same purpose and objectives of the ancient markets and the World Fairs- **advancing sales.**

The book will also focus on the US cities, the convention centers, exhibit suppliers, and the associations THAT fueled the fire to forge the growth and success to create this Invisible Industry. Enjoy!

CHAPTER ONE

Before the Beginning

From Persian Markets to Crystal Palaces

Wherever there are crowds, there is the possibility to sell products and make money. This face-to-face opportunity is one of the common threads linking fairs, expositions, and tradeshows.

Trade shows impact the world around us, but they are not a new phenomenon. At their most basic, they are a gathering of people, ideally both buyers and sellers, coming together in the same place at the same time. By this definition, such happenings have been occurring in marketplaces for thousands of years: from Persian bazaars located outside city walls as far back as 3000 BC... to street vendors in Athens and Rome before the time of Christ... to roaming caravans of merchants during the Middle Ages... they all have one thing in common: they were there looking to sell, trade, or buy goods. These markets became the predecessors to modern-day trade shows.

The word "fair" is derived from the Latin "feria." One definition of the word is "a market festival, often in observance of a religious holiday." Festivals drew crowds, which in turn attracted merchants.

One of the earliest documented festivals, "The Champagne Fairs," traveled to different towns in northeastern France during the 12th and 13th centuries. They evolved into six celebrations a year, usually centering on religious dates and lasting a month or longer. Selling animal skins, fur, leather, spices, textiles, and other merchandise, they attracted large crowds. These fairs began to diminish in the late 1400s as major commercial hubs developed permanent markets.

Possibly the first trade fair in Europe, based in a single town, was in Frankfurt in 1150. It was legally recognized in 1240 by Emperor Frederick II and became an annual event called the "Autumn Fair." This was followed, ninety years later, with an annual "Spring Fair." Copying Frankfurt's success and attempting to increase their own business, Vienna and Munich established "December Markets" in 1298 and 1310. In 1365, the Holy Roman Emperor Charles IV, desirous of establishing new trade routes, granted a trade fair license to Hamburg. Not to be outdone by competing regions, Frankfurt instituted a December market in 1393, adding to their two annual fairs. The first "Christmas Market" was in Dresden in 1434. In addition to traveling merchants, these fairs attracted entertainers: jugglers, acrobats, troubadours, and occasionally a trained bear. Local bakers and cooks would also set up tables.

Trade shows work. Frankfurt holds the record for the first trade fair and also for the oldest trade show—one in existence for more than 550 years.

Frankfurt Book Fair 2019.   Credit: Arielson. Licensed under Creative Commons.

The Frankfurt Book Fair officially dates back to 1462 and reportedly had 40,000 visitors that year. Today, that same show is the biggest book fair in the world, in terms of the number of attendees, publishers, and exhibiting companies. In 2019, the show ran for five days and attracted 286,000 attendees and 7,300 exhibitors. Book fairs in Kolkata and Cairo have recorded significantly larger numbers of visitors but are judged to be a different type of event.

Across the English Channel

Fairs were not exclusive to the continent of Europe. In 1204, King John of England licensed an agricultural fair in Ireland. Located on the south side of Dublin, in the religious district of the Church of Saint Broc, the "Donnybrook Fair" lasted for more than 650 years. By the late 1700's, it had become more of a carnival and gained a reputation for drinking, fighting, and "hasty marriages." The phrase "donnybrook," meaning a brawl or argument, lived on even after the last fair was disbanded in 1866.

Between 1608 and 1814, whenever the Thames froze over, there were a series of "Frost Fairs" in London. Activities on the ice included dancing, football, puppet plays, horse racing, coach rides, bull-baiting, fox hunting, ox roasting, elephant walking, nine-pin bowling, and of course ice fishing, ice skating, and sledding. Barbers, shoemakers, fruit sellers, tavern keepers, pub owners, and other tradespeople set up tents and booths to peddle their wares. There were hot food stands, tobacco stands, bars, brothels, and printers selling personalized certificates of attendance. Fires, food, and drink were plentiful. The last "Frost Fair" commenced on December 27, 1813. The ice began breaking up unexpectedly on February 5, 1814; several people drowned, but the fair continued for another two days, ending on the 7th of February.

Early Industrial Expositions and Fairs, 1798 – 1849

The focus of emerging trade exhibitions is on Europe and, to a lesser degree, America, because Europe is where the Industrial Revolution began. It was industries and the need to promote and sell products that propelled these shows. There were at least thirty expositions in the first half of the nineteenth century, and that number increased more than eightfold in the second half of the century.

Although there were minor industrial meetings in Genoa in 1789 and Hamburg in 1790, the first industrial exhibition was in Prague in 1791, at the coronation of Leopold II. The first public show, "L'Exposition Publique des Produits de L'Industrie Française," was held in Paris in 1798, and it would prove to be the first of eleven French industrial expositions held between 1798 and 1849. They were intended as celebrations and designed to promote French products. Only, and exclusively, French products: If it wasn't made in France, it could not be displayed at any of the expositions.

The first Paris exposition showcased 110 exhibitors. This number doubled in 1801 and increased to 540 exhibitors in 1802. The fourth exposition in 1806 had 1,422 exhibitors. Political and military events delayed the next show until 1819. That show and the next two, held in 1823 and 1827, had between 1,642 and 1,695 exhibitors. Clearly, interest from exhibitors and attendees was steadily increasing. The 1827 show attracted 600,000 visitors in 60 days.

Exposition of Products of French Industry. 1801.

The Paris Exposition planned for 1832 had to be cancelled due to local rioting (think Victor Hugo, Les Misérables, and mobs). That same year, a cholera epidemic killed 2.5% of the population of Paris. Shows were held in 1834 and 1839 and continued to increase in size. The 10th Exposition in 1844 restricted the number of exhibitors, yet it still set a record with 3,960. A new display hall of 240,000 square feet was built for the 11th Exposition, held in 1849. 5,494 exhibitors participated, necessitating separate buildings to house the overflow exhibitors and the larger machinery. The show was known for its photographic displays.

The 1844 Exposition is credited as the inspiration for Prince Alpert in the planning and financing of the Great Exhibition of 1851. The Paris expositions are also credited as the basis for the five Turin industrial expositions from 1829–1850, the three in London in the late forties, as well as the expositions in Bern and Madrid in 1845, Genoa in 1846, Brussels and Barcelona in 1847, St Petersburg in 1848, and the 1849 expositions in Lisbon and Birmingham.

Trying to rival the French, Berlin hosted three early industrial expositions. The first, in 1822, lasted for one and a half months; it had 182 exhibiting companies displaying 998 products and attracted 9,514 visitors. The second was in 1827, and the third was in 1844— that one had 3,040 exhibitors "displaying a large variety of German industrial goods" and registered 260,000 attendees.

---

*__The steady growth and popularity of these shows clearly
indicate a need for them and foreshadow their popularity
in trade shows and convention centers in the United States
and Europe in the twentieth and twenty-first centuries.__*

Looking across the Atlantic, there was nothing as grand as what was
happening in Europe. The first agricultural fair in North America
occurred in 1765 in Windsor, Nova Scotia, although the first
community fair may have been in Hardwick, MA, in 1762. The first
county fair in the US was a "cattle show" in 1810 in Pittsfield, MA,
initiated by Elkanah Watson, who first brought two sheep to show
in Park Square in 1807. By 1811, the fair was a competition; it had
demonstrations and offered prize money. The show continued to
grow in size and prize money throughout the decade.

The American Institute Fair, New York, 1829-

The American
Institute Fair,
launched in New
York City in 1829,
attracted 30,000
people that year and
continued as an
annual event until
1897. It was
founded "for the
encouragement of
agriculture,
commerce, manufactures, and the arts." Inventors like Thomas
Edison displayed products and showcased new technologies there.
Considered by some to be the first world's fair in the United States,
it did not attract the crowds that the expositions in Europe did.

Most consider the 1876 Centennial Exposition in Philadelphia to be the first "official" world's fair in the United States, although some bestow that honor on the New York 1853 exposition.

The first state fair in the US was "The Great New York State Fair" (September 29–30, 1841). By various accounts, it attracted between 10,000 and 15,000 people. Events included speeches, animal exhibits, a plowing contest, and samples of manufactured goods for both the farm and the home, and of course there was food and alcohol. In 1849, an attraction was added: a 50-foot-tall manually powered oak and iron wheel with wooden buckets that could hold adults or children; it was a forerunner to the Ferris wheel, which premiered at the 1893 World's Fair in Chicago. The second state fair in the United States was in Michigan in 1849, and the third opened in California in 1851, the same year as what is generally recognized as the first modern trade show—London's "Great Exhibition.".

That exhibition and its venue, "The Crystal Palace," would soon be copied and spread to cities around the world.

Trade shows work. There are many precursors to the modern-day convention, ranging from agrarian and industrialized events to state fairs and "world" expositions. They evolved, sharing common attributes:

- Part community. A gathering of people, usually having a good time.
- Part education. An offer of learning or speeches.
- Part demonstration, A display of new products and/or technologies.
- Part brand awareness. Promoting name recognition.
- Part entertainment. Creating memorable experiences

- Part sales oriented. Offering immediate and deferred opportunities.

During the first half of the nineteenth century, from Barcelona to Brussels, and from Berlin to Bern... from France to Russia, and from England to Italy—no matter what city or what country—all of the European Expositions were provincial events, displaying only "home-country" products. That was about to change. And the exposition industry would never be the same.

CHAPTER TWO

The First Modern Trade Show 1851

The Great Exhibition

The Industrial Revolution created a new manufacturing economy. Increased production required an increase in sales, which, in turn, necessitated the display and promotion of products.

On May 1, 1851, "The Great Exhibition of the Works of Industry of All Nations" opened in London. The crowd size that day outside the building was estimated to be over 300,000 people.

The Great Exhibition was a seminal event of the Victorian era as well as a defining moment in trade show history. As a show, it was huge, international, inspiring, breath-taking, unique, enormous, and excessive. The building was four times larger than the largest exposition hall in the world at that time; the event was global in scope and hosted industries from 44 countries; the show displayed over 100,000 exhibits and attracted over six million attendees in five and a half months.

The exhibition exceeded all expectations and proved to be a colossal success. It was specifically designed to be a large, international event and to showcase Great Britain as the industrial leader in iron, steel, textiles, and machinery. One of the stated goals was that technology (especially British technology) was the key to a better future. Nothing like the building or the show had ever been seen before in London, or, for that matter, anywhere in the world. The London press, and much of Parliament were initially opposed to the exposition and its proposed location in Hyde Park. But halfway through construction, the press crowned the building "The Crystal Palace," and once the show opened, they proclaimed it to be "The Eighth Wonder of the World."

One hall of The Great Exhibition. The elm tree is over 100' tall.

Over the years, many words have been written to describe this show: "Biggest," Best." "Monumental." "Historic." "Trendsetting." "Colossal." "Transcendent." "Enormous." "Awe-inspiring." Maybe the most accurate description is in the name itself, the word "Great." And was it ever! The exhibition shattered the competition and created the model for future expositions, fairs, and trade shows. and the Crystal Palace did the same, laying the foundation for future venues.

Perhaps the best way to understand the magnitude and significance of this show is to review the number of records it established, many of which still stand today:

➢ **First international exposition.**
  o Brought countries, businesses, and products together from around the world. Literally.

➢ **First show to make a profit.**
  o 186,346 pounds. Equivalent to 32,602,182 pounds in 2024.
  o Possibly the most profitable tradeshow ever.
  o The next profitable large show is the 1889 Paris Exposition.

➢ **First show with no government funding.**
  o All public funding. No private companies were involved.
  o Money was accumulated through subscriptions, donations, dinners, and fund-raising events.

➢ **First show to charge admission to a construction site.**
  o Thousands a day paid to tour during construction and in the weeks before the show opened.

➢ **First show to sell tickets.**
  o Included are differential pricing and season ticket holders.

- o Used turnstiles to count and record the number of visitors.
- o Prices were lower during the week and later in the season.

> **First glass and metal convention center.**
  - o Glass was not a common construction material at this time.
  - o This building inspired hundreds of future convention center designs.

> **First large-scale modular construction.**
  - o Prefabricated and pre-tested prior to installation.
  - o Designed to shorten the build time.
  - o Unique and necessary due to very tight time constraints.

> **First show to exceed 1,000,000 visitors.**
  - o 6,039,722 paid attendees in five and a half months.
  - o Ten times the previous published record, and almost a third of the population of England.

> **Largest show opening crowd, until 1876.**
  - o 25,000 entered on day one.

- o Over 300,000 stood outside, watching.

- ➢ **Largest one day attendance.**
  - o 109,915 people on October 9, 1851.
  - o Held record for exactly 25 years (until October 9, 1876 at the Philadelphia Exposition).

- ➢ **Largest Exhibit space in the world in 1851.**
  - o 990,000 square feet of exhibit space.
  - o Four times larger than any previous building.

- ➢ **Largest building in the world in 1851.**
  - o 33,000,000 cubic feet.
  - o Over 1/3 mile long.
  - o Covered 19 acres.

- ➢ **Largest construction project at the time.**
  - o 10,080,000 pounds of iron.
  - o 293,655 panes of glass. 30 miles of gutters.

- ➢ **Largest number of exhibitors and exhibited products.**
  - o Over 14,000 exhibitors.
  - o More than 2.5 times the previous record.
  - o Over 100,000 exhibits.

- **First public flush toilets.**
  - George Jennings volunteered structures, toilets, and labor.
  - Charged a penny. Made 1,769 pounds (304,546 pounds today).

- **First show to sell a sponsorship.**
  - Schweppes paid for a beverage and food sponsorship. Made 45,000 pounds (7.7 Mil today).
  - Three refreshment centers sold a total of 1,927,337 beverages.
  - Established a brand.

- **Most number of countries exhibiting.**
  - Businesses from 44 countries travelled to England, many at the expense of their governments.
  - Previous record, 1. New record, 44.
  - This number would not be equaled or exceeded for the next forty-two years (not until Chicago hosted 46 countries in 1893).

- **First World's Exposition.**
  - More than 100 in over 20 countries since 1851.
  - Called World's Fairs in the United States.

- **First modern trade show.**
  - Perhaps the most important designation of all.
  - Drew the blueprint for shows for next one hundred and seventy years.

A place to see and be seen:
Queen Victoria visited the show on forty-one different days.

How huge was this event?

> **"I was there for five days, and still did not see it all."**
>
> Horace Greeley, Founder and Editor, New York Tribune

To put the size into perspective, compare it to centers and shows in the United States. The Crystal Palace, if it still existed, would be one of the ten largest exhibit halls in the US, although Chicago, Vegas, and Orlando do have show floors more than double their size. The ceiling of the Crystal Palace was twice the height of the highest ceiling at McCormick Place. No show would have more exhibitors—not even close—and very few would have the same or larger footprint (ConExpo, CES, SEMA, and Pack Expo are four that are larger). And when it comes to attendance, there is no comparison. Only two B2B shows (Music Merchants and SEMA) had more total (multi-day) attendance than the highest one-day attendance at this event, and even huge consumer shows rarely draw more than a million people for the entire show.

A larger than a life show – unlike anything seen before.

Another way to picture the size of this show: All the conventions in Las Vegas in 2019 combined attracted a record-setting 6.6 million visitors to the city. In twelve months and thousands of meetings, Vegas attracted only ten percent more than London did in one show in five and a half months, one hundred and sixty-eight years earlier. Admittedly, it is not an apples-to-apples comparison. The Great Exhibition became a cultural phenomenon; it was a must-see event; it was the first world's fair.

But again, to keep it in perspective, the event drew over 6,000,000 people at a time when the population of Greater London was 2,650,000. The population of all of England was less than 18 million.

So how did this happen? What were the origins of the show? Who were the principal players involved? How did it all come together?

It takes a team to create any type of success. And that is definitely true here: show site construction required one to two thousand workers, six days a week, every week, for over half a year. There was the Royal Society, there was the Building Committee, and there were all the contractors involved. The list could go on.

But the three heroes of this story have to be the Queen, the Prince, and the Gardener. Certainly, Henry Cole and Charles Fox played instrumental roles, but lacking any one of these first three, it is unlikely that the Exhibition would have happened.

Queen Victoria rarely receives credit for the Exhibition. But without her involvement, it is doubtful the show would have happened. No doubt, without her determination, it would not have been as successful.

Queen Victoria in 1843

Queen Victoria proved instrumental in bringing the Exhibition to reality in several ways: 1) she appointed Albert to chair the Commission that created the Exhibition; 2) the building was constructed in Hyde Park, which was royal land and needed her permission and approval; 3) her support was beneficial in priming the subscription funding; and 4) she insisted—against much political pressure and advice – she insisted on being present and opening the Exhibition on Day One. There was a valid reason to suggest the Queen should fear going out in public in the midst of such a large crowd: There had been six assassination attempts on her life between June 10, 1840, and June 27, 1850. Her announced presence at the Exhibition dramatically increased support for and attendance at the show. The last reason, maybe the most compelling reason of all, is that had she not married Albert, he would not have been there to proclaim the advantages of an international exhibition.

Victoria ascended the throne on June 20, 1837, at the age of eighteen. She proposed to Albert in October of 1839, and they were married on February 10, 1840. Albert was not a favorite of the press or Parliament, as many felt the Queen had married a lesser royal. It was an arranged marriage, but she had several options, and she chose Albert. It appears to have been a happy marriage, as they had nine children (and, surprisingly for the period, all the children survived to adulthood). Upon Albert's death in 1861, Victoria went into mourning and stayed dressed in black for the next 40 years, until her death in 1901.

Prince Albert. 1840. Portrait by John Partridge.

Prince Albert is the visionary and driving force behind The Great Exhibition. He wanted an international show, one focusing on the benefits of technology, and he wanted it to be the biggest and best show in the world—one befitting and promoting Britain's image and stature. He sought to "build a cathedral to free trade" and "invite every country to send its creations." Although his ideas were not initially popular, he was persistent in stating them. He would not be deterred by criticism from Parliament or from the press.

In 1843, Albert was elected President of the Society of the Arts. In 1846, Henry Cole, editor of the *Journal of Design* and creator of the first commercial Christmas card, joined the society shortly before the name was changed to "Royal Society for the Encouragement of Arts, Manufacturers and Commerce." Both men were familiar with the 1844 Paris Exposition and wanted to do something similar in England. They developed three expositions in 1847, 1848, and 1849; they were not major shows, but attendance increased each year from 10,000 to 73,000 to 100,000 in 1849.

These shows did not attract governmental interest or support for a proposed larger event. However, once it was determined that the show would be self-financing, Parliament was less antagonistic.

Still, there were obstacles: the xenophobic press and many members of parliament feared an event like the Exhibition would be an invitation to revolution and that bringing foreigners onto the soil could lead to more disease. This fear was not totally unwarranted: the revolutions of 1848 across western and central Europe and the Chartist Movement in England were recent memories; second, there had been a cholera epidemic in London in 1848, and 52,000 people perished from the disease (the epidemic in Russia killed over a million people between 1847 and 1851). Another obstacle was that many people did not want a large structure built in Hyde Park, destroying the ground's pristine beauty. Lastly, there was the problem of what to build and how to build it. The building had to be temporary and inexpensive, but it also had to be huge, impressive, and able to be constructed within a limited time frame.

Joseph Paxton.

Joseph Paxton would solve the "build" problems. He was the designer and builder of the Crystal Palace.

Although the press referred to him as "a gardener," he was a landscape designer, architect, and builder. At the age of twenty, he became Head Gardner for the Duke of Devonshire. His public garden designs and work at Birkenhead Park directly influenced the design of Central Park in New York City. But more importantly for this story, he was a pioneer in working with glass and metal. Between 1833 and 1848, he designed and built three large greenhouses for the Duke.

The Great Conservatory at Chatsworth, finished in 1841, was 227 feet long, 123 feet wide, and 61 feet high. At the time, it was the largest glass building in the world. In 1846, Paxton completed the construction of the Chatsworth Lily House. He knew where to find craftspeople and contractors, specifically ironworkers and glaziers, and he would use these contacts in the construction of the Crystal Palace. Paxton knew Robert Chance. Chance was a pioneer in glassmaking technology, and his company, Chance Brothers, is the leading glass manufacturer in England. Paxton persuaded Chance to produce glass in four-foot lengths (the previous lengths were a maximum of three feet long). Paxton also worked with Charles Fox, of Fox and Henderson. They were a railway equipment company specializing in structural iron for railway bridges, stations, and roofs. Chance Brothers and Fox and Henderson would prove to be essential contractors.

The Crystal Palace revolutionized building design.

The design of the Crystal Palace projected a unique spatial look, one befitting the technological advances that the Exhibition showcased. The blueprint was a daring plan, and one that Paxton executed brilliantly. Once construction started, he proved to be a masterful magician who managed to bring the project in ahead of schedule. Not all future expositions would open on time, but this one did.

Paxton's input was critical because one year prior to the show opening, the Great Exhibition was still only an idea—there was no land, no design, and no approval. In fact, even ten months before the show opening date, there was still no consensus on a design, let alone an approved bid. How it all came together is fairly unbelievable. Preliminary work would start on July 30, 1850. But before that could happen, a lot of problems had to be overcome. Getting other countries to buy into the idea of an international exposition wasn't a problem. Getting Britain to do so was.

But resistance in Parliament and in the British press wasn't nearly as challenging as finding a way to build a structure in time.

The Great Exhibition was a spectacular show of historic proportion. It helped shape and define Britain's position in the world, and it demonstrated the superiority of British technology. It would draw the blueprint for success for future shows.
But one year prior to the show opening, there was no structure in which to hold the show. Or even an approved building design.

Countdown to Show Opening

Imagine planning the largest event the world has ever seen, but first you have to build a structure to house it ... and one year out, before the show opens to the world, you haven't even broken ground.

"The Crystal Palace," home to The Great Exhibition of 1851, was a glittering glass and iron structure with 990,000 square feet of exhibit space. It was 1,850 feet long, 408 feet wide, and 128 feet high—tall enough to enclose existing trees within the interior of the building.

Viewing the Great Exhibition today, the show seems almost inevitable. The idea was brilliant: invite countries from all over the world; make it big; make it the best; promote technology; showcase British products; and include goods from other countries. It sounds like a great idea—it seems destined to happen, doesn't it? But looking at this show through the lens of the present distorts the reality of the past. The Great Exhibition was not inevitable. Far from it. At the time, there was a lot of negativity in Parliament and pessimism from the press. "England was an island for a reason," some said. "An island is meant to keep out foreigners," others added.

There were many objections and obstacles that nearly prevented this show from happening. And there were valid reasons for people to be concerned: the revolution on the continent; the Chartist movement in England; the cholera epidemic in London—these were recent and very real memories. However, the biggest problems were that, fourteen months before the show opening date, there was no design, no land, no consensus, and only limited funding for the project.

The Crystal Palace covered 19 acres of Hyde Park. It was modularly built and completed in an astonishing nine months and five days. That time was not just for the construction! No, that was **nine months and five days from verbal acceptance of the contract, to ground breaking, to venue completion, to show move-in, and finally to show opening.**

Approximately six and a half months prior to show opening

The Palace interior, six weeks before show opening.

COUNTDOWN TO THE EXHIBITION.

The Great Exhibition would open on May 1, 1851. At the start of 1849, it was barely a glimmer of an idea. And even a year later, sixteen months prior to the eventual opening, there had been little progress. At that point in time, there was no reason to believe this "Great" show might actually happen. So how did this exhibition materialize? How was the Crystal Palace designed and built? What was the time frame?

1849, January. At the beginning of the year, Prince Albert proposes hosting an international event. Thanks to Albert and the Royal Society, there was already a scheduled British Industrial Exposition planned for that summer; it would be the third one in three years and would attract 100,000 visitors. But Albert was envisioning something more spectacular. Something "Great". Something international. Unfortunately, except for Albert and Henry Cole, no one believed this was a good idea.

1849, June. At the beginning of June, Henry Cole and three other Royal Society of the Arts committee members attend the 11th Paris Exposition.

At the end of June, Prince Albert summons the committee to elaborate on a plan for the next London exhibition. The Society discusses having an international exposition, and appointing a Royal Commission to be headed by Albert. Four potential locations for the exhibition are discussed; Hyde Park is again recommended as the preferred site. No decision is made. Except for some minimal fund-raising, nothing happens for six months.

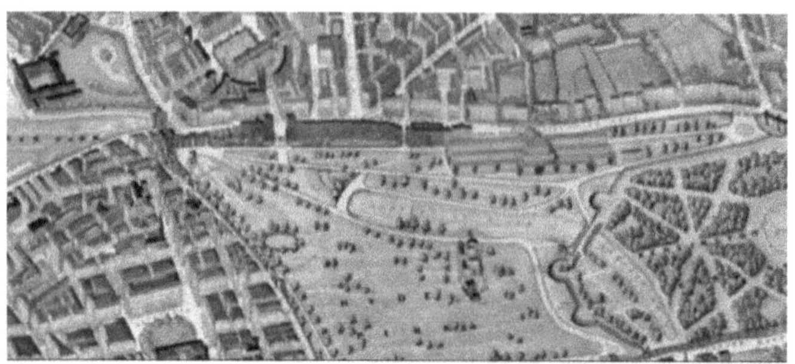

Hyde Park, London, 1851. Location of the Crystal Palace and the Great Exhibition.

Map of Hyde Park. Hyde Park would prove to be the eventual location of the Crystal Palace. In this 1851 drawing, Buckingham Palace (the Queen's residence) is located on top, left. The bottom center and right are Hyde Park. The structure at the top of the park, drawn to scale, is the Crystal Palace. It is one-third of a mile long and located approximately two miles from Buckingham Palace. The river Thames, not shown, would be slightly above the top of the map. Hyde Park was, and still is, a majestic place.

Prince Albert and some committee members meet.

January 3, 1850. After a six-month delay, Albert receives his appointment as President of the Committee. Later in the month, an "Executive Building Committee" is appointed; it includes renowned architects and engineers. Multiple delays and objections continue.

FOURTEEN MONTHS TO SHOW OPENING.

March, 1850. The Committee meets and again discusses various locations. Hyde Park seems to be an obvious choice. It is close to the palace. It is royal property and controlled by the queen. It is close to a train station, which will help in the transportation of construction materials and also aid in getting people to the show.

Members of the Committee express concern about permanent and irreversible damage to the park (this concern would be intensified in Parliament and in the press, especially in the London Times). Again, no decision is reached on the location.

The May 1, 1851, date is announced. Countries are invited to participate.

March 15. An international design competition is announced, and architects are invited to submit proposals. Per the design specifications, the building should be **"temporary, simple, inexpensive as possible, and able to be built within the allotted time frame."** Most of the designers would end up ignoring these specs.

The deadline to submit renderings and proposals was three weeks.

THIRTEEN MONTHS TO SHOW OPENING.

April 8, 1850. 233 design entries are received (plus 12 more after the deadline); 38 proposals are international, including submissions from seven European countries.

SHOW OPENS IN ONE YEAR.

May 1, 1850. The Building Committee evaluates the submissions. They like only two designs, both are from renowned architects: Englishman Richard Turner, and Frenchman Hector Horeau. Both designs, interestingly enough, were for cast iron and plate glass structures. But all the designs are rejected as too expensive, too permanent, and taking too long to build. After the Building Committee creates their own group design later in the month, Richard Turner is furious and demands payment for his design work (probably because he thinks their design looks a lot like his, although he does not accuse them of theft).

Criticism of the Exhibition continues in Parliament. One of the more outspoken critics there, the popular Colonel Charles de Laet Waldo Sibthorp, calls the idea *"one of the greatest humbugs, frauds, and absurdities ever known."* To give the Colonel his due, he also thought railways were a passing fad, and he was opposed to all foreign influences. *"England's an island for a reason, don't you know?"*

There is still no confirmed location. But there is a definite outcry over the potential destruction of Hyde Park. Members of Parliament express their concerns and fears: concern trees would be cut down; fear the exhibition would attract too many people; concern crowds might get rowdy; fear crowds destroy the Park; fear the crowds might riot; fear the crowds might bring disease to London and spread a new plague. And besides, one MP asked, where will all these people relieve themselves? (As amusing as that sounds, it was a valid concern.). As it turned out, the Crystal Palace became the first building to have public flush toilets.

Iron and glass designs by Hareau above, and Turner

Committee design for the Great Exhibition. The public hated it.

Mid-May. The Building Committee releases its own design. In addition to this being highly unethical (they looked at 245 designs and took elements from several of them), the design was highly impractical—it would require nearly 15 million bricks; it was not temporary; it was not cheap; and it would miss the show opening deadline by at least 3 months. Perhaps some or all of these objections could be overcome, but the biggest obstacle of all could not: the design was ridiculed and mocked in the press, and the public hated it. Apparently, "Design by Committee" doesn't work very well.

ELEVEN MONTHS TO SHOW OPENING.

Still no land and no design. June 7, 1850. Joseph Paxton travels to London and talks with an acquaintance, John Ellis. Ellis is a Member of Parliament and chairman of Midland Railway. Paxton learns that the plans for the Great Exhibition are not going well. Ellis believes they are still searching for a building design. He takes Paxton to the Board of Trade and introduces him to Henry Cole.

June 9, 1850. Paxton walks the grounds of Hyde Park, envisioning possibilities. He imagines that a giant greenhouse would solve many of the potential problems. It would be temporary. It would be modular and pre-fabricated. It could be built quickly. It would have limited internal walls (allowing for more exhibit space), and it would not need to be heated (saving construction time). However, there was one major challenge: the scope of the project dictated that the building would be thirty times the size of the largest structure Paxton ever built. Thirty times! Wow.

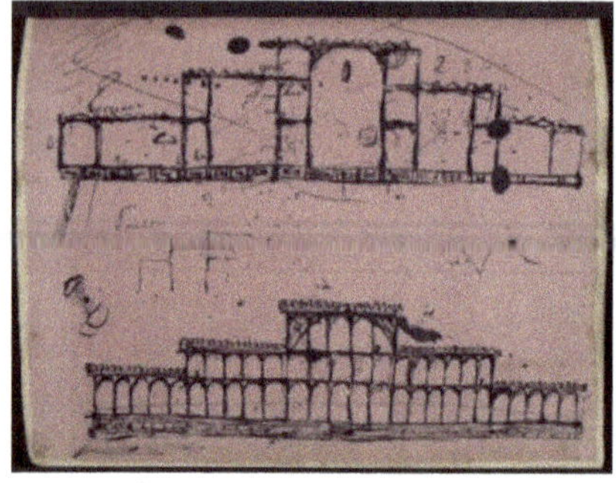

Paxton's rough sketch for a modular solution.

June 11, 1850. In addition to his duties as Head Gardener, Paxton is a Director of the Midland Railway Company, and during a board meeting, he doodles a rough preliminary sketch. It is a glass and metal modular design for a giant greenhouse. It would be cheaper and faster to build than other designs. Paxton's eventual build will cost 72% less than the estimated cost of Turner's design. Plus, it will be larger.

Mid-June. Paxton's design met with resistance from members of the building committee. "He's a mere gardener." "He's not an architect." Several of the architects on the committee will continue to question the structure throughout construction, causing roadblocks and delays.

June 21. Paxton takes ten days to develop ideas. He creates a more finished rendering. He talks with Charles Fox about construction costs and challenges. Fox-Henderson was a railway construction company with whom Paxton has worked previously. Paxton works the numbers. The committee pushes back.

TEN MONTHS TO SHOW OPENING

Paxton's next rendering met with public acclaim.

July 6. Paxton realizes he has to force the issue. He has his new rendering published in the "Illustrated London News." The public, and much of the press, love the design. Under pressure, the committee realizes it is running out of time. But still, there are many objections, including some questions regarding the safety of glass (a relatively new construction medium).

This particular design called for the pre-fabrication of modules with a 24" x 24" base. The modules were constructed on the limits of a single pane of glass; the largest piece of glass in 1851 was 10" wide by 49" long. Because it was modular and pre-fabricated, the structure of the Crystal Palace could be assembled and dismantled relatively quickly.

July 9. John Henderson (of Fox-Henderson) suggested adding a "Barrel" to the center hall, eliminating the need to cut down existing trees that grew within this section of the proposed building.

Punch Magazine calls the design "an example of an early English shed," probably a polite British architecture term meaning, "I think it's ugly."

July 15. The Commission decides to accept Paxton's design but says the final proposal must be due in eleven days—that includes construction drawings and all costing and final numbers. After months of inaction and delays, now they are in a hurry!

Friday, July 26, 1850. Paxton meets the deadline. The proposal is verbally accepted, although the contract will not be signed until October. Paxton and Fox-Henderson (now hired as the general contractor) have no choice, however. If they are to build a structure in time for the show, they have to gamble and start immediately. They cannot tolerate any more delays or wait on a formal, signed contract.

NINE MONTHS AND TWO DAYS TO SHOW OPENING.

Initial work is to begin. Finally!

Tuesday, July 30, 1850. On-site work kicks off with 30 men on the first day. They plot locations for the bases of the columns and start to level the ground where necessary. The perimeter of the building is 1,848' x 408'. Starting the following week, crews will work Monday through Saturday, every week, until the show opens. Being in Victorian England, there is no working on a Sunday. Crew sizes will vary and slowly increase, dictated by the amount of work possible in a given week.

Strictly controlling labor numbers reigned in the cost of the build.

August. A perimeter fence of 45,000 square feet is installed. The fence will later be dismantled, and all the lumber will be recycled and used for the interior flooring. The daily crew size in August ranges from 43 to 60 men.

A perimeter fence was installed. This illustration was from late October.

From his experience building greenhouses, Paxton designed an innovative ridge and furrow system with hollow iron columns for drainage. He believed he had a "kit of parts," which would make design and assembly easier and quicker. In some ways, constructing the Crystal Palace was like building a giant erector set. Or, more precisely, assembling a huge system exhibit.

The initial materials begin to arrive. The building will need: 4,500 tons of iron, 3,230 iron columns, 2,224 trellis girders, 30 miles of gutters (Paxton created specially designed ridge and furrow greenhouse gutters), 202 miles of sash bar, 60,000 square feet of lumber, 293,655 panes of glass (978,850 square feet of glass, nearly as many square feet as both floors of exhibit space), and sixteen very large laminated timber arches (the semi-circular ribs of the transept). Materials are transported by train to London, then loaded onto horse-drawn wagons and hauled to the construction site at Hyde Park.

During August and September, off-site, materials are being produced and modules are assembled.

September. On-site, daily construction crews will increase to 293 a week by the end of the month.

September 14. First delivery of cast iron columns.

September 26. Erection of columns begins. First girder goes up. The frame will take nine weeks to complete.

October. Crews increase from 467 a week to 843 at the end of the month.

There were many benefits to a partially prefabricated building. The parts could be quickly and cheaply mass-produced in large quantities. Assembly was quick, and the structure was easy to erect. It was self-supporting; as a result, the shell, with minimal interior walls, maximized exhibition space. Its light weight meant there was little need for heavy machinery. Another benefit is that the relatively light concrete footings could be left in the ground after the dismantling.

But the biggest advantage was that it could be assembled section by section, multiple modules at a time. Glass could be installed, and the roof was worked on in smaller sections at one end, long before other work was even started. And since the building would be temporary and open from May to October, no heating system was required.

SIX MONTHS TO SHOW OPENING.

Crews in November steadily increased from 1,538 a day to 2,129.

November 7. Glazing starts, while construction of the frame continues.

293,653 individual panes of glass will need to be installed. Each pane of glass is 10" wide by 49" long. Each module, in fact, was based on these dimensions. The entire exterior surface could be glazed using identical panes; this reduced production costs as well as installation labor, time, and expense. A crew of 80 glaziers installed 18,000 panels in the first week. If they can keep that pace up, with no crew changes, working six days a week, and no holidays, they will finish in 16 weeks and two days. So, the scheduled completion date would be March 1, 1851—two months ahead of the show opening. But still, the hall must be prepped, the freight moved in, and the exhibits set.

This sounds great. Finish the installation of the glass two months before the show opens. But Paxton determines they must do better. And they will.

Some shows don't open on time. New York in 1853 opened two and a half months late; Chicago, forty years later, opened seven months after the original date. But the Great Exhibition would open on time.

November 28. Except for the transept and the glass, the exterior frame is complete. The arches still need to be raised, although that will be surprising quick, and the glazing will continue for months. Plus, a lot of work still needs to be completed on the interior, and that does not include detailing the flooring, the fountains, the overhead banners, the freight, or the exhibits.

To the degree possible, work is completed on the ground (or as close to it) before structures are raised into the air.

FIVE MONTHS TO SHOW OPENING.

December. Crews vary from 2,128 a day to 2,035. There was one death: Timothy Byrnes, a carpenter, fell from the scaffolding. Two other injuries occurred that month. These three are the only ones reported for the entire project.

Death is tragic at any construction site. But only three accidents in nine months are fairly remarkable for a project this size in the mid-1800's. While exact numbers of British industrial deaths in this decade are difficult to determine, the press reported workers dying in factories, children dying in mines, and house painters dying from lead poisoning.

December 4. The first arch is raised. The sixteen circular arch ribs were made of laminated timber and took one week to install.

December 11. The frame is completed.

Punch, a weekly British magazine, likes the light and airy look and calls the structure a "Crystal Palace." This is the same magazine that called the rendering a "shed.".

FOUR MONTHS TO SHOW OPENING.

A rolling trolley speeds the glass installation.

January. Labor goes from 2,145 a day the first week down to 1,417 at the end of the month. But the labor call will increase to 2,128 in April. The installation of the glass continues.

Paxton designed a moveable trolley system to speed the placement of the glass on the multiple roof sections.

THREE MONTHS TO SHOW OPENING.

February. Paxton and Fox continue to control the labor call, and work only the number they believe is necessary. The labor calls each week this month fluctuates from 1,333 to 1,210 to 1,244 to 1,353, before steadily increasing every week in March.

After the roof is completed, portions are tarped with canvas to limit the amount of light and heat. The interior of the south hall is paneled in wood, also to lessen the effects of the greenhouse heat.

Architects on the Building Committee continued to raise concerns and force added work and delays. They were concerned that excess rain water would cause the glass to shatter and fall upon crowds at the Exhibition. Paxton had anticipated this problem in his previous greenhouses; his special gutters and ridge and furrow roof system channeled water away; this was not a problem. The architects were concerned about excessive heat. Again, Paxton anticipated this concern and had already planned on tarping sections of the roof and paneling one wall of the interior. He created a ventilation system that allowed for the cool air to rise from spaces between floor boards and for the hot air to escape from open windows near the roof. The Building Committee was concerned the roof would leak. It did leak in places, but not significantly, and, in any event, additional caulking helped. Some on the committee were concerned that excessive noise would shatter the glass; that did not happen, not even after moving to a new location and standing for the next eighty-four years.

The Building Committee was concerned about safety and structural integrity, and rightly so. Modules were pre-tested before assembly and before going up in the air. One of the more comical tests was testing the structural integrity of the floor. Before erecting the floors inside the palace, sections were built outside with the iron modules and the wood planking on top. A squad of soldiers was ordered.

First, to march in place on top of the floor, and then to run in place. Finally, they were told to jump—all of them jumped off the floor and into the air at the same time. Ready. Set. Jump!

The fencing around the entire perimeter of the building has to be removed. The horizontal boards are re-used and become the flooring inside the structure. The boards are spaced about 3/8" apart to allow for debris to be swept below (which was cleaned daily) and to allow for cooling air to rise.

Unloading of exhibit properties.

February 10, 1851. First day to receive exhibits.

Freight had been accepted into the country as early as mid-November

First move-in of exhibits in some areas, would occur this month.

TWO MONTHS TO SHOW OPENING.

March 1851. The entire structure is finished, except for the exterior painting.

A show floor axiom: if there are days left before the show opens, there will be people who will want the extra time. And they will use that extra time. It doesn't matter what country, what show, or what period of time in history. Work fills the schedule.

The basic work is done, but the labor calls increase. The labor call in March steadily surges from 1,613 men a day the first week to 2,071 the last week of the month. There were cost overruns, which Fox-Henderson was able to bill for and collect.

April 1851. There are still crews of over 2,000 men working six days a week for the entire month of April. 2,128 men worked the first week in April, and 2,149 worked the week ending May 2. The labor call decreases to 1,697 the next week in May and to 542 the following week. Work continues through July, but in steadily decreasing numbers, with 103 people working the final week, the week ending August 1, 1851.

April 15. Deadline for receiving all shipped products. Russia missed the deadline (and missed the show opening) because the Baltic Sea was still frozen, which prevented ships from sailing from port.

April 19. The exterior four-color painting is complete. The final detailing inside the hall continues.

April 30. The Queen is advised, yet again, not to attend the show for fear of violence. This was not entirely unfounded, as there had been six attempts on her life between June 10, 1840, and June 27, 1850. But she had made a commitment to open the show, and that is what she was determined to do.

SHOW OPENING DAY

7:00 AM. A gorgeous morning. The News calls it, "the Queen's weather". Crowds are already arriving in the Park.

10:00 AM. The streets are packed with people.

11:00 AM. Queen Victoria is advised to enter through the rear of the building because of the size of the crowds – later estimated to be

"Crowds who were familiar with magnificent spectacles, who had seen coronations, and fetes … (had seen) nothing to compare with the Queen's arrival."   London Times

between 300,000 and 500,000 people! She insists on entering through the main entrance, in full view of the public.

May 1, shortly before noon.

*Queen Victoria arriving at the Crystal Palace,
prior to opening the Exhibition.*

As the Queen's carriage rolls through the crowds and moves closer to the Crystal Palace, ***"bursts of cheering broke out from every side"***, according to the Times. (From the beginning, the London Times had been one of the harshest critics of the idea of this exhibition).

May 1, 1851. Noon. The building is complete, the exhibits are in place, and the doors are now open. Victoria and Albert led a procession of 25,000 fans who paid the equivalent of 350 pounds to view the Exhibition on opening day.

Time to tour the interior of the building... Walk down the aisles. View some of the displays ... and see if it was worth "All this hullabaloo", to use one of Colonel Sibthorp's phrases.

A Tour of the Great Exhibition of 1851

"Those who are so fortunate to see it hardly know what to admire. Around them, amidst them, above their heads, was all that was beautiful and useful in nature and in art. Above them rose a glittering arch, far more lofty and spacious than even our noblest cathedrals."
London Times. May 2, 1851.

Queen Victoria opened the show on May 1, 1851, with her husband, Prince Albert, and two of their children. She was accompanied by 25,000 VIPs who paid a premium for the privilege to be there on day one. Estimates of the size of the crowd standing outside varied from 300,000 to 500,000 people, depending on the publication (the Times reported 300,000).

On day two, May 2, the show opened to the public, and 16,560 people paid to enter the exhibition. Word-of-mouth increased attendance. On October 9, 109,915 people paid to view the Exhibition (probably not the best day to walk the floor and tour the show). The show attracted over 6,000,000 attendees—more than a third of the entire population of England at the time.

So, what was the show like? Why did so many people choose to visit this first international exposition?

What would one see walking the floor?

Visitors to the Exhibition first passed through a turnstile at the main entrance. The largest fountain, and one of the elms was directly ahead. Before arriving at the fountain and the main exhibition areas, there were pavilions on either side. On the left, fragrant smells of colonial produce from Trinidad assaulted the senses, and on the right, tents from Tunis displayed the skins of leopards and lions. The British area, including India, Canada, and other colonies, was to the left of the fountain, and the foreign exhibitors were to the right. The United States pavilion was to the right of the fountain and at the end of the foreign nave. Beyond the fountain were more exhibit areas, refreshment stands, and comfort stations.

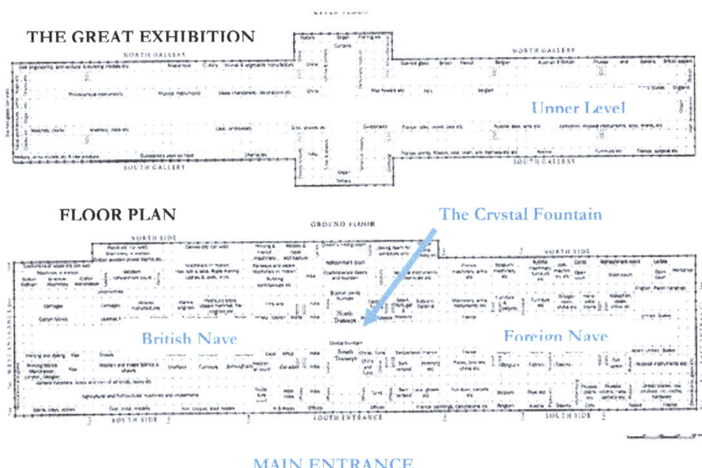

Do not be deceived by the small floor plan—the building was over one-third of a mile long!

The British Nave.

Exhibits were on two levels, but most of the major displays were on the ground floor. There were 14,000 exhibitors (almost half from counties other than Britain) and over 100,000 exhibits. Forty-four countries had their own display areas, including Russia, France, Germany, Italy, Spain, Portugal, Switzerland, Sweden, China, India, Turkey, Holland, Ceylon, Canada, and the United States. Great Britain occupied half the exhibit hall; after that, France and then the United States had the largest display areas.

Initially, there was a grand organ located in the gallery above the crystal fountain. But the performances created too many people stopping and listening in the center of the hall. To reduce the congestion, the organ was moved and placed above the American Pavilion.

"It looks like a fairy land."   Lewis Carroll

Technology and working equipment were popular. Exhibited items at the show included ironwork, firearms, repeating revolvers, fabrics, steam engines, hydraulic presses, printing presses, telescopes, an electric telegraph, a reaping machine, microscopes, telegraphs, vulcanized rubber, the first voting machine, musical and surgical instruments, as well as the precursor to the fax machine.

Walking into the British Nave, there were pavilions from India on both the left and right sides, followed by displays from other colonies, before arriving at British products and technology.

Downstairs, still in the British area, were displays of linens, cotton, flax, furs, woolens, hardware, agricultural equipment, furniture, and machinery. There was a folding piano, a piano with a collapsible keyboard, and a locomotive that required 22 horses to drag it in place.

Printing presses were producing thousands of copies of the Times and the Illustrated News in an hour. There was a voting machine, an envelope folding machine that also glued the envelopes, and a cigarette machine. There were artificial teeth made out of hippopotamus, as well as teeth that could swivel so the user could yawn, and furniture made out of coal. There was a hydraulic press where one man could move thousands of pounds of iron. There was a bed with a timer that would stand the sleeper upright. A revolutionary lens for lighthouses and a carriage drawn by kites were also highlights.

British hardware and furniture displays.   *British machines on display.*

One of the benefits of a trade show is the ability to compare products side by side. It can also be a drawback: although British furniture was well made, it lacked the detail and design of French furniture.

Upstairs, there were medicines, surgical tools, musical instruments, toys, embroidery, linens, pottery, and a gallery of stained glass.

Leaving the upstairs, visitors could pass through several Fine Art Courts, on their way back to the Crystal Fountain.

> *"It is a wonderful place … vast, strange, new and impossible to describe. Its grandeur does not consist of one thing, but in the unique assemblage of all things. Whatever human industry has created you find there. … It seems as if only magic could have gathered this mass of wealth from all the ends of the earth."* Charlotte Bronte

The United States exhibition area. The middle display was vulcanized rubber.

The organ above was British, and moved there after show opening.

At the far end of the Foreign Nave was the United States area, or the American Pavilion Display; it was the third largest exhibit area on the floor. Unfortunately, there was so much empty space that Punch magazine joked that the Americans should rent space as a bed and breakfast or use it as an additional waiting room for the toilets. The show did not charge for exhibit space, and the anticipated number of American entries did not materialize. Unlike many of the countries, the United States did not sponsor or pay for the delegation in any way. The exhibitors' shipping costs were donated, and they were fortunate that upon arrival in London, an American banker, George Peabody, paid to have the exhibit properties unloaded and transported to the hall.

Major US product displays included: Cyrus McCormick's Virginia grain reaper (which modernized harvesting and was the foundation of the International Harvester Company); Charles Goodyear's revolutionary vulcanized rubber (the large display in the middle of the photo above); I. M. Singer's sewing machine (Singer manufactured the first straight stitch sewing machine in Boston in 1850); a collection of daguerreotypes by Mathew Brady; a patented double grand piano for four pianists; a cotton gin; Cincinnati pickles; Virginia honey; and Samuel Colt's "formidable revolving charge pistols". And of course, no area in the hall would be complete without at least one marble nude. The Greek Slave" by Hiram Powers was critically acclaimed and one of the best-known American artworks of the nineteenth century.

Elsewhere in the hall, other objects of interest, in addition to the Koh-I-Noor diamond, weighing 186 carats, were "the giant telescope" and a cotton production demonstration going from spinning to finished cloth. The show had the first paid public toilets, at a cost of a penny. The first America's Cup competition was held in conjunction with the show.

The Great Exhibition was a huge success, viewed from any vantage point. Biggest. Monumental. Historic. Trend setting. Profitable. It laid the groundwork for the design, concept, and function of future trade shows. It became one of the defining points of the nineteenth century. And despite initial fears, it was a peaceful event.

The show excelled and set records in terms of numbers of attendees, exhibitors, and square feet. Perhaps most impressively, it made a profit. It didn't just cover the operating expenses; it made 186,000 pounds. In 2024, that would be 32,541,647 pounds. Now, that's a successful show!

Was the show a success from an individual, or company, sales standpoint? Hard to say. The show wasn't designed to write orders but rather to display technology and sell products at a later date. Prices could not be displayed, but exhibitors were allowed to discuss prices if asked. Except for the three sponsored refreshment centers, no sales were allowed on the show floor (although deliveries were made after the show); however, outside, there were myriad vendors selling souvenirs and food in Hyde Park. Still, there were individuals and companies that made a name for themselves: Americans Brady, Colt, Goodyear, McCormick, and Singer are a few easy examples: they promoted their brands and established their products.

Alfred Krupp is another entrepreneur who benefited from exhibiting at the show. He displayed a solid steel, flawless ingot weighing 4,300 pounds; he also displayed his first steel cannon, a six-pounder. Already a pioneer in steel fabrication and no-weld railway tires, the company was just getting started exhibiting at expositions and building a munitions business.

The power of trade shows: As part of the US delegation, Samuel Colt traveled to London for the Exhibition to present firearms display and demo. He owned a manufacturing company in Hartford, CT, named "Colt Armory." Long before the assembly lines of H. J. Heinz or Henry Ford, Colt's factory utilized a production line to assemble interchangeable parts. At the Exhibition, Colt displayed his repeating revolvers.

Sales were not allowed. But show floor gifts were.

Attracting crowds with a live demonstration, he disassembled ten revolvers and then reassembled them using parts from different guns. He delivered a lecture on mass production techniques to the Institute of Civil Engineering. Colt was the first US company to open a branch overseas; he built a factory in London in 1852 and sold 23,000 revolvers to the British Army and Navy. (Pictured here is a Colt "show floor giveaway" provided to Prince Albert and other distinguished attendees.) Colt's revenue in 2022 was $270.9 Million.

After May 1, the show was open for 140 days; it was closed on Sundays. Queen Victoria enjoyed the show so much that she returned 40 more times. (But then she was allowed to enter before show opening hours, and she did have her very own, private "retiring room").

Joseph Paxton, designer and architect of the Crystal Palace.

Charles Fox of Fox-Henderson; the primary building contractor.

After the show closed to the public, it remained open for three more days. The first two were for exhibitors and their families only. And day three was the closing ceremony. Joseph Paxton received 5,000 pounds (the equivalent of approximately 875,000 pounds today) and was knighted along with Charles Fox, on October 23, 1851. Henry Cole received 3,000 pounds

Victoria and Albert

The question became: What to do with the Crystal Palace? Paxton wanted to leave it there and turn it into a "Winter Park and Garden under Glass." Parliament granted a reprieve on a decision until May 2, 1852, but one of the initial and strongest opponents of the Great Exhibition, Colonel Sibthrop, demanded in Parliament that it be removed by April 29th. The Palace was dismantled—it took only three months—and rebuilt in a different location—at the top of Penge Peak, next to the affluent Sydenham Hill area. It opened in 1854, and was demolished by fire in November, 1936.

A Blueprint for the Future

Find the right location.

Maximize participation.

Display new products.

Promote technology.

Show live demos.

Solicit sponsorships.

Print show brochures.

Distribute floor plans.

Create pavilion areas.

Charge for admission.

Have attractions.

Include public facilities.

Fashion it as fun.

Style it as "must see".

Trade Shows Work. Some of the profit from the show was used to purchase land and build museums in London. The first ones were the Victoria and Albert Museum and the Science Museum, which opened in 1857. That was followed by the opening of the Royal Albert Hall in 1871. Henry Cole was the first director of the Victoria and Albert Museum. Other properties built from the Exhibition's profits included the Natural History Museum and the Imperial College, London.

Among its many successes, in addition to making a profit, The Great Exhibition spawned at least 240 additional shows during the second half of the century. Immediate examples include The Cork Exhibition of 1852; the Dublin Exhibition of 1853; the New York Exhibition of 1853; and the Munich Exhibition of 1854. The last three all had their own Crystal Palaces. The number of shows steadily increased each decade: (15) expositions in the fifties; (27) in the 60s; (44) in the 70s; (82) in the 80s; until a slight decrease to (72) exhibitions in the 90s.

They showed others a blueprint for how to make it work. One of the few things they didn't do that would happen in the future was charge exhibitors for the exhibit space. And that would have been very unwise to do at this time. They did not charge, but there were 7,000 exhibits donated after the show.

The reason for this tremendous and fantastic growth in the numbers and sizes should be obvious: **exhibitions work; they work very well.**

It made political and economic sense for other cities and countries to follow London's lead. If a city could attract a million, or ten million, visitors, then it would have millions of opportunities to sell ideas and promote products—in other words, potentially millions of opportunities to make money. Fairs quickly began popping up in other cities, other countries, and on other continent

CHAPTER THREE

New Horizons.

1852-1876.

New Shows. New Ideas.

After the Great Exhibition in 1851, expositons travelled across the water to Ireland and America, then back across the Atlantic to London, Paris, and other major commercial centers in Europe.

In the days before radio, television, and social media, fairs and expositions were the main avenue to drive publicity and awareness. Industries and individuals exhibited at shows for a variety of reasons: to showcase a new invention; to display a new product; to increase brand awareness; to promote new foods. The bottom line was that manufacturing was exploding, companies needed to sell products, and exhibitions were an avenue to success.

Entrepreneurs and companies that made a name for themselves during this period included: Singer; Steinway; Krupp; Colt; Edison; Bell; Remington; Goodyear; McCormick; Otis; Heinz; Lippincott; Smith and Wesson; Pratt and Whitney; and Yale Lock. Some new products released this quarter century included:

- the telephone
- the typewriter
- the sewing machine
- the passenger elevator
- vulcanized rubber
- underseas communication cables
- the first elevated train
- reinforced concrete
- the Colt revolver
- the repeating rifle
- the Gaitling gun
- plastic

At Expositions, some newly promoted foods included ketchup, root beer, sugar popcorn, waffles, soda water, ice cream sodas, and the first bananas in North America.

Many countries tried to imitate the Great Exhibition. Few did it as well, and none in this period were profitable. Many new exhibition halls were iron and glass builds, similar to London's Crystal Palace, but smaller and designed to be permanent. Three immediate examples were in Dublin and New York in 1853, and in Munich in 1854. (The appeal of glass builds for convention centers continues today: no matter where in the world one looks—from Shanghai to Hannover, Vancouver to Boston, or from Sydney to Rio de Janeiro to New York—beautifully designed glass convention centers are in most major cities.).

The list of expositions below is not all inclusive (there were almost 70 shows between 1851 and 1876), but this list highlights some specific shows based on year, location, size, and/or the technology displayed.

1852. The Irish Industrial Exhibiton. Cork.

Taking place, a year after the Great Exhibition and two years after the Great Famine, this fair was intended to revive local industries for whiskey, slate, gingham, and hydraulic presses. In addition to three halls of industrial exhibits, there was also a hall dedicated to the fine arts. The show was small; it attracted only 129,000 people, but it foreshadowed bigger things to come.

1853. The Great Industrial Exhibition. Dublin.

A year later, still in Ireland, the Dublin Expo attracted over a million visitors. Queen Victoria and Prince Albert attended during the summer. Colt and Singer were two American companies with exhibits. William Dargan, an Irish railway developer, donated $400,000 for this show and hoped his seed money would jumpstart the Industrial Revolution in Ireland.

Several elements of the interior Crystal Palace design were incorporated into the main hall. Despite the design and Dargan's donation, Dublin could not duplicate London's magic. The show lost a million dollars. Dublin would try again and host a Fair in 1865, but it attracted barely 900,000 people that year.

1853/1854. The Exhibition of the Industry of All Nations. New York.

Another attempt to duplicate the Great Exhibition, both architecturally and financially. But despite having their own Crystal Palace and running for 16 months, New York could not replicate London's success. It is remembered today for two things: allowing sales directly from the show floor; and the origin of the Otis elevator.

The show opened two and a half months behind schedule. And even then, the buildings were not complete. The delays were caused by the Commission members and the architects arguing over designs and cost overruns (a recurring dispute in other cities and future venues). Partially due to the delayed opening, only 600,000 people attended the show in 1853. To boost attendance and generate more revenue, P. T. Barnum was hired, and the show was extended by a year. Barnum enticed entertainers to promote new products (including the world's first quadracycle and a steam washing machine), added new attractions, and suggested exhibitors sell items directly off the show floor. This was the first time for direct sales off a trade show floor; it would not be the last.

Barnum also paid an unknown inventor, a man named Otis, $100.00 to perform a twice-daily death-defying demonstration. Drum roll, please.

Trade Shows Work. Otis Elevator. 1854.

Elisha Otis designed and constructed the first safety brake for elevators. and in doing so, he changed the future of high-rise construction. In 1852, there were no passenger elevators, only freight ones, and workers were too scared to ride with the freight because of the repeated accidents.

At the New York Exposition in 1854, P. T. Barnum, ever the showman, paid Otis to create a performance and attract crowds. At the show opening, in the center of the hall, the inventor stood on a platform with freight.

New York Expo, 1854.
"Is it safe?" "Should I cut the rope?"

"Ladies and gentlemen. Ladies and gentleman," he shouted. *"Gather around; gather around."*

A winch moved the platform upward at the agonizingly slow speed of twelve feet per minute.

"Look at me, folks," he hollered. "Look at me!"

Crowds gathered.

Otis' platform moved higher.

Then stopped.

"Should I cut the rope?" he yelled.

People looked up. They moved closer.

"Should I cut the rope?" he yelled again. "Do you think it's safe?"

Some in the crowd protested, "No! No!" "Don't!"

Others cheered, "Yes." "Do it!" "Do it!"

And so, at the age of forty-two, Elisha Otis did just that: he grabbed an axe from atop a crate and severed the hoisting cable. The platform dropped... and the safety brake kicked in.

"All safe!" Otis smiled, raising his arms. "All safe!"

First there was a stunned silence, then, suddenly, wild cheering. Otis' safety brake worked. And it continued to work, day after day. Three years later, the first passenger elevator was installed at Haughwout's department store on the corner of Broadway and Broome in New York City.

Passenger elevators today are so safe that people take them for granted. In New York City alone, there are over 30 million elevator trips daily. But without safe passenger elevators or some similar invention, the world as we know it would be very different. Think about it: There probably would be no buildings over six or seven stories high; there certainly would be no skyscrapers without some type of safe, vertical transportation.

Paris 1878

After Elisha's death in 1861, his two sons took over the business, and understanding the importance of tradeshows, they exhibited in numerous capitals throughout Europe. They demonstrated the elevator in Paris at Expos in 1867 and 1878; they built the Washington Monument elevator in 1880. At the Exposition Universelle of 1889, Otis manufactured and installed elevators at the Eiffel Tower (despite the Fair's initial stipulation that only French companies could be used for any construction). Then, at the turn of the century, again at an

Exposition in Paris, the Otis Elevator Company unveiled the world's first escalator.

Today, there are over 2.6 million Otis elevators and escalators worldwide, moving two billion people daily. When Elisha Graves Otis first exhibited, that tradeshow lost money; however, the company he founded did not. In 2023, Otis employed 71,000 people and generated revenues exceeding $14.2 billion. In March 2024, the company had a net worth of $39.9 billion.

1854. The General German Industry Exhibition. Munich.

First General Germany Exhibition, Munich, 1854

The Glaspalast in Munich was another iron and glass Crystal Palace inspiration. Again, there are similarities between the interior and exterior looks. It was smaller, 768 feet long, 220 feet wide, and 82 feet high, with 37,000 windows. It was built to showcase German industry to the world. Prior to the opening of the show on July 15, there was a cholera outbreak. 90,000 people visited on opening day, but fewer than half a million people attended the three-month show.

1855. Exposition Universelle des produits de l'Agriculture, de l'Industries et des Beaux-Arts. Paris

Emperor Napoleon III and others in France were upset that the British had taken France's idea of an industrial exposition, and made it better. They wanted to outdo England. They came close with 5.1 million attendees and businesses from twenty-seven different companies. But it did not focus on technology, and it was not as successful.

This year was the first time a French exposition would charge admission. The show lasted six months and was known for its works of art and photography, but not for innovative technology. It developed the significant "Bordeaux Wine Official Classification" and displayed a 10-foot-high percolator that brewed 2,000 cups of coffee an hour.

One novelty at this expo: price tags. Displayed items could be purchased on the spot or ordered for later delivery. It's estimated that the Fair lost about $4.5 million. But money was spent on hotels, restaurants, the theater, other live entertainment, and, of course, on the items purchased on the show floor.

Having failed to beat Britain this time, Paris would host four more Expositions between 1867 and 1900, attracting crowds of twelve to fifty million attendees. Huge numbers in any era.

Trade Shows Work. Singer Sewing Machine Company. 1855.

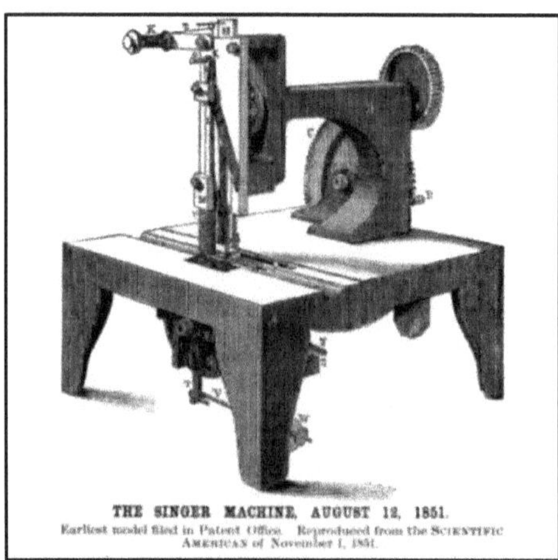

THE SINGER MACHINE, AUGUST 12, 1851.
Earliest model filed in Patent Office. Reproduced from the SCIENTIFIC AMERICAN of November 1, 1851.

Issac Singer won a gold medal at the 1855 Paris Exposition. Five years earlier, he manufactured the first straight-stitch sewing machine in Boston. In time, his invention would revolutionize the clothing industry and make Singer a fortune, but first he had to find a way to market his product.

He couldn't sell what people or companies didn't know they needed.

Singer exhibited in London in 1851. Between 1852 and 1854, the company sold 810 machines. After winning a gold medal in Paris, Singer's business took off. By 1860, through patents, word of mouth, and mass production, Singer had become the largest manufacturer of sewing machines in the world. They continued exhibiting at tradeshows and founded the world's first multi-national company. By 1875, the Singer Manufacturing Company had over 50,000 employees worldwide and had produced over two million units—quite an increase from the 810 machines manufactured in the early fifties!

At the 1876 Centennial Exposition in Philadelphia, Singer exhibited a variety of new models in the main hall. They also constructed a separate "Singer Pavilion" (an entire building) on the Exposition grounds and provided their employees with an all-expense-paid round-trip to the Philadelphia Fair. On June 22, 1876, the company rented six trains to transport over 4,000 employees from the New York office and the Elizabeth, New Jersey, manufacturing plant. It was reported that Singer spent $15,632 (equivalent to $384,246 today) on the excursion.

Continuing to innovate and display at tradeshows, Singer demonstrated the first electric sewing machine at the International Electrical Exhibition in 1885. They exhibited at the Columbian Exposition in 1893. In 1895, Singer manufactured and sold over 13 million sewing machines. In 1950, celebrating 100 years, Singer generated sales of $307.8 million. In the early 1990s, Singer had annual revenues exceeding $1.2 billion. Platinum Equity acquired a controlling stake in SVP Singer Holdings in 2021.

1862. The International Exhibition of Industry and Art. London.

Babbage's pre-computer.

London came close to matching the 1851 show, with 6 million visitors and exhibitors from 39 countries. New inventions included the electric telegraph, submarine communication cables, plastic, and Babbage's analytical engine, the precursor to the modern-day computer. The machine was built from plans Babbage was prohibited from presenting at the Great Exhibition eleven years earlier.

Trade Shows Work. Steinway and Sons. 1862.

Henry Steinway won "First Prize" at the International Exhibition in London in 1862, but it wasn't his first exhibit or even the company's first award. Steinway, at Barnum's behest, first exhibited at the Crystal Palace in New York City in 1854. A year later, at the annual American Institute Fair, the company won their first gold medal. Later that same year, they came in first at the Metropolitan Institute Mechanics Fair in Washington, DC. Between 1855 and 1862, Steinway would receive 35 gold medals at events of varying sizes. Demand was so great for the pianos that he had to move to a larger factory in the 1860's. At the time, he employed 350 men and was hand-crafting 500 pianos a year.

Steinway and Sons was founded in New York City in March 1853, and they sold their first piano for $500 (about $20,000 today). Henry's father, Heinrich, had a factory in Germany and had built 482 pianos during the previous quarter century. Heinrich emigrated to America with his family in 1850. His pianos had a reputation for quality and innovation (Steinway has 139 patents, with the first one coming in 1857).

Henry Steinway knew that in addition to building a great product, the product needed great awareness. And it didn't matter how great he told people the piano was; it was more important what others said.

In 1867, at the Paris Exposition, Steinway won three gold medals, including "The Grand Gold Medal of Honor." The company had arrived! In 1876, at the Centennial Exposition in Philadelphia, they won

two gold medals plus a "Certificate of the Judges," showing a top rating of 95.5 out of a possible 96. (There were rumors at the time that Steinway bribed judges in order to win, but it was also reported that the company was an innocent victim of an extortion attempt.) Additional gold medals included two in 1885 in London. The first one was at the International Inventions Exhibition. That exhibition was a smaller World's Fair and attracted slightly more than three million visitors in six months. Later that year, Steinway won the "Grand Gold Medal" at the Royal Society of the Arts.

Over the decades, Steinway continued exhibiting and winning awards. Still in business today, Steinway produces 2600 pianos annually, with typical prices ranging from $75,000 to $129,000 for a new piano (although some can range as high as $585,000). In 2015, Steinway produced their 600,000th piano and sold a special edition one for a record $2.4 million. Steinway and Sons most recently exhibited at the National Association of Music Merchants annual show in Anaheim.

A bit of trivia: John Lennon bought a used, weather-worn Steinway Model Z upright in 1970. He said it was his favorite piano. Lennon also bought a new, white Steinway Grand Piano for Yoko Ono for her birthday in 1971.

1867. Exposition Universelle. Paris.

Fifteen million visitors and fifty thousand exhibitors from 42 countries came to Paris for fun and business. This Exposition brought a carnival atmosphere to the city, with activities in the park. Previous expos had been more serious; this one was the first to have restaurants and amusements on the grounds, ringing the main building.

The English Lighthouse Paris, 1867.

New inventions included reinforced concrete, an electrical tower (the English Lighthouse, predating the Eiffel Tower by twenty-two years), and a hydrochronometer (a water clock), which is still working today. Bonds to finance the Suez Canal were sold from a display at the show. Krupp exhibited at this event with a 10,000-pound cannon, far larger than his first cannon in 1851. He would also exhibit in Vienna in 1873 and in Philadelphia in 1876 (not to mention all of the major expositions in the last quarter of the century). The Otis Brothers demonstrated the safety of the elevator by repeating their father's stunt from years earlier: in front of a throng of disbelieving journalists, they loaded thousands of pounds of block onto the elevator and severed the cable. They only had to do it once, until a generation later, when they had to prove it all over again at the Eiffel Tower, prior to the opening of the 1889 World's Fair.

1871 and 1872. London, Moscow, and Copenhagen.

These were two uninspiring years for expositions, possibly due to the smallpox pandemic. Still, people traveled.

London attracted 1,142,159 visitors from 35 countries at their 1871 show. Moscow had 750,000 visitors and over 12,000 exhibitors in 1872. Copenhagen attracted 600,000 people to their Exhibition that same year.

1872. Chicago.

The Interstate Exhibition Building in Chicago was another Crystal Palace inspiration. Built to demonstrate the city's rebound from the Great Chicago Fire, the "Glass Palace" was the largest structure in North America at the time, with 220,000 square feet of exhibit space.

Constructed in an astonishingly fast ninety days, the venue dominated the lakefront and increased revenue at adjacent hotels and restaurants. It did not house an international exposition, but it did hold industrial events for twenty years, until it was torn down prior to Chicago's 1893 Exposition.

1873. Weltaustellung. Vienna.

This was not a good year: smallpox was lingering, cholera was spreading, and the financial panic of '73 triggered a depression in both Europe and America. Nevertheless, Vienna entertained over seven million visitors and attracted 42,584 businesses from 35 countries, including 643 companies exhibiting from the United States. Despite the crowds, the exposition lost $9 million.

Philadelphia sent a delegation to observe the show in advance of their own exhibition. They wanted to learn from Vienna's successes and also from their mistakes. Based on their pre-show intelligence, Philadelphia improved upon both transportation and lodging and lowered overall costs.

1876. The 1876 International Exhibition of the Arts, Manufactures, and Products of the Soil and Mine. Philadelphia.

The City of Brotherly Love thrilled 10 million visitors and 14,420 exhibitors from 35 countries. Significant numbers, considering the Exposition was held across an ocean and on a different continent. It was the first official World's Fair in the United States and the first show to write sales orders on the tradeshow floor. Prominent displays included: Bell's telephone; Remington's typewriter; Krupp's cannons; Edison's telegraph; and the Monorail.

America's First Trade Show:
The Centennial Exposition of 1876

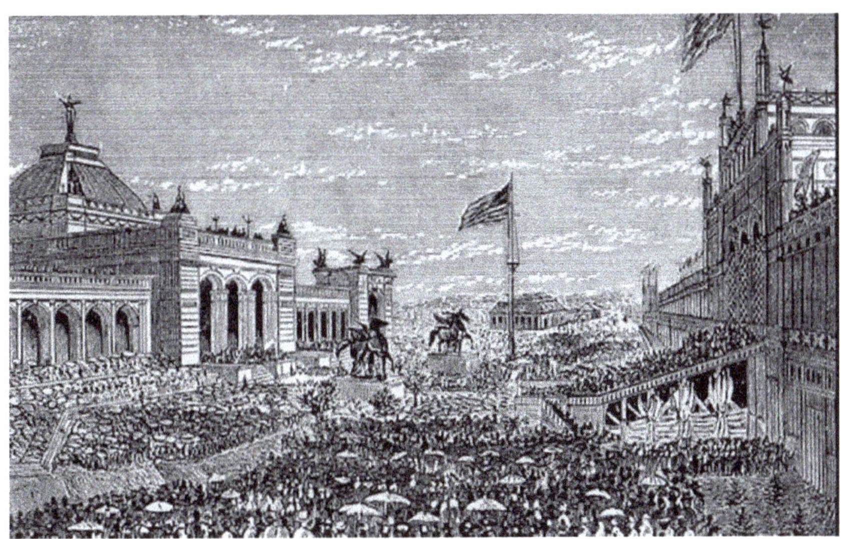

To commemorate the 100th anniversary of the signing of the Declaration of Independence, the United States presented a birthday party to the world. "The 1876 International Exhibition of the Arts, Manufactures, and Products of the Soil and Mine" showcased American industry and innovation; it promoted patriotism, promised entertainment, and produced the country's first modern tradeshow.

Viewed through the lens of the present, both the show and the location seem inevitable. It should have been a no-brainer. Only it wasn't: it wasn't inevitable; it wasn't unanimous; and it wasn't without controversy. New York, Boston, Cincinnati, Chicago, and St. Louis battled for three years for the privilege to host the exposition. At the same time, politicians, pundits, and members of the press voiced their concerns:

- They cried; it couldn't be done.

- They complained that it would be too costly.
- They claimed no one would attend (at least not from overseas).
- They carped that US products might be viewed as inferior goods when seen side-by-side with European ones.
- They campaigned for their city … and if it couldn't be held there, some didn't want it to be held at all.

Fortunately, the naysayers and critics were proved wrong, and the show was a stunning success. The Exposition attracted nearly ten million people at a time when Philadelphia's population was 817,000. From New Zealand to Norway, North and South America, England, Egypt, India, Istanbul, Australia, and Japan, businesses and fairgoers flocked to Philadelphia from across the globe. It was the highest-attended event of the nineteenth century (outside of Paris) until the 1893 "World's Columbian Exposition."

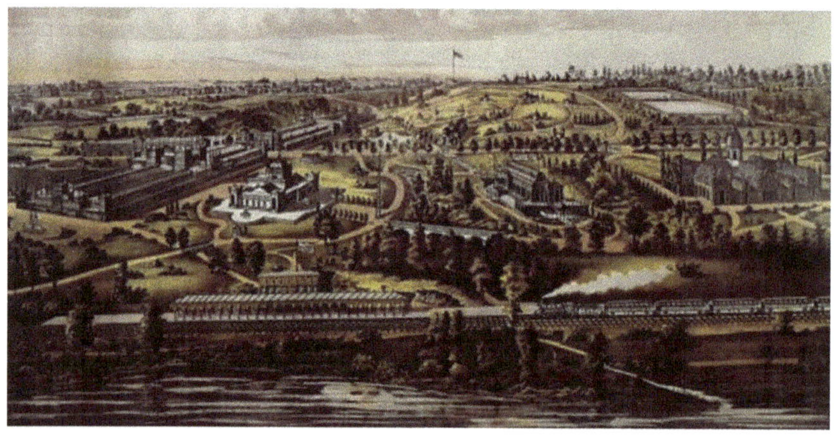

The Fairgrounds were huge. Sprawling across 285 acres in Fairmont Park, it was the largest expanse of land for a World's Fair at the time. Workers constructed a temporary town of over 200 buildings, including multiple halls dedicated to machinery, agriculture, horiculture, and art.

The centerpiece, the "Main Exhibition Building," enclosed a record-setting 21 acres under one roof. Separate structures were erected for each of the 35 countries exhibiting and for 26 of the then-37 individual United States. Over fourteen thousand businesses occupied almost two million square feet of exhibit space. The show was open from May to November, and visitors paid fifty cents for an experience of a lifetime.

New products. New ideas.

Wherever one looked, the Exposition displayed a series of firsts … from the monorail above … to the telephone and Lady Liberty's arm … to imported bananas and kudzu … there were new technologies, new food, new ideas, new products, and new sales.

Alexander Graham Bell displayed his recently patented invention. It went mostly unnoticed for forty-seven days, until a Brazilian monarch stopped by the booth and, after being handed a receiver, exclaimed, "My God, it talks!"

Edison exhibited his automatic telegraph and his electric pen. The battery-powered pen instantly created multiple copies and won a bronze medal. Edison sold over 60,000 pens in four years and discontinued them prior to inventing the "mimeograph.".

Remington revealed the first commercial typewriter and sold typed souvenir letters. Sholes and Glidden designed the typewriter in 1874, and a division of Remington's firearms company manufactured it.

Pratt and Whitney showcased tools for manufacturing machine-made fasteners and interchangeable parts.

The Waltham Watch Company demonstrated the first automatic screw-making machine, showcased machine-made watches, and won a gold medal. Swiss watchmakers displayed hand-made pieces and then returned to America in 1893 with machine-made ones.

The Wallace-Farmer Dynamo.

The Wallace-Farmer dynamo powered a system of arc lights at the Exposition and inspired Thomas Edison's work on incandescent illumination. Moses Farmer patented an early light bulb and is credited with lighting the first house with electricity. His inventions were used to light the Wannamaker department store in Philadelphia with the first Christmas lights.

Roebling and Sons exhibited a revolutionary 5¾ inch-thick cable (the same cable used in the construction of the Brooklyn Bridge, which opened in 1883).

Krupp unveiled the world's largest cannon, an 81-tonner.

The Grant Difference Engine, a pre-computer, foreshadowed the future. Elsewhere in the hall was a large travel bag that doubled as a portable bathtub (not every invention on display was successful).

Henry Heinz, Charles Hires, and Stephen Whitman offered new products (ketchup, root beer, and boxed chocolates); two others making future fortunes selling new food items were J. W. Tufts and I.

L. Baker (surprisingly popular and profitable were the sales of soda water and sugar popcorn).

Bananas were a tasty novelty that fairgoers enjoyed eating with a knife and fork.

Up in the air, moving between two buildings, a steam-powered locomotive transported sixty cushioned passengers in a lavish saloon car.

More Firsts.

Thanks to Elizabeth Duane Gillespie, the granddaughter of Benjamin Franklin and an early woman's rights advocate, the influence and accomplishments of women were recognized for the first time at a World's Fair. The Women's Pavilion displayed over 80 newly patented items, including interlocking bricks, a dishwasher, and a cold handle for a hot iron.

The first International Art Exhibition in the US opened at the Fair; a separate building presented photographs. The American Library Association originated at the show.

Singer, the largest manufacturer in the world, sold multiple models of sewing machines in the main hall, built a corporate pavilion, and sponsored the first corporate retreat. The company manufactured its two millionth machine at the end of 1875 and displayed it prominently on the exhibition floor. Their first machine was built in 1850.

Attracting Crowds and Selling Products.

A sample exhibit: Wilson Sewing Machines.

America was an expanding national marketplace, with shopping becoming an increasingly popular activity. The Exposition, the first successful B2C and B2B event in the United States, turned into a major consumer spectacle and was the first show where writing orders on the exhibit floor was commonplace. It was also the largest and heaviest show to date, with over fifty-seven million pounds of freight.

The Fair showcased everyday items: hand tools, furniture, wagons, stoves, fabric, textiles, clothing, and lanterns, as well as some less-common ones: Yale locks, Tiffany jewelry, Doulton pottery, Schumacher pianos, and suspenders with one's name custom woven into the fabric. Other items on display included sewing machines, pianos, printing presses, hydraulic and pneumatic power machines, trains, steam engines, dynamos, reapers, and windmills. DuPont displayed gunpowder, and arms manufacturers selling new items included Colt, Remington, Smith & Wesson, Gatling, and Krupp.

The organizers of the Exposition visited Vienna in 1873 to learn from that Fair's successes and failures. They wanted to increase attendance and create an enjoyable experience. For this show, the Philadelphia Committee added cars and improved railroad and trolley service. They built new hotels and offered both high-end and inexpensive restaurants. Gardens and fountains dotted the landscape, along with displays and dioramas showing life around the world. And on the outskirts of the

Fair, a shanty town evolved with beer parlors, sideshows, can-can dancers, and brothels.

Built specifically for the Exposition and stretching over three hundred feet into the air, the Sawyer Observatory was the tallest structure in the United States at the time. Visitors moved to the top via a round glass elevator that held up to thirty adults. It was the tallest exhibit, but not the most popular one. The two most popular and well-attended displays were Liberty's Torch and the Corless steam engine. Both were fifty feet high.

Lady Liberty's arm was the first piece of the Statue of Liberty to arrive on America's shore. For fifty cents, one could climb to the torch balcony and view the fair. The admission fee was designed to be a fundraiser for the base of the future statue.The 1400 horsepower Corliss steam engine—the largest in the world—powered the hundreds of other machines at the show: machines printing newspapers and wallpaper; machines spinning cotton and combing wool; and machines pumping water, sawing logs, and making shoes. These dynamic devices simultaneously showcased technology, entertained fairgoers, and generated sales orders.

Trade Shows Work: Hires Root Beer. 1876.

Before Dr Pepper (1885), before Coca-Cola (1886), before Pepsi-Cola (1893), there was Hires Root Beer, the first national "soft drink" in the United States. It was offered free of charge at the Philadelphia show in 1876, and the company began national distribution in 1884.

In the United States, during the mid- and late 1800's, sanitation was poor in big cities, and water literally stank. Alcohol was the beverage of choice, and per capita consumption in 1875 was four times what it is today (or at least what it was in the year 2000). It is no coincidence that four pharmacists, in different locations of the country, independently created non-alcoholic tonics intended to improve one's health.

Charles Hires came up with the idea of a popular, non-alcoholic drink while tasting "root tea" on his honeymoon in 1875. He was a pharmacist, but also an entrepreneur. He believed in temperance and wanted to create a drink with a long shelf life that both looked and tasted good. He researched making root tea less bitter by blending sixteen herbs, berries, and roots. He market-tested the drink among friends and was told the word "tea" would not appeal to men. He gave his beverage the look of beer and began selling packets of a powdery mix in grocery stores—without much success.

He knew he had to let people know his drink existed and that it tasted good!

He paid for a sponsorship and a space at the Centennial Exposition and began giving away free glasses of his special root beer. He continued selling it as a powdery concentrate (a 25-cent packet created five gallons) and then began producing a liquid extract and syrup for use in soda fountains. He started shipping kegs nationwide in 1884, incorporated in 1890, and by 1891 was selling over a million bottles of root beer annually. Soda fountains in the United States served over 65 million glasses of his root beer in 1909, a year when the population in the country was 90 million people.

Charles Hires believed in promoting his product, both at tradeshows and through advertising. One of his favorite sayings was, *"Doing business without advertising is like winking at a girl in the dark. YOU know what you are doing, but nobody else does."*

In 1960, the Hires family sold the company to Consolidated Foods. Over the ensuing decades, the brand moved to Crush, Proctor & Gamble, and then onto Cadbury Schweppes before production was stopped in the twenty-first century.

Trade Shows Work. Bell Telphone. 1876.

FIRST BELL TELEPHONES, PHOTOGRAPHED FROM THE ORIGINAL INSTRUMENTS IN THE PATENT OFFICE AT WASHINGTON

When the Philadelphia Centennial Exposition opened on May 10, 1876, Aleander Graham Bell was in Massachusetts, employed as a professor at Boston University. Two months earlier, on March 7, he received a patent for the telephone. In mid-May, after the Philadelphia show had already opened, Bell demonstrated his invention at the American Academy of the Arts in Boston. It was a success, and his future father-in-law convinced him to exhibit in Philadelphia. Bell had his day job and responsibilities and could not travel to the show at that time. He sent a modified version of his phone to display; it did not create a sensation and was initially passed over by the judges and the rest of the visitors at the show.

After classes concluded at the university, Bell traveled to Philadelphia. He was in his booth on June 25 when judges were reviewing the technology exhibits. They were running behind schedule and were only considering previously reviewed products. They were walking past Bell's booth when Emperor Don Pedro of Brazil paused. He recognized Professor Bell from a previous meeting in Boston and stopped to ask him why he was there. Don Pedro was handed a receiver; he listened and said," My God, it talks!"

Bell won the gold medal for technology, and his instrument became the talk of the show.

The Bell Telephone Company was founded the next year, and in 1878, the phone was displayed across the ocean, a continent away, at the Paris Exposition. The rest, as they say, is history: More shows. More awareness. More sales.

Bell Telephone became the world's largest corporation until it was broken apart by the U.S. Justice Department in 1984. At the time, it employed over one million people, with assets worth approximately $379 billion. Impressive growth for 108 years... and like the success of many other companies, it all started at a trade show.

Trade Shows Work. Singer Sewing Machine. 1876.

As mentioned previously, Issac Singer was a believer in the efficacy of trade shows. Studying Samuel Colt's production process (something he became aware of at the London Exhibition in 1851), he lowered costs by using interchangeable parts and mass-producing his machines. He increased business by exhibiting at shows and by instituting an original idea: sales on the installment plan. In 1876, his company rewarded thousands of employees with an all-expense-paid trip to America's first World's Fair. The Singer Pavilion housed food, lounges, comfort rooms, and some of the latest sewing machines. Most of the product and all of the sales took place on the floor of Machinery Hall.

Did the Centennial Exposition increase brand awareness and propel future sales for Singer? The answer seems to be yes: Singer produced 120,000 units in 1875 and 120,000 units again in 1876. Then, in 1877, the year after the Exposition, demand and orders increased, and Singer manufactured 630,000 machines.

The Fair's Legacy

The Centennial Exposition was a thought-provoking place to see and be seen. Current and future inventors included George Eastman, George Westinghouse, Moses Farmer, Thomas Edison, Alexander Graham Bell, and a young 16-year-old named Elmer Sperry (the "father of modern navigation technology" and inventor of gyroscopic compasses). The show boosted the cross-pollination of ideas and created an incubator for inspiration—over 10,000 US patents were issued in the first four years after the close of the show!

Looking back, what was the legacy of America's first modern trade show?

- It sold products, developed businesses, and created fortunes.
- It illuminated the dawn of a new American manufacturing age.
- It displayed the country's industrial power and future potential.
- It launched 27 major Expos in the US over the next 28 years (including the World's Fairs in Chicago, Buffalo, and St. Louis).
- It transformed the global image of the United States.

Philadelphia's Centennial Exposition brought people, money, ideas, and businesses together; like the Great Exhibition, it unfurled a blueprint for the future and proved exhibitions and tradeshows work.

Tradeshows focus brand awareness on a targeted audience. They make money for exhibitors, save time for attendees, and display extraordinary inventions that change the world.

CHAPTER FOUR

Electrifying the World

1876-1901

From Argentina to Australia, Barcelona to Buenos Aires, Calcutta to Cape Town, Madrid to Moscow, and from San Francisco to Vienna, Expositons Expanded Worldwide.

Forward-thinking leaders around the globe viewed the popular success of previous World's Fairs and wanted to share the experience and the wealth. During the last quarter of the nineteenth century, fairs and international expositions criss-crossed six continents, averaging more than seven events a year. Dozens of countries and tens of thousands of businesses exhibited in foreign locations because it made financial sense to do so. These dynamic shows attracted crowds, displayed technology, electrified audiences, and were a platform for inventors and businesses. These events increased spending in cities and boosted trade for countries. Thirty-six individuals Expositions attracted over a million attendees, including three in Australia, ten in the United States, and twenty-two in Europe. Three separate shows registered more than twenty-five million attendees and over 60,000 exhibiting businesses. Read that last sentence again, and consider the size and impact of those numbers: twenty-five million people and 60,000 businesses, all paying for the privilege to be at a show. Wow!

Paris Leads the Way

The French believed they invented industrial expositions and were irritated that the British dared to improve upon their concept. Between 1876 and 1901, Paris produced three of the five largest events of the century, culminating in 50 million attendees and 76,112 exhibitors in 1900.

Exposition Universelle de 1878. Paris.

The Palace of Industry.

"Bigger is more magnificant" exclaimed Gustave Eiffel.

His words became the theme of the Exposition, and it was here that Eiffel established his reputation. He had been involved with construction at the 1867 expo; here he was responsible for the design and construction of several structures, including the Palace of Industry and the Statue of Liberty's head. His reputation was enshrined at the 1889 Exposition with his signature landmark. Eiffel used iron extensively in both the exterior and interior design of his work, and the structures were intended to be permanent. Other structures at this Exposition were temporary and made of "staff," a low-cost building material consisting of jute fibers, plaster of Paris, and cement. "Staff" was invented in Paris in 1876 for the construction of these temporary buildings; it was later used extensively at many other Expositions.

After their last Expo in 1867, France exhibited at shows in Vienna and Philadelphia. City leaders, politicians, and show organizers wanted to observe and learn from those exhibitions, but most of all, they wanted to outdo their own 1867 event—they wanted to dazzle the world! And dazzle the world they did—with street lights, ice machines, elevators, hydraulic pumps, solar energy, an underground railroad, a "Street of Nations," and many popular new products on display.

The 1878 Expo attracted 12,623,847 attendees, with participation from 36 countries. The Fairgrounds covered sixty-six acres and spread across both sides of the Seine. It was larger and more impressive than the 1867 event, and it showcased several noticeable differences. First, instead of small family businesses, there were now larger corporate, national and international firms. Second, at the 1867 expo, the emphasis had been on steam engines and the arts; in 1878, the emphasis was on machines and products that could help people. Third, the engineering was majestic: four giant hydraulic pumps moved water through twenty-three miles of pipe, creating the energy necessary to muscle machines, move elevators, flow fountains, feed aquariums, cool buildings, and entertain crowds. Fourth, a sight here-to-fore unseen anywhere in the world, were the sixty-four electric arc lamps that lit parts of the Fair and a section of the Avenue de l'Opera in Paris. These "Yablochkov Candles" created a dazzling display far beyond what could be lit by conventional gas lights.

Displays. Attendees marveled to see Bell's telephone, Edison's phonograph, the typewriter, and rubber tires (which created smoother carriage rides). People stood in line at the telephone pavillion. The instrument was a major hit and vastly improved with new technology in the past two years. Edison displayed a phonograph and a megaphone used to help the deaf. It was hard to imagine their impact on audiences at the time, but the megaphone could increase sound up to fifty times and truly help the hard of hearing hear. When the phonograph debuted, many in the audience suspected a ventrilquist to be behind the sound emanating from Edison's machine.

Muchot's solar powered generator. 1878

Solar power was used to turn water into steam and power a refrigeration unit, which produced ice. The display won Augustin Muchot a gold medal. The Singer Sewing Machine Co. and the Wheeler and Wilson Sewing Machine Company had both exhibited in Paris in 1867; they returned in 1878 with more machines and won more medals. Another returning company, the Otis Brothers displayed an elevator and demonstrated their safety brake. Other American companies included: a watchmaking assembly line demonstrating mass production and the efficiency of interchangeable parts; and a cordwainer demonstrating semiautomatic boot making.

A precursor to the movies displayed at this Expo was the praxinoscope, an early animation device using mirrors to produce the illusion of motion. In 1882, it was used to project pictures onto a screen. This instrument possibly led to the invention of cinema by the Lumiere brothers and later improvements by Thomas Edison. For amusement, visitors could climb inside Liberty's head or ride in hot-air balloons.

Expositon Universelle de 1889. Paris

France wanted to celebrate the 100th anniversary of the French Revolution. Because of that decision, many European countries with monarchies refused to participate in the event. Still, the show was a success, with 35 countries participating and over 32 million people attending. The organizers wanted a memorable entrance, and

Gustave Eiffel won the competition for designing a landmark. The competition commenced in 1884, with more than one hundred designers, engineers, and architects submitting drawings. Eiffel was awarded the contract in 1886. (Some claimed he won because he allegedly had advance knowledge of the design specifications). Construction took two years, two months and five days. Prior to the show opening, many did not like the landmark. One writer called it "unnecessary and monstrous." There was talk about tearing it down after the show, but, of course, that did not happen.

All the previous Expos in Paris honored the arts, and this year was no different. But in addition to a building focusing on the arts, there were buildings devoted to exhibits on medicine, music, teaching and photography. Curiously enough, none of the Paris Expos from 1867–1900 displayed paintings by any of the impressionists (even though many of them started painting in the 1860's.). With each successful Exposition, there was more and more emphasis on technology, machinery, and products. A stunning, record-setting 61,722 businesses chose to spend money to exhibit at this show. (This record for the extraordinary number of businesses would be broken in Chicago in 1893 and again in Paris in 1900).

The "Gallery of Machines" was the biggest building at the Exposition. Another iron and glass structure, it covered 830,000 square feet of interior space with almost 375,000 square feet of glass. It was the single-longest interior space in the world at the time.

Different forms of electric lighting and displays dotted the fairgrounds, but the centerpiece—the newly constructed Eiffel Tower—was lit with gas lamps. Bell and Edison had their own pavilions. The Otis Company installed elevators carrying passengers up the legs of the Eiffel Tower. Prior to the show opening, Otis had to demonstrate once again the safety of their machines. Similar to what they had done previously at two earlier expositions in Paris, Otis prepared a demonstration for the disbelieving audience, this time a gang of journalists. Otis placed 6,600 pounds of lead inside an elevator—much heavier than any group of passengers—an d then, with some fanfare, proceeded to cut the cable. Once again, the safety brake kicked in and the elevator stopped safely, much to the amazement of some in the audience.

Expositon Univeselle de 1900. Paris.

The Palace of Electricity

This was the fifth fair in Paris since the London Exhibition in 1851. It was the largest event in Europe or America in the nineteenth century. It welcomed almost 51 million visitors from 58 countries and hosted 76,112 businesses (some sources state there were 83,047 businesses present). In terms of size of the footprint, it was the second largest in acreage (Chicago in 1893 was larger). That summer, Paris hosted the first Olympic Games of the modern era, outside of Greece. The games ran from May to October, while the Expositon started in mid-April and ended in mid-November. The Olympics helped boost attendance, but despite record numbers, the Expositon lost money, and Paris would not host another one until 1937.

The Palace of Optics

This fair was more focused on science and technology than the French ones in the past. Popular tech pavilions included the Palace of Electricity, the Palace of Optics, and the Palace of Illusions. Some of the popular attractions and products were: The French Ferris wheel (the Grande Roue); moving sidewalks; an electric trolley line; escalators; diesel engines; electric cars; electric fire engines; an audio recorder; dry cell batteries; an early version of talking films; the largest refracting telescope in the world (it enlarged the image of the moon to a magnification of 10,000 and projected it onto a 1,550-square-foot screen in an auditorium with 2,000 people); a giant kaleidescope attracted 3 million paid visitors; and even more people watched dancers performing in phophorescent costumes. Campbell's soup won a gold medal at the show, which is still displayed on their labels today. A hall of mirrors with electronic lighting created optical illusions, and the world's largest aquarium could be viewed from underground. An electric passenger train toured people around Lake Daumesnil, and the first passenger trolley bus line debuted at the fair. The International Electrical Congress met for a week in August.

A Million and More

During this time period, there were thirty-six separate expositions that attracted a million people or more. Some of the shows were bigger than others. Some emphasized the arts, others technology. Some opened on time, some were still under construction on opening day, and a few postponed their show opening date. Some made money; many did not, but they all brought revenue into their cities and furthered brand recognition. And they all attracted one million visitors, or more.

Excluding Paris, the top three events during this time period were in the United States: Philadelphia in 1876 with 9.9 million attendees, Chicago in 1893 with 27.5 million, and Buffalo in 1901 with 8 million visitors. But there were numerous other shows that broke the one million attendance mark. For example, Great Britain had ten separate expositions that attracted more than one million visitors between 1884 and 1890; the United States had six such shows between 1893 and 1901.

A million is a big number. But how big is a million people, really? Here are a few modern comparisons:

- The top ten college football stadiums in the US, if each sold out on the same day, would total less than a million (995,926).
- In 2023, the Dallas Cowboys led all NFL teams in attendance with a total of 1,378,743 for 17 home and away games.
- Rod Stewart had a free New Year's Eve concert in Rio in 1994, which attracted an estimated 4.2 million people.
- In 2023 and 2024, Taylor Swift will likely sell twelve million tickets.
- In 2022, Disney's Magic Kingdom attracted 17,133,000 people to lead all amusement parks worldwide.

But even these comparisons are misleading.

The world population today is six times larger than it was in 1880. That doesn't mean that attendance at nineteenth-century shows would have been six times larger, but it is likely that if the population were larger, then the individual numbers at most of those shows would have been greater.

Twenty-two of the events with a million or more people during this period occurred in Europe. But the largest event of the nineteenth century occurred across an ocean, a continent away. It was the largest in terms of size and the third largest in terms of attendance. It changed the image and perception of a country, and it moved the world quicker into the future.

The Fair That Changed America

Once upon a time, a magic city appeared on a lakeshore, rising out of a swamp. It was temporary and didn't last long. But for a brief flicker of time, millions of people from around the globe flocked to be there.

Part Mardi Gras, part Consumer Electronics Show, part Disney experience, it was the largest event of the nineteenth century. Impressive, exotic, and immense, it covered nearly 700 acres and showcased the world's newest technology. Newspaper reports from the day said it would take over three weeks and walking more than 150 miles in order to see everything. This fantasy land was so large that it was known by several different names: "The World's Columbian Exposition", "The White City" and as most know it today, "The 1893 Chicago World's Fair".

'CHICAGO 1893 -- THE FAIR THAT CHANGED AMERICA'

On May 1, 1893, President Grover Cleveland pressed a gold telegraph key, closing an electrical circuit. Slowly, generators buzzed. engines whirred... Spotlights swirled in the sky. Colors bathed cascading fountains. A hundred thousand incandescent lights flared. As the Exposition energized to life, crowds stared silently at first and then began cheering wildly.

Nothing like it had ever been seen before in the history of the world!

Building a Neo-Classical City.

Initially proposed during the mid-1880s to commemorate the 400th anniversary of Columbus' arrival in the "new world," the show opened six and a half months late. But that was understandable since decisions were delayed because New York City, Washington, DC, St. Louis, and Chicago all clamored to hold the event. Each location wanted to promote their region, generate revenue, and boost real estate values. Chicago eventually won Congressional consent because they had the space, they had the money, and they had the railroads. An all-star team of architects, led by Daniel Burnham and Frederick Law Olmstead, designed the space. Construction began late in the summer of 1891.

In eighteen months, 40,000 workers transformed the space and constructed 200 buildings. Materials included: 75,000,000 board feet of lumber; 64,000,000 pounds of iron and steel; 30,000 tons of staff (staff was a mixture of plaster, cement, and hemp). Because of the tight time constraints, the buildings were metal skins clothed with wood, covered with staff, and painted white. They were designed to be temporary, and inside, they looked like empty sheds. The exteriors were spectacular, and each main building was designed by a different prominent architect.

Six miles from downtown Chicago was the entrance to the Fair. There, sixty-one acres of recovered swampland morphed into lagoons, ponds, waterways, and islands. Surrounding "The Grand Basin" were the main exhibit halls; they totaled 3,780,318 square feet of space (over a million square feet larger than today's McCormick Place). "Manufacturing," with 1,327,669 square feet, was the largest building in the world. Beyond the White City, the fairgrounds included pavilions from forty-six countries and 34 states.

Attracting Attendees.

The organizers of the Fair wanted to outdo the Paris Exposition of 1889. They wanted to attract massive crowds and make their event memorable. Daniel Burnham, the Fair's director, challenged a group of American engineers to create a landmark that would *"out-Eiffel the Eiffel Tower."* George Washington Ferris accepted the challenge. He proposed a rotating wheel revolving high above the fairgrounds. A giant wheel, 250 feet tall, and "carrying a thousand, maybe two thousand people.".

The idea shocked the Fair's organizers. They had never heard of such a thing!

One board member called him "a crackpot".

Another laughed and said, "Ferris has wheels in his head."

Undeterred, Ferris spent $25,000 of his own money to have the blueprints reviewed. After safety certification and Board approval,

Ferris raised $400,000 from investors. Crews commenced construction on December 16, 1892, 135 days prior to the show opening.

It was winter in Chicago, and the ground was frozen solid. Workers heated the soil, drilled down, then lowered and exploded sticks of dynamite—all before driving wood and steel bars thirty-two feet deep. As they poured concrete over the rods to form pillars, they steadily steamed the cement to keep it from freezing. Each of the eight massive reinforced pillars measured

20'x20'x35'. These footings, covering three hundred and twenty square feet, rose three feet above the ground and formed a massive foundation.

This base was critical, but the key to the wheel was the axel. Constructed by Bethlehem Ironworks, the hollow-core axel was the largest piece of steel ever forged up to that time. At 45 feet long and 33 inches wide, it weighed 89,320 pounds. Two cast iron circles on either side of the axel added another 53,031 pounds.

The Fair opened on May 1, and the Wheel welcomed passengers on June 21. Scientific American published a cover drawing of the wheel in its July 1 issue; the magazine called it "a modern mechanical marvel".

A Parade of People.

In 1893, Chicago was the second-largest city in America, with a population of 1,099,850. In six months, the Fair attracted 27,500,000 visitors.

A partial list of dignitaries includes: Henry Adams; Jane Addams; Susan B. Anthony; Philip Armour; L Frank Baum; William Jennings Bryan; Buffalo Bill Cody; Alexander Graham Bell; Grover Cleveland; James J Corbett; Clarence Darrow; John Dewey; Elias Disney; Frederick Douglass; Theodore Dreiser; Anton Dvorak; Thomas Edison; Little Egypt; Archduke Franz Ferdinand; George Ferris; Marshall Field; Henry Ford; Carter Harrison; Milton Hershey; Harry Houdini; Scott Joplin; Helen Keller; Eadweard Muybridge; Annie Oakley; Ignacy Paderewski; Bertha Palmer; John Philip Sousa; Nikola Tesla; Louis Tiffany; Frederick

Jackson Turner; George Westinghouse; Woodrow Wilson; and Frank Lloyd Wright.

It was truly a place to see and be seen.

A World of Firsts.

The Exposition was a place to network, to display products, to conduct business, and to have fun. It showcased original items as well as some existing ones that became popular after the fair. Ten "firsts" in 1893 included:

- The First World's Fair building designed by a female architect.
- The first practical electric automobile.
- The first commercial movie theater.
- First automatic dishwasher.
- First electrical transit system in the US.
- First moving sidewalk.
- First indoor ice-skating rink.
- First-time event numbers exceeded 750,000 attendees in a single day.
- For the first time, a single company's tradeshow promotional giveaways topped 1,000,000 items.
- The most important first is the one most easily overlooked: it was the first demonstration to a national audience of the widespread potential of electricity.

Other items debuting at the Fair included: zippers; fluorescent lights; aerosol sprays; the first spray paint machine; Cream of Wheat; Wrigley's Juicy Fruit; Quaker Oats; Shredded Wheat; Aunt Jemima pancake mix; Cracker Jack; Vienna sausage; diet soda; the first US coin bearing the portrait of a woman; souvenir post cards; commemorative stamps; and squished pennies. Items at the fair existing before and becoming popular afterwards included: Pabst (which won the Blue Ribbon for beers); hamburgers; peanut butter; carbonated beverages; and brownies.

It is believed that the writings of "America the Beautiful" and "The Wizard of Oz" were both influenced by the Fair, as were the ideas behind Disneyland and Epcot Center. Milton Hershey was inspired by the fountains of flowing chocolate from Europe; after the Fair, he sold his Lancaster Caramel Company and started Hershey Chocolate.

The Midway.

The first dedicated amusement area at a world's fair, Chicago's Midway, was the moneymaker of the Exposition. Located "on the other side of the tracks" from the White City, it offered rides, food, entertainment, and a glimpse into other cultures. Attractions included: villages from around the world; Hagenbeck's zoo; an ice-skating rink; a tethered 1,500-foot hot-air balloon ride; a movie theater; an ice-railway and toboggan slide; the "World Congress of Beauty"; the "wild man of Borneo"; and a belly dancer named "Little Egypt".

The centerpiece of the show was George Ferris' original "Great Wheel". It stood 265 feet high and had 36 cars, each the size of a bus, measuring 27' x 13' x 9'. Fully loaded, the Wheel rotated 2,160 people up 25 stories into the sky for an unforgettable view of the city of Chicago. Ferris' Wheel grossed $25,343,916 (in 2024 dollars) and saved the Fair from bankruptcy.

Displays.

There were over 65,000 exhibits at the Exposition, displaying over a million individual pieces. Countries, and some companies, had their own pavilions. Edison spent over half a million dollars on his displays (equivalent to about $17 million today). Westinghouse, General Electric, Bell Telephone, Western Electric and HJ Heinz had multiple exhibit areas. Tiffany and Krupp had their own pavilions. There was an art museum housing over 10,000 pieces of art, an aquarium, and the world's largest selection of wine.

Not including the buildings, some of the largest items at the Fair included: the Ferris wheel (weighing 1,433 tons—without people!); Krupp's cannon (44' long, weighing 122 tons, with a record-setting firing range of 15 miles); the Yerkes telescope (61' long, weighing 75 tons); and an eleven-ton/22,000-pound wheel of Wisconsin cheese. Other unique items attracting crowds included: Edison's 150-foot light tower; a clock tower 120 feet high; 16,000 varieties of orchids; a tower of 14,000 oranges; diamonds, ostriches, and Egyptian cigarettes; and William Morrison's electric vehicle (which had speeds up to 20 mph and a range of 50 miles).

The Exposition's Legacy.

The 1893 Fair was one of the most impressive in history. It demonstrated the enormous power of expositions. And its influence impacted many areas of life:

- Architecturally, it triggered the "City Beautification" rebuilding movement in Chicago and spurred the Beaux Arts and Classical revival in other parts of the country.

- Culturally, it displayed lifestyles from around the globe; the Women's Pavilion recognized the achievements of women and sped the movement towards emancipation.
- Scientifically, there was a wealth of inventions and products; the World's Congress Auxiliary showcased experts and published nearly 6,000 articles.
- From a business standpoint, the Fair attracted the largest number of countries and exhibitors of any event in a century; it provided a space for international networking and for closing business deals. The Fair made a significant profit (despite the Panic of 1893 and the ensuing depression).
- It fostered international cooperation and promoted recognition of the United States as a potential world power.
- Most of all, the 1893 Chicago World's Fair sparked the electrification of America and propelled the country into the future.

The Columbian Exposition electrified the Chicago skyline, and powered America towards the future. The country, and trade shows, would never be the same again.

Are Expositons Trade Shows?

Some claim that Expositions and World's Fairs are not truly trade shows; they are spectacles, a once-in-a-lifetime event. And to a degree, it's true: historians tend to focus on the architectural and cultural aspects of these events. People traveled to these Fairs to learn about the world at large because they didn't have exposure to televisions or computers. But each major exposition in the nineteenth century had an active tradeshow floor, as was evidenced in shows in London, Paris, Philadelphia, and, in this case, Chicago.

The 1893 Chicago World's Fair had something for everyone – culture, architecture, education, excitement, entertainment, and jobs. At its core it was a trade show. It had displays, inventions, promotions, giveaways, contests, conferences, products, and networking. It had exhibitors. It had sales. It made a profit.

Businesses came to the 1893 Chicago World's Fair to show their inventions, display products, and most importantly, to sell items. They sold to consumers and businesses on the show floor and made contacts for future sales after the show. A partial sampling of familiar brands making a name for themselves at this show includes:

Quaker Oats	General Electric
Pabst Blue Ribbon	Westinghouse
Aunt Jemima	Heinz
Cream of Wheat	Tiffany
Shredded Wheat	Libbey Glass
Juicy Fruit	Graybar
Cracker Jack	Chase & Sanborne

But that's only part of the story. There were over 65,000 exhibitors in Chicago, with a total show footprint of nearly 30 million square feet. Eleven main buildings totaled 3.8 million square feet of exhibit space. These buildings were devoted to specific themes. Individually, they created a series of smaller, vertical trade shows within the Exposition.

The "Manufacturing" building housed 1,327,669 square feet of exhibit space on one level, with exhibit galleries above; it was the largest building in the world at the time. The main aisle was fifty feet wide, and throughout the building, one could view achievements in science, art, and industry. Exhibits from around the world included: shoes, clothing, textiles, glassware, jewelry, musical instruments, scientific instruments, medical supplies, medical devices, pharmaceuticals, bicycles, ceramics, metal work (including a massive wrought-iron gate from Germany that sold for $25,000 after the show), furniture, literature, research instruments, breads, beer, pens, chocolate, Egyptian cigarettes, Cuban cigars, and much, much more.

Machinery Hall, with almost a half million square feet of space, housed the giant Allis Corliss quadruple expansion steam engine. It weighed 135,900 pounds and powered the dynamos that electrified the show. Displays in the earsplitting hall included motors, pumps, hand tools, power tools, sewing machines, boilers, printers, and packaging machines. One machine boxed three tons of coffee into individual one-pound bags daily, and then those bags were sold onsite.

The Electricity Building, Chicago, 1893.

While not the largest building—only 314,550 square feet of exhibit space—the Electricity Building housed some of the most important, impressive, and future-centered products and inventions of the Fair:

alternating current; Edison's "Tower of Light", the first seismograph; a primitive motion-picture machine; search lights; incubators, stage lights, arc lamps, elevators, fire alarms, dynamos, switchboards, incandescent lights, generators, wires, phonographs, heaters, drills, batteries, fans, phones, and more motors. The Board of Judges awarded two hundred and twenty "Best Exhibit in Class" awards in this building to seventy-four domestic companies and thirty-seven foreign businesses.

Trade shows are business events that bring buyers and sellers together in one place at one time. Visitors attended the Exposition because it was the place to be, and they were "wowed" by what they saw.

Why did companies exhibit at the Exposition? Simple: it made money and sense to do so. Below are sixteen exhibiting companies from the summer of 1893, a small sampling of success stories from the show.

Trade Shows Work. Exhibits in Chicago, 1893.

Edison's "Tower of Light"; 18,000 bulbs.

General Electric. J. P. Morgan and Thomas Edison spent over a half million dollars ($17.3 million in 2024 dollars) to display their new company at the show. GE won 32 best-in-class awards, including one for Edison's Kinetoscope (an early motion picture film projector).

American Bell Telephone offered free long-distance calls to the east and hooked up phonographs to broadcast to distant concert halls.

Western Electric. One of two companies co-founded by Elisha Gray, it became a major manufacturer for American Bell. For one of their three pavilions, they built an electrified replica of an Egyptian temple from 1800 BC. They won eight "Best" awards.

Graybar. At the fair, Elisha Gray's "telautograph" transmitted handwriting over distances via a two-wire circuit; Gray called his transmission a "fac-simile."

H J Heinz. With multiple displays, Heinz was the largest commercial food exhibitor at the show. The company offered free samples, gave away watch-chain charms to select customers, and offered over a million green pickle pins to booth visitors—possibly the largest trade show give-away in history.

The Westinghouse Exhibit 1893,

Westinghouse. Nikola Tesla and George Westinghouse won the current wars, beating out Thomas Edison and selling electricity to the Fair. Alternating current lit the Exposition, producing ten times the power of the 1889 Paris Expo. Tesla enthralled visitors with the magic of lightning bolts, neon lights, and a magnetically spinning "copper egg." The company won 14 "Bests."

Venice Murano Glass, the original company, from Italy, provided glass-blowing demonstrations to attract crowds and then sold their product on the show floor.

Gulden's Mustard, from New York City, won a gold medal. They had won previous awards in New York in 1883 and would win a medal in Paris in 1900.

Remington displayed forty typewriters, each one designed for different languages, including one that was all numbers and numerical symbols.

The "Remington Typographic Machine," also known as the "Sholes & Glidden Typewriter," is shown in the photo.

Libbey Glass. Thousands of people paid ten cents each to watch glass-blowing demonstrations from this small Toledo, Ohio, company. The admission price could be applied towards purchases, which most people did. One hundred and twenty-five years later, Libbey Glass had revenue of $797.9 million.

Part of one of Tiffany's Pavilions.

Tiffany. Although already successful, Louis Comfort Tiffany further separated himself from his father's jewelry company when he started a new business in 1892. His Tiffany Pavilions displayed large glass screens and panels, as well as a selection of lamps.

U.S. Wind Energy and Pump Company exhibited outdoors, displaying windmills that powered Midwest farms.

Chase and Sanborne. Chase & Sanborn's "Seal Brand" coffee was the official coffee of the Columbian Exposition. A machine boxed three tons of Chase and Sanborne into individual one-pound bags daily. and then these bags were sold onsite.

The McCormick Exhibit, Chicago, 1893.

McCormick Harvesting Machine Company. The McCormick Reaper revolutionized farming by allowing more crops to be harvested in less time, and with fewer people. Cyrus McCormick founded his Chicago based company in 1847 and exhibited in London in 1851, where his reaper won several competitions and became a "must-see" invention. The company exhibited in New York in 1853, Paris in 1868, and Philadelphia in 1876. Sales increased from fewer than 500 before 1850, to 4,000 by 1856, and over 25,000 a year by the late seventies. After exhibiting in Chicago in 1893, they showcased their product in Paris in 1900. The company became International Harvester in 1902, and exhibited under that name in St Louis in 1904, San Francisco in 1915, and in later expositions. During the 1980's several divisions were sold, and others became part of Navistar International. **McCormick Place** is named after Cyrus' great nephew, Robert McCormick, owner and publisher of the Chicago Tribune, and a long-time advocate for a new Chicago convention center. Who would have ever imagined that the power of this brand would influence the world of trade shows!

Adams Express Company. One of the oldest companies listed on the New York Stock Exchange, it became Adams Funds decades after the show.

Garris-Cochrane Company. You may not know the company's name. But you probably know the name of the company it became.

At the fair, this company won the prize for "best mechanical construction, durability, and adaption to its line of work".

The invention? The first automatic dishwasher. The inventor? Josephine Cochrane, a Chicago socialite.

When her husband unexpectedly died, leaving her nothing but debt, she designed, patented, and produced a pressurized hot-water, compartmentalized dishwashing machine. She showcased it at the Fair, sold the appliance to nine restaurants, and took show-site orders for future business. In 1897, she opened a new factory and renamed the company "Cochran's Crescent Washing Machine Company". It was acquired by KitchenAid in 1926.

Trade Shows Work. H. J. Heinz.

At the time of his death in 1919, Henry John Heinz was worth the equivalent of $1.45 billion. His twenty-two-acre Northside Pittsburgh factory employed 4,600 people and produced millions of bottles of ketchup a year. Today, that company sells over 650 million bottles of ketchup annually, plus an additional eleven billion squeezable ketchup packets. To say he was a successful innovator, entrepreneur, visionary and businessman would be an understatement. But that was not always the case. In 1875, his company declared bankruptcy, and Henry Heinz was arrested for fraud. His road to riches is a fascinating one, but it depended on a couple detours and stops at Expositions along the way.

From Bankruptcy to Billions.

In 1869, at the age of twenty-five, he founded his second business, producing horseradish and other condiments in his father's basement. That company, "Anchor Pickle and Vinegar," soon became Heinz Noble. Heinz sold bottled horseradish sauce as a convenience food to hotels, restaurants, and grocers. They employed 150 people during peak harvest time and produced 500 barrels of sauerkraut, 15,000 barrels of pickles, and 50,000 barrels of vinegar. In 1873, Heinz took out loans to expand production, and he purchased farmlands. Then the financial Panic of 1873 hit. Food was suddenly dirt cheap, and his products weren't selling. Heinz, overextended, could not pay his creditors. Although the fraud charges were dropped, he lost everything, including his parents' house. But Henry John Heinz was a proud and ethical man; he was determined to make things right and pay all his creditors.

In the 1870s, the state of food was deplorable. There was no refrigeration. Food was stored in vermin-infested barrels. Meat was tainted and often smelled bad. Catsup was used to mask the smell and change the taste of meat, as well as other foods. Depending on where it was made, catsup might include soybeans, fermented fish, walnuts, celery, spices, and even sawdust as a thickener (not cellulose fibers, but actual sawdust).

Driven to restore his reputation, Heinz sold bottled pickles and started a test kitchen in his brother's house. He believed he could develop sauces that could sell—sauces that people living in cities did not have the time or the ingredients to make. He developed a new condiment, a red sauce. He first added salt, onion, and garlic to a tomato base; then he added distilled vinegar and brown sugar. The resulting combination was both sweet and sour, with a touch of tartness and a hint of acidity. He tested it on family and friends. Everyone seemed to like it a lot! He packaged it in clear glass bottles so people could see its purity (a radical idea at the time). Heinz realized he had a great new product... but he had to get people to notice it. He decided to go to the Centennial Exposition in Philadelphia. But first, he had to name his sauce. He chose "ketchup" to differentiate it from the existing "catsup". He knew his condiment was better-tasting and purer than anything else on the market.

Heinz began selling his bottled ketchup in stores and restaurants across Pennsylvania. He also marketed his pickles and horseradish sauce, then expanded his condiments to include apple butter, pepper sauce, and mincemeat. He believed he could mass-produce food products and then sell them nationally.

Heinz built a factory on the north side of Pittsburgh, adjacent to railroad lines. By 1892, the company was shipping over sixty different products nationwide. During a trip to New York that year, Heinz spied an elevator advertisement promoting "21 Styles" of shoes. He liked the phrase, thought it was catchy, and wanted to do something similar for his company. He chose his and his wife's two favorite numbers, a "5" and a "7", and created the now-famous logo tagline, "57 Varieties".

1893.

Heinz wanted to make a statement at the Chicago World's Fair. He contracted space for multiple exhibits and was the largest commercial food distributor at the show. Unfortunately, his exhibits were located on the second level of the Agricultural Building, an area that required people to climb almost one hundred steps. Not surprisingly, the number of visitors on the second floor was limited.

Heinz' solution for attracting people to his booth was simple: he would offer free gifts to anyone stopping by his exhibit. Today, we would say his solution was obvious, but in 1893, the idea was both original and brilliant. Heinz hired young boys to distribute a "promise card" that could be exchanged in

The Heinz Exhibit, Chicago, 1893.

his exhibit for a "free souvenir". Over the summer, Heinz gave away over one million items—possibly the largest promotional give-away in history—and in another brilliant move, Heinz tied his promotion to his product: the give-aways were small green pickle pins, embossed with the Heinz logo, and could be used as a bracelet charm or attached to a key chain.

His promotional campaign was so successful, attracting so many people, that there was structural damage to the second floor of the building. According to an article in the New York Times that fall, "the galley floor of the Agricultural Building has sagged where the pickle display of the HJ Heinz Company stood."

Prior to 1893, Heinz was already a national concern. The Columbian Exposition launched the company internationally, so of course they would exhibit at the next major international exposition, in Paris.

1900.

The company won two gold medals at the Paris Exposition of 1900: the first for product quality and the second for exemplary factory conditions. Henry Heinz accepted the awards in person. The following year, Heinz exhibited at the 1901 Pan-American Exposition, with an even larger booth space and display.

He went on to exhibit in St. Louis in 1904, with a central display in the Palace of Agriculture and ten smaller exhibits around the fairgrounds offering regional tastings. He proceeded to exhibit at smaller shows throughout the decade. At the 1915 Exposition in San Francisco, Heinz added a movie theater adjacent to his main exhibition building.

The Heinz Exhibit, Paris, 1900.

Heinz was an innovator. He was the first to power a full industrial plant with electricity. Like many others in 1893, he had been impressed with the electrical lights and displays in Chicago. But unlike others, he took action to electrify and light his manufacturing plant. He did it first: before Andrew Carnegie, before JP Morgan (who co-owned General Electric), and even before George Westinghouse or Thomas Edison. Heinz also developed "a continuous flow system" in his factory, utilizing an assembly line to enable workers to perform one simple task over and over again. Heinz' assembly line predated the automobile assembly lines of Ransom Olds and Henry Ford.

Unlike many of his contemporaries, Heinz had been concerned with food safety and purity all his adult life. He and his son were a force behind the passage of the Food and Drug Act of 1906 (the first significant Congressional consumer protection act). Heinz' factories were so clean, sanitary, and well-lit that he offered public tours, and over 20,000 people walked his factory floor annually. His factories had stained glass windows, electric ventilation systems, and were designed to be completely fire-resistant, with an electric fire-proofing system that closed doors and sounded alarms.

In February 2013, not quite one hundred years after the founder's death, Berkshire Hathaway, coupled with 3G Capital, purchased Heinz for $23 billion. Two years later, the company merged with Kraft Foods.

Electrifying the World

For over two hundred years, expositions and trade shows have showcased merchandise and promoted products, all designed to attract crowds and sell goods. Many of the innovations displayed at shows changed the world. Examples include the elevator, the telegraph, the telephone, the phonograph, the television, and the computer, as well as movies, munitions, medicines, and medical devices. But perhaps the biggest world-changing display was that of electricity. Electric lights illuminated new possibilities and forever changed the way people lived.

It didn't start out that way, and it didn't occur overnight or solely at expositions. The first electric coil was patented in 1851. In 1868, Moses Farmer lit a house in Boston, MA. The electric-lit Souter lighthouse first appeared on the English coast in 1871. The first public demonstration of outdoor electrical lighting in America was in Cleveland, Ohio, in April 1879. In March of the following year, using Charles Brush's dynamo and his electric light system, Wabash, Indiana, became "the first town in the world generally lighted by electricity". Thomas Edison opened the Pearl Street Power Station in New York City in 1882, brightening parts of Manhattan.

Electricity and lighting didn't start at expositions. But expositions did focus the product on the public. It may have started in Philadelphia in 1876 or in Paris in '78. Whatever the date or the location, once it started, it quickly intensified. Electricity appeared at more and more shows; then something extraordinary happened—there were expositions exclusive to electricity!

The first world's fairs showcased horizontal tradeshows—all types of businesses and industries exhibited on the show floor. Electrical expositions became the first "vertical" shows, where industries were limited to one type of trade. But prior to the first vertical show, there was an event in Berlin. It did not draw a million people, but it did showcase an inventor who electrified his city with excitement.

1879. Industrial Expositon Berlin.

This Exposition displayed technology with an amusement park feel. The world's first electric streetcar was built by Werner Von Siemens and debuted at the Berlin Industrial Exposition on May 31. It may look like a kiddie ride taken over by adults, but the concept was original and revolutionary. Over 86,000 people rode the train around the short, circular track, and the Siemens electric ride became the talk of Berlin.

At the time, inside cities, people traveled by foot, by horse, or by horse-drawn transportation. but all that was about to change. After unveiling the first electric streetcar, Siemens built the first electric tramway in 1881. He built the first electric locomotive. He proposed an elevated railway but had to abandon plans because landowners thought it would lower their property values. He continued pushing boundaries and developed a number of firsts: an electric tram, an electric trolley, an electric mine locomotive, and an underground electric railway. Others took notice of his inventions.

Banishing the Darkness

Before electricity could light up the night, its benefits had to be demonstrated to the public. The concept worked. An added advantage of these exclusively electrical exhibitons, was an exchange of ideas. Networking and chance encounters stimulated thought and new products. The International Electrical Congress and the American

Institute of Eletrical Engineers developed from these shows. But the main focus was showcasing electricity as the future and how light and lighting products could be utilized.

1881. International Expositon of Electricity. Paris

This was the first Exposition dedicated solely to electricity; it would not be the last. The show illuminated advances in technology since 1878. Several types of electric lighting with incandescent lamps were displayed. The lighting instruments of Swan, Lane-Fox, Maxim, Edison, and others were compared. Edison's high-resistance lamp design was declared the most efficient and won first prize. Exhibits at this show included: Gramme's dynamo (which powered Yablochkov's arc lamps); Bell's telephone; Siemen's tram; Touve's electric boat; plus distribution, lighting, and incandescent lamp displays by numerous inventors, including Deprez, Edison, Siemens, and Swan.

This Exposition was the co-located site for the first International Electrical Congress. Participants presented technical papers, agreed to specific definitions, and established international standards. The Congress would also meet for one week during the 1893 Chicago Fair, the 1900 Paris Exposition, and the 1904 St. Louis Fair.

1882. International Electrical Exhibiton. Munich.

This was the first major electrical engineering event in Germany. It was held in the 1854-built Glaspalast. Dynamos, electric lamps, models of hydroelectric power stations, and measuring instruments were prominent displays. For the first time, electricity was transmitted over great distances. Deprez conducted current for over 35 miles, though it only worked for a few hours. Schuckert transmitted power a few miles for the duration of the show.

1882. The Electrical Exhibition. London.

After the Exhibiton of 1851, the Ctyrstal Palace was dismantled and moved to Sydenham, an affluent section of London. Shows continued to exhibit at this venue until it was destroyed by fire in 1936. For this exhibit, visitors were dazzled by the lights and maybe even more by the possibilities.

One journalist at the time wrote: *"Few visitors can look around the huge hall without experiencing that electricity is the great force of the future... Apparently, there is no limit to its usage. It can drive a tram or a sewing machine; it can play a piano*

or fire a cannon. It can reproduce a far-off speaker's voice. It has brought electric lighting within the range of public and domestic use, and we should recommend all disbelievers in the future of lighting by electricity pay a visit to the Palace."

1883. The International Electrical Exposition. Vienna.

Vienna hosted the world's fair ten years previously. This event did not attract as many people, but it focused more on technology. The large roundabout was illuminated spectacularly with electric light, and an exterior tower was lit at night for non-fairgoers to see. One new invention displayed here was an electrical wind turbine.

1883. International Fisheries Exhibition. London.

While not a true "vertical" show, this exhibition featured widespread use of electric lighting and attracted higher-than-expected numbers, with 2.6 million people.

1885. Interntional Inventions Exhibiton. London.

This show drew 3.75 million visitors and attracted inventors from around the world. One new item was the Cardew voltmeter.

1891 International Electrotechnical Exhibition. Frankfurt.

The show demonstrated the "first long-distance transmission of high-power three-phase electric current."

It transmitted three-phase power over 100 miles, established best practices, and enabled three-phase to become commercially viable. An electrically powered waterfall was visible beyond the buildings.

1896. The Great Industrial Expositon of Berlin.

This show required so much electricity that it needed a dedicated power plant on the Fairgrounds. With a footprint of 9.7 million square feet, it was one of the three largest European events of the nineteenth century, in terms of size. The Expo attracted over 7 million visitors and hosted 3,780 exhbiting businesses.

An X-ray machine was on display and attracted curious crowds. The show highlighted German culture, food, and products. The faigrounds were dotted with multiple beer gardens, accessed by the many electric trams. Otto Lilenthal displayed his steam engines, gave a lecture on flight experiments, but was not allowed to demonstrate his air plane. Lilenthal died in a glider accident later that year.

The United States Lights the Way

Two of the five largest shows of the last quarter of the nineteenth century were in the US. More importantly, those two and others played a prominent role in both developing tradeshows and expanding electricity.

1876. The Centennial Exposition. Philadlephia.

Two years before Yablochkov's candles dazzled Paris, the Wallace-Farmer dynamo powered three arc lights in Philadelphia, shining so brightly as to inspire Thomas Edison.

1883. The Southern Expo. Louisville.

Louisville displayed the largest installation of incandescent light bulbs to date. With 4,600 bulbs in the exhibiton hall and another 400 lamps in the art gallery, it shined more light than all of New York City at the time. The event attracted 971,000 people in three months. This show continued showcasing electricity and attracting crowds for the next four years, with shows lasting 100 days each summer.

1884. The World Cotton Centennial. New Orleans.

The main hall was lit with ten times the amount of light in all of New Orleans—now that's an impressive demonstration. There were electric elevators in the observation hall and multiple experimental electric street cars to move people around the fairgrounds.

The first commercial electric street car was built in Cleveland in 1884. The first fully-functional electric trolley system was built in Richmond,

VA, by Frank Sprague. He was in Paris in 81, at the same time as Seimens and Edison, and at the Crystal Palace Expo in 1882, where he was a judge, awarding medals to exhibitors. Sprague invented the inverted type of dynamo in 1881. He began working for Edison in 1883. After he left Edison, he developed regenerative braking for use in trolleys and elevators. Expositions proved to be a great place for networking and the exchange of ideas.

1884. International Electrical Exposition. Philadelphia.

The first great electrical exhibiton in the United States hosted 196 businesses displaying 1,500 exhibits. It attracted over 300,000 visitors to the Franklin Institute in just 39 days.

Electricity powered trains, printing presses, sewing machines, and the first ever "search light." Edison displayed dynamos and showcased power distribution systems that could be used in the future for lighting houses, hospitals, hotels, and factories. Edison had exhibits with a lit floor, lit flowers, and a pyramid with 2,600 flickering, colored bulbs. The biggest attraction was a fountain ablaze with electric lights.

This show laid the foundation for what would become the American Institute of Electrical Engineers.

1893. The World's Columbian Expositon. Chicago.

Prior to 1893, the world relied on daylight, candles, oil lamps, and gas lights. The transition to a possible illuminated world seemingly

happened in an instant... Shortly after noon on May 1, 1893, President Grover Cleveland turned a switch and illuminated 100,000 incandescent lamps. Later in the day, as nightfall descended, the sight was unlike anything anyone had ever witnessed before, anywhere in the world. By Fair's end, over 27 million people would witness the miracle of electricity... and the world would never be the same again.

The first world's fair ever to be powered by electricity, it brought an end to the current wars and showcased the first commercial movie theater, the first moving walkway, the first Ferris Wheel, and the first practical electric automobile. The electricity building was the second largest of the 200 specially built buildings for the Fair, and included an electric kitchen with an automated dishwasher.

The Fair hosted the 1893 International Electrical Congress in August.

1894. The California Midwinter Intl Expositon. San Francisco.

The show opened in Golden Gate Park in late January and closed on July 5. After the Panic of 1893, it was planned specifically to energize the local economy. Financed entirely by donations, with no government funding, it made a profit of $344,320.

The Expo lit up the night sky, a sight previously unseen in the state.

1896. National Electrical Exposition. New York City.

The highlight of the show – and one of the major forgotten events of the decade -- was New York Governor Morton (at show site in New York City) turning on the power plant in Niagara Falls and sending electricity to select cities all over the country. Niagara Falls was the first major hydroelectric power plant in the world. Power generated at the Falls that day, was transmitted as far away as San Francisco, New Orleans, St. Paul, Augusta Maine, and oh yes, New York City. Simultaneous telegrams from those cities, sent immediately back to New York, proved the transmission had been successful. The electrical signal also fired cannons in four of the five cities.

This exhibition was housed in New York's Grand Central Palace Industrial Building, located at 43rd Street and Lexington Ave. The event was produced by the National Electric Light Association, whose first show was in 1885. The show occupied three floors of the Palace: the first two floors were for exhibits, and the top floor was for lectures and an electrical laboratory. The show required two weeks to install and prepare for its opening. On May 4, Commodore Perry Vedder spoke before an opening crowd of 7,000 people and proclaimed electricity *the mighty miracle of the nineteenth century.*

The show floor displayed new inventions and promoted the practical uses of electrical products. There were 163 booth spaces on the first floor and sixty-five on the second. In the middle of the hall was a model of the Niagara Falls Power Company. The Westinghouse Co. had a large exhibit in the back corner of the hall; it displayed Tesla's sound generators and his disconnected incandescent lights.

Edison had two companies exhibiting. The first, the Edison Electric Illuminating Company, displayed electric cooking, electric irons, radiators, bed warmers, lights, and other items, showing no unpleasant odor or risk of fire, as with gas. This exhibit space was 10' wide by 84' long and could be viewed from the second floor. It attracted the largest crowds because it demonstrated the practical use of electricity in everyday life. His second company, General Electric, displayed a room lit with "invisible" lighting. Edison was present on different days and drew crowds wherever he went. He also displayed his fluoroscope, with its x-ray magic.

1897. Tennessee Centennial and Intl Exposition. Nashville.

Located on the shores of Lake Watauga, the Exposition housed a hundred buildings and attracted 1.8 million visitors. Electricity was a theme, and President McKinley opened the Fair from the White House when he pressed a button and energized the machinery building.

McKinley visited the Fair in person and had better luck than he would in Buffalo. Designed to celebrate the 100th anniversary of statehood (1796), the Fair opened a year late, not an uncommon occurrence with Expositions. What was uncommon was that this Expo did not lose money.

1898. Trans Mississippi and International Exposition. Omaha.

Another dramatic skyline showcasing the magnificence and magic of electricity. This Exposition drew 2.6 million people, including President McKinley.

1899. The Electrical and Kindred Industry Exhibitiom. New York City.

On May 8, 1899, more than two years before the auto show motored into Madison Square Garden, the National Electric Light Association moved their exhibiton from the Palace to the Garden.

The NELA was a trade association that represented operators of power stations, electrical engineers, scientists, electrical supply companies, and some universities. Their first convention was in Chicago in 1885, with

ninety electrical enthusiasts in attendance. The second convention was in New York, the third in Baltimore, and the fourth in Philadelphia. The NELA promoted and helped expand the US electrical industry. The 1895 show sponsored a conference that produced the first edition of the US National Electrical Code. This 1899 event was their 22nd convention (some years had multiple shows). In 1904, the NELA had a membership of 588 members; by 1921, memberhip had increased to over 11,000. The association was dissolved in 1933.

A plan showing the exhibit spaces on the floor of Madison Square Garden.

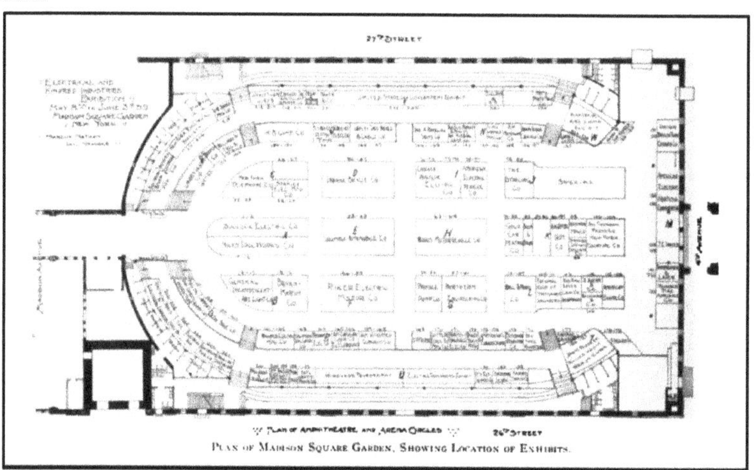

Tesla presented a paper at he 1893 NELA St Louis convention. He, Edison, Brush, and Westinghouse were honorary menbers and frequent exhibiors. At the 1899 show, Edison displayed a new alkaline battery, and showed a short "movie," one considered controversial and scandalous at the time.

1901. The Pan-American Eposition. Buffalo.

Of all the electric exposition skylines, Buffalo's was the most enchanting and impressive.

After the success of the 1893 Exposition and having finally won the current wars, Nikola Tesla and George Westinghouse built the first commercially viable hydroelectric power plant in 1895. Located at Niagara Falls, the plant's power was displayed at the Pan-American Exposition in Buffalo six years later.

Affordable, long-distance transmission of electricity was becoming a reality, thanks in large part to exhbitions and conventions.

Expositions and world fairs in the nineteenth century were the settings for mega-tradeshows, with each location building on the previous event. Each wanted to be bigger, better, and more excting.

CHAPTER FIVE

The Start of Trade Shows in the United States

The Expositions of the nineteenth century displayed technology and hosted businesses. They laid the ground work that developed the concept for the trade shows of the twentieth century.

The nineteenth century was a time of innovation and scientific advances. Expositions in Europe and America promoted original ideas, displayed amazing technologies, and exhibited manufactured goods. However, an invention alone—no matter how original the idea—was not sufficient for success. No, success necessitated promotion, awareness, interest, and, most importantly, sales. Many commonplace items of today became commonplace items because of their introduction at expositions and trade shows.

During the last two decades of the nineteenth century in the United States, there were electrical shows, bicycle shows, food shows, and regional industrial expositions. In 1884, Philadelphia's Franklin Institute hosted the first vertical electrical show in the country, with displays from 196 different businesses. The show attracted 285,000 people over thirty-nine days. During the second week of the show, the National Conference of Electricians held their first national convention, co-locating it with the much larger event. A year later, halfway across the country, the National Electrical Light Association held their inaugural event. Between 1885 and 1899, the NELA sponsored twenty-two separate conventions in various locations. The first five were held in Chicago, New York, Baltimore, Philadelphia and Boston. As interest and attendance increased, the problem soon became finding venues large enough to hold all the exhibitors that wanted to participate. NELA hosted events at New York's Grand Central Palace, and at Madsion Square Garden. Only companies associated with the electrical industry were allowed to participate – whether exhibiting or attending.

New York Bicycle Exhibition, 1890.

The earliest recorded bicycle show in America is the 1883 Bicycle Camp and Exposition in Springfield, Massachusetts (home of Frank and Charles Duryea, two bicycle mechanics who designed the first successful American gasoline automobile). The New York City Bicycle Exhibition started in the mid-eighties. It became an annual event and attracted more than 100,000 people in 1890. Huge crowds continued to attend the show every year, even after the recession hit in 1893. That same year, bicycle companies presented prominent exhibitions in the Transportation Building at the Chicago Exposition. Chicago, like New York, hosted annual bicycle shows, and the 1897 Bicycle Manufacturer's Exhibition, held at the Chicago Coliseum, was one of the largest trade shows in the country up to that time.

The First Auto Shows.

The New York Auto Show, November 1900. 160 different cars on display.

The popularity and crowds at bicycle show influenced the start of the first auto show in New York City, with cars first appearing at the New York Bicycle Exhibition in 1897. Encouraged by the reception, the New York Automobile Club of America hosted the first stand-alone car show in the country. It opened on November 3, 1900, inside Madson Square Garden, with 160 different cars on display. There were thirty-four companies displaying cars and thirty-five ones displaying ancillary products (once again proving the interest in trade shows for all types of businesses within a vertical market). Over a seven-day period, 48,000 people paid the fifty-cent admission to view these "horseless carriages." There were electric-powered cars, steam-powered cars, and gasoline-powered cars, with the latter having the fewest number of vehicles. At the time, there was one horse for every four people in the United States and one car for every 10,000 people. The NY Auto Show continued every year until 1942, when the war took precedence. At the end of 1941 -- after decades of car shows in multiple cities -- there was one car on the road for every four people living in the United States.

There were other auto shows around the turn of the century. The first Chicago Auto Show opened in March of 1901, five months after New York's opening. Detroit displayed "a few cars" at a sporting goods event in 1898. The first stand-alone Detroit show was held in 1907, the same year as the first LA auto show. In Europe, Paris had a show with four cars in 1894, and London had one with a half dozen vehicles in 1895. But the 1898 Exposition Internationale d'Automobiles (aka, the Paris Motor Show) is considered the first major automobile exposition in the world. The show moved to a larger venue in 1901 and changed its name to the "International Automobile, Cycle, and Sports Exhibition" in order to expand the display of products and attract more people. London hosted a large auto show at the Crystal Palace in 1903.

Paris Motor Show, 1908.

Later in the decade, the Paris Motor Show included other forms of transportation, including hot-air balloons and planes. That part of the show floated on its own in 1909 and attracted more than 100,000 visitors; it is now the largest air show, aviation, and aerospace exhibition in the world. In 2019, the Paris Air

Show had 2,453 exhibiting companies from 49 countries; the show spanned 1,350,000 net square feet of exhibit space and attracted 316,470 visitors. Orders written on-site at the show totaled more than $140,000,000,000. That's $140 billion, with a "B". From bicycles to cars, and from cars to airplanes, new technologies would exhibit at one event and then spin off into an event of their own. Trade shows work.

The Pan-American Exposition. Buffalo. May 1 to November 2, 1901.

The largest event at the start of the new century was in upstate New York.

Planning for the Pan-Am started with the energy and excitement of the 1893 Chicago World's Fair. The anticipation increased when Westinghouse began building generators for the proposed Niagara Falls power plant. Buffalo wanted the thrill, the brand recognition, and the revenues that a world-class exposition would bring. Believing that limiting participation would increase interest, the planners decided to welcome only businesses from the western hemisphere and called the event "The Pan-American Exposition.".

Buffalo was the eighth largest city in the country in 1900 (population 352,387), and over half of the country's populace was within a day's travel by rail. Thanks to the Niagara power plant, the town had streetlamps everywhere. Nicknamed "The City of Light," Buffalo was primed for a world-class international event: it had the space; it had the transportation; it had the desire; it had the money; it had the electrical power; and it would have the President of the United States.

The Exposition displayed the newest scientific, technological, and material accomplishments of the day. Nineteen countries attended. Thousands of companies exhibited, including many well-known names that had exhibited at previous expositions:

Baker's Chocolate.	Bell Telephone.	Westinghouse.
General Electric.	Western Union.	Heinz.
Otis Elevator.	Pabst Blue Ribbon.	Singer.
Shredded Wheat.	Western Electric.	

Other prominent and familiar companies exhibiting for the first time at a major exposition included:

International Paper.	Crane Brothers.	Doubleday.	Fisher.
Funk & Wagnalls.	Nickel Snake Oil.	Ingersoll.	NCR.
Kellogg Telephone.	Maxwell House.	US Playing Card.	Vaseline
Quaker Oats.	Statler Hotel.	Waterman.	Arrow.
Gillette.			

Washburn Crosby—while the name might be unfamiliar, it was one of the two companies that merged to become General Mills in 1928.

There were also businesses displaying incubators, acetylene products, and a lot more.

Buffalo wanted to outshine Chicago's Fair and planned their buildings to be brighter, more electrifying, and more colorful. Theirs would be "The Rainbow City" versus Chicago's "White City." To entice attendees, they occasionally offered free food, free drinks, and free souvenirs. Buffalo's Midway was an entertainment complex: it had concerts, foreign villages, the "House Upside Down," "Cleopatra's

Temple," and to rival Chicago's "Great Wheel," Buffalo designed its own "Aerio-Cycle," a giant 140-foot-long seesaw, elevating to 275 feet in the air, with two spinning cages, each carrying 72 passengers for a fantastic view of the fair.

Art, entertainment, electricity, exhibits, technology, transportation—Buffalo believed they had it all! The expectation was that the Pan-Am would be the best Exposition in the United States in the last fifty years.

"'The Pan' could not fail," it was said.

Death at the Exposition

William McKinley addressed an Exposition record-setting crowd of 116,000 people on September 5, 1901. The president spoke about trade reciprocity and ending American isolationism. It was said to be one of his finest speeches. He also gave one of the great summations on the efficacy of events:

"Expositions are the timekeepers of progress. They record the world's advancement. They stimulate the energy, enterprise, and intellect of the people and quicken human genius. They go into the home. They broaden and brighten the daily lives of people. They open mighty storehouses of information. Who can tell the new thoughts that have been awakened, the ambitions fired, and the high achievements that have been wrought through this exposition?"

The next day, on the morning of September 6, the President and his wife breakfasted and briefly visited the Exposition. Then, he, Pan-Am President John Milburn, and the Fair's Chief Medical Doctor, Roswell Park, traveled to tour Niagara Falls and the power plant. Park, the Chief Trauma Surgeon in Buffalo and a proponent of antiseptic practices,

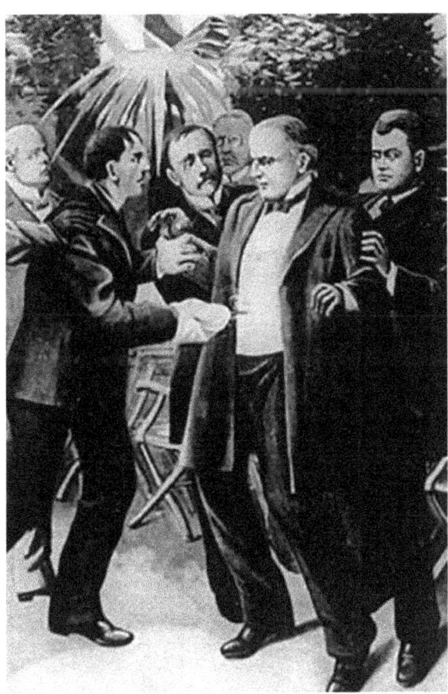

Artist rendering by T. Dart Walker

stayed behind in Niagara Falls for a scheduled surgery that afternoon. McKinley headed to the Temple of Music. Had Park stayed with the president, perhaps his life could have been saved.

September 6, 1901, was a hot day in Buffalo, and some people used handkerchiefs to wipe their sweaty brows. An assassin stood patiently in line. He wasn't sweating, but he did have a handkerchief in his hand; it concealed a handgun. At 4:07 p.m., two shots rang out in quick succession. One bullet deflected off a coat button and caused a superficial chest wound. The second bullet entered the president's stomach. The third shot was prevented by the heroic actions of James Parker, a tall waiter standing in line to meet the president. Parker punched the pistol out of the assassin's hand and tackled him to the floor—all before the 75-person security force reacted.

The ambulance arrived in six minutes. Instead of being rushed to Buffalo's General Hospital, the President was taken to the Emergency Hospital on the Fairgrounds. It was closer, but not as well equipped. As the best surgeon in the city was unavailable, Mathew Mann, a gynecologist, decided to do the surgery, even though he was not familiar with abdominal wounds. Despite the vast amount of electricity at the Fairgrounds, there were no electric lights in the emergency room. Dr. Mann operated with the waning sunlight reflected from a metal bedpan. Mann could not find the bullet; he removed some cloth from the wound, probed with his ungloved finger, then sewed up the patient without draining the wound. The operation was neither sterile nor sanitary. Ironically, one of the inventions displayed at the Exposition was an x-ray machine; it was not used at the time of the operation nor later.

While initially appearing to recover, McKinley was fifty-eight and overweight, and his wounds had not been cleaned properly. Gangrene set in and slowly poisoned his blood. He died a week later, at 2:25 a.m. on September 14. Teddy Roosevelt was sworn in as president shortly afterwards.

Some would say it wasn't the bullet that killed McKinley; rather, it was the lack of proper medical attention. Others say the single bullet not only killed the president but also killed Buffalo as well.

With McKinley's death, the bright lights of the fair began to fade. At Expositions in the past, attendance increased dramatically during the last two months of operation. But at the Pan-Am, daily attendance peaked on September 5. Initially, fair-goers visited the emergency hospital as a sort of macabre tourist attraction, but overall attendance quickly faltered. By mid-October, it was clear the fair had severe financial problems: expenses exceeded revenues by more than a 2:1 margin. Total attendance was recorded as 8,120,048, but the total paid attendance would prove to be only 5,306,859—well below the initial projections of ten to twenty million. The Exposition closed in the afternoon of November 2. By early spring, the Fairgrounds were being demolished. Bankruptcy was avoided when Congress provided a partial bailout, but while some mortgage holders received money, contractors lost over a million dollars in money owed to them. Some city leaders moved away almost immediately after the fair; others stayed but invested their fortunes elsewhere. John Milburn, the President of the Fair and in whose house, McKinley died, moved to New York City in 1904.

In 2022, the population of Buffalo was 276,807—a decrease of 75,000 people from 1900—and the city's rank nationwide dropped seventy spots to the 78th largest city in the country.

After the Pan Am.

The bullet that killed McKinley and damaged Bufalo's reputation did not kill international expositions, but the world's fairs did begin changing around this time. While the number of countries attending an exposition would increase, the number of businesses exhibiting at those events dramatically decreased. For example, the 1900 Paris Exposition had 40 countries with pavilions and 76,112 businesses exhibiting; Expo 2015 in Milan had 145 countries and 21 businesses; Expo 2020 in Dubai (which opened in 2022 due to the pandemic) had 192 countries with pavilions and fourteen exhibiting businesses with pavilions.

During the first forty years after the Pan-Am, there were four major international expositions in the United States, occurring in St. Louis, San Francisco, Chicago, and New York.

1904. St Louis. The Louisiana Purchase Exposition" hosted 60 countries, with almost 20 million visitors attending. Like Paris in 1900,

the Exposition was co-located with the Olympics, which helped to draw additional crowds. Electric light displays were still an attraction, and the Exposition buildings at night out lit those of previous expos in Buffalo and Chicago. The Fair featured electric street cars, a wireless telephone, a fax machine, incubators, x-ray machines, windmills, and Chicago's original Ferris Wheel. It displayed yachts and 140 models of cars, hosted an "Airship Contest," and showcased companies wanting to exhibit their products.

The exhibits were immense and impressive; many were two-story structures. Exhibiting companies included: National Cash Register; Singer; Universal Typewriter; Gillette; Bethlehem Steel; ATT; General Electric; Puffed Rice: Jello; Webster Dictionary; Ralston Purina; Baker Chocolate. Automobile companies were Studebaker, Ford, Olds, and Rambler. Edison had multiple exhibits; Westinghouse used motion pictures to attract visitors. Heinz had a huge central display in the "Palace of Agriculture" plus ten smaller exhibits in individual state pavilions, each offering a sample catering to regional preferences.

ATT and General Electric combined forces and introduced a wireless "radiophone". Harvey Hubbell showcased his pull-chain electric light socket, and introduced his patented electrical power plug and receptacle.

1915. San Francisco.

"The Panama-Pacific International Exposition" hosted twenty-four countries and attracted almost nineteen million visitors, even though a war was raging in Europe. The show celebrated the building of the Panama Canal and the rebuilding of San Francisco after the devastating 1906 earthquake. It showcased, "aero-planes," cars, and the original Liberty Bell; it demonstrated long-distance phone calls, held auto races, and displayed myriad products.

Exhibiting companies included: International Harvester; Waltham Watch; Hearst (demonstrating the largest color printing press in the world); Sperry Flour (with international chefs cooking and offering free tastings); US Steel; Union Oil (which became Unocal 76 and was acquired by

Chevron in 2005); Columbia Graphophone Co. (which became EMI and Columbia Records); and of course, Heinz, GE, and Westinghouse. Henry Ford constructed a working factory, where Exposition attendees could watch a single car being assembled every ten minutes – eighteen Fords in three hours every day, Monday through Saturday.

1933. Chicago.

In one hundred years, Chicago grew from a small wilderness settlement on the western frontier, to the fourth largest city in the world. Designed to celebrate that growth, the Fair also gave the depression-era city an economic boost with twenty-one thousand new jobs, and an influx of millions of tourists.

"A Century of Progress International Exposition" was the first exposition in the United States to receive the official designation of "World's Fair" from the new Bureau of International Expositions. Forty-eight million people attended this event, despite the great depression. In addition to showing "Dream Cars," a well-attended highlight of the Fair was the "Homes of Tomorrow Exhibition," which provided a future look at construction and appliances. Some companies exhibiting at the Fair included: GE; Westinghouse; ATT; RCA; Firestone; A&P; Sinclair; and Heinz. IBM displayed over seven hundred products. Goodyear offered "airship" rides for a fee. General Motors had a fully functional Chevrolet assembly line – with cars being paraded onto the Fairgrounds at the end of each day. Chrysler sponsored the "Hell Divers" with stunt crashes and rollovers – all designed to show the durability of Chrysler vehicles.

Originally intended as a one-year event, the Fair was extended through October of 1934. The Exposition lost money in the first year but made a total profit of $160,000 by the end of year two. Ford Motor Company did   not have a presence that first year, but after seeing the attendance at the General Motors Pavilion, Henry Ford spent $2.5 million on exhibits, and employed over 800 people.

1939-1940. New York. "The New York World's Fair" focused on the future, taking a look at "the world of tomorrow." Held from April 30, 1939, to October 27, 1940, it attracted forty-four million people,

despite a war breaking out in Europe on September 1, 1939. RCA introduced the television at this show and promoted sales of the sets in various stores in New York City. DuPont introduced "Nylon" at this show, and Westinghouse debuted the Nimatron, "the first fully-constructed computer game." Carrier built a seventy-foot high, igloo-shaped pavilion and invited guests to experience air conditioning in the summer, and central heating in the winter. Borden's promoted a "Dairy Farm of the Future, with an electric rotating carousel for milking cows. The General Motors' "Futurama" exhibit looked twenty years into the future, and correctly predicted the interstate highway system. Costs prevented many small businesses from participating in the Fair, but major corporations built impressive pavilions promoting their brands. In addition to the ones noted above, a partial list includes: Ford, Chrysler, Kodak, NCR, Nabisco, Kraft, Coca-Cola, Wonder Bread, Beech Nut, Carrier, Elgin, Swift, Schlitz, Schaffer, and Lucky Strike.The first world science fiction convention was held in conjunction with the Fair.

From Fairs to Emerging Trade Shows

As the number of companies choosing to exhibit at the world's fairs decreased, the number of conventions in the United States increased. In 2019, according to an EIC/Oxford Economics study, 270 million people and 1.7 million exhibiting companies participated in approximately 10,000 business events in the US.

The big business news over these decades was the emergence of business-to-business and business-to-consumer events. Listed below are some prominent twenty-first century trade shows that first opened between 1900 and the start of World War Two. This is a list of large, national shows that have thrived for the past 100 years or so. (It does not include smaller shows like the Boston Food Fair in 1908 or The Candy Show in Philadelphia in 1910—industries that would launch their own vertical tradeshows.) The specific show statistics listed below are from 2019, unless otherwise specified.

These are some of the largest trade shows in the United States, in terms of net square feet of exhibit space. And each show had over 1,000 exhibiting companies and tens of thousands of attendees. Some shows had over 100,000 attendees; others had 2,000; even as many as 4,000 companies paying for the privilege to exhibit their products. These numbers are remarkable, but what is even more impressive is the staying power of these events—most being around for more than one hundred years!

1900. The International New York Auto Show. While official numbers are not publicly reported, it has been estimated that, in some years, these shows have drawn close to a million visitors. The 2019 New York Show covered 950,000 square feet of exhibit space. There were dozens of brands, hundreds of cars, test tracks, and specialty exhibits.

1901. NAMM. The National Association of Music Merchants. In 2019, it was the nineteenth-largest trade show in the country (in terms of net square feet). It hosted 1,917 exhibitors, 115,303 attendees, and covered 616,065 net square feet of exhibit space.

1902. The Toy Fair. It was the thirty-third largest show in 2019 and attracted 1,039 exhibiting businesses.

1903. PPAI (Promotional Products). In its first year in Cincinnati, it was called the National Association of Advertising Novelty Manufacturers and hosted twelve companies. The second show was in Chicago in 1904. It was the 59th largest convention in 2019 and attracted 1,236 exhibiting companies.

ConExpo. The Road Show. 1926. Chicago.

1909. ConExpo. Their first meeting, called "The Road Show," was in Columbus, Ohio, in 1909. The photo is from the 1926 "Road Show," held in the Chicago Coliseum. It became CONEXPO-CON/AGG and was the largest B2B event in the United States in 2023. The show hosted about 2,400 exhibitors from 36 countries, covering nearly 3 million square feet of space. It also set a show-best record of 139,000 attendees. The show is a triennial event; there was no show in 2019, and the 2020 show was cancelled due to COVID.

1918. IAAPA (Amusement Parks). Twenty-third largest, with 1,144 exhibitors.

1919. National Restaurant Show. The sixteenth largest show of 2019 had 42,544 attendees, 2,364 exhibitors, and over 725,000 net square feet.

1923. NAB. National Association of Broadcasters. Originally the

NAB, 2007.

"National Association of Radio Broadcasters," it became the "National Association of Television and Radio Broadcasters" before finalizing the name "National Association of Broadcasters" in 1958. It was the eighth largest show in 2019 with 40,111 attendees, 1,632 exhibitors, and 924,876 net square feet of exhibit space.

1933. MAGIC. Men's Apparel Guild in California. It is so popular today that it is held twice a year. In 2019, the August show welcomed 76,819 attendees and 4,697 exhibitors; it was the 13th largest show of 2019 in terms of net square feet.

1939. Housewares. 34,500 attendees and 2,203 exhibitors. Eleventh largest B2B show in 2019.

After World War II, there was an increase in economic activity, coupled with the ease and availability of travel due to advances in interstate highways and commercial aviation. Trade shows became more popular, expanded into more industry sectors, and increased in size, with some shows exceeding a million square feet of exhibit space. ("Net square feet of exhibit space" is the total leased booth space in the exhibit hall; it is approximately half of the total, or gross space in the exhibit hall). To put this size into perspective, the largest trade show of 2019 was the size of fifty football fields.

As trade shows increased in number and size, it was necessary to find ways to produce them, set them, and service the attendees and exhibitors. How did this happen?

The Early Years of Trade Show Labor

Prior to World War I, excluding the world's fairs, exhibits were found at farm shows, state fairs, museums, in department store windows, and in some hotels and other venues as trade shows became more prevalent. Installation labor was provided by the show organizers, the contractors constructing the convention halls, the venues, or sometimes by the companies building the exhibits—cabinet makers, window dressers, decorators, sign makers, flag makers, and sometimes retail display builders.

Hotels held small events in meeting rooms and banquet halls. Larger arenas, like Madison Square Garden and the Chicago Coliseum, primarily hosted sporting, entertainment, and political events, although they did hold bicycle and automobile shows. Large, single-purpose trade show centers weren't built until the late fifties: LVCC opened in 1959 and McCormick Place in 1960. These centers spurred the growth of larger in-person events, which led to more centers being built in more cities. But the "origin" stories start both before and after that time.

The Early General Contractors.

1898. Brede. Possibly the first General Service Contractor in the country, Brede started in Minnesota in 1898. The founder's son, Bill, opened a rental furniture business in the 20s and is credited with inventing "pipe and drape" on the show floor. Brede purchased Exhibit Aids in the '70's, partnered with Allied Convention Services in the 80's, and was acquired by The Expo Group in 2020.

1901. Hale. George Hale had a floral business in Buffalo in 1901 and provided decorating services at the Pan-American Exposition. The exposure there led to a request for services in other cities in the East and Midwest. After World War II, Hale moved from decorating to events and onto general contracting.

1905. Shepard. Shepard Decorating was started by Virgle Shepard in Atlanta in 1905. Their initial projects included parade floats, Christmas decorations, and department store window displays. In 1939, Shepard created the Gone with the Wind premiere celebration. During the sixties, they became the first US contractor to manage conventions in China, and in 1976, they produced the first trade show at the Georgia World Congress Center. Originally a family-run business, Sherman Wade and Carl Mitchell took the reins in 1982; the company became an ESOP in 2012. Today, Shepard produces shows nationwide, with warehouses and offices spread across the country. Carl Mitchell is the Executive Chairman.

1909. Fern. "George E. Fern Decorator" was first listed in the Cincinnati Business Directory in 1909, but an earlier decorating company under his father's name dates to 1901. Fern produced the Ohio Valley Exposition in 1910 and is credited with the first use of a standard rental booth. In the teens and twenties, Fern produced the Cincinnati Auto Shows and the annual Ohio Food Show. In 1919, they provided show-floor electrical services, and in 1927, at the Home Beautiful Exposition, they built the first indoor two-story structure. During the 20s and 30s, they produced shows in all regions of the country. In 1962, they were purchased by Budig Trucking and then sold in 1985 to focus strictly on events. Freeman purchased Fern in 2011, then the employees re-acquired it one year later. In July 2023, Fern was acquired by MSouth Equity Partners.

1927. Freeman. "Buck" Freeman started his career in college, planning fraternity parties and parades. He founded the "New Idea Service Company" in Iowa City and then established Freman Decorating in Des Moines in 1927. World War II necessitated changes, and in 1950, he opened the Dallas office. The company purchased Sullivan Transfer in the early sixties, and by 1963 it was making a million dollars in revenue (equivalent to over ten million dollars today). Don Freeman Jr. became president in 1972, expanded the company regionally, and then acquired six east coast GES offices in 1981. Acquisitions of Fern, Champion, and Immersa Marketing came in 2011. Over the decades, Freeman has evolved from a local decorating company to a national general contractor to a worldwide live event agency. The company has 30 domestic locations, and according to Forbes, it employs 39,000 people.

1939. GES. GES' roots stem from Manncraft, a business that started as a sign and window company in Kansas City in 1939. They began selling exhibits in the Southeast in the 50s. Greyhound Corporation purchased them in 1969 and changed the name to Greyhound Exposition Services. When GES sold off offices in 1981, Freeman focused on the eastern US, and GES produced shows in the west. In 1993, GES purchased United Expo and Andrews Bartlett (including their labor division, ECC) and then expanded back east. Headquartered in Las Vegas, GES owns ExhibitGroup/Giltspur, is part of Viad, and is second only to Freeman in terms of revenue and numbers of employees.

1946. Hargrove. Before commercial television and the advent of online advertising, Earl Hargrove created animated department store window displays for his father's business, Hargrove Display Decorators. The company provided patriotic flags and banners and holiday-themed props of all types, including parade floats. Located ten miles from DC, Hargrove participated in their first of many inaugural parades in 1949 and became the general contractor for all official inaugural events during the Clinton era. They started a sixty-plus-year run installing and trimming the National Christmas Tree in 1955. Earl created a division, Hargrove Convention Services, to provide decorating equipment to hotels. He purchased Shenandoah Caverns in Virgina (the largest such site on the east coast) in 1966 and built attractions and displays. Over the years, in addition to the inaugural events they are famous for, Hargrove has produced the DC Auto Show and myriad Miss America pageants. Today, Hargrove services trade shows and events, builds exhibits, and designs environments.

Post war expansion.

There were some early display houses before World War II: for example, George P. Johnson in 1914, Ohio Displays in 1919, Taylor in 1933, and Jack Morton in 1939. But things would change dramatically after the war ended. Businesses retooled from military to commercial production. Consumer spending ignited the economy and propelled a marketing boom. Brands became more prevalent. Trade shows sprang up in hotels. At this time, show floor labor was typically supplied by the general contractor, supported by local unions. Display houses and newer convention centers began populating the country. With the expansion and growth of trade shows, exhibitors wanted greater choices in their exhibit design, site locations, and show floor labor.

Trade shows in the United States in the latter half of the twentieth century increased in complexity and size, propelling economic growth and creating new opportunities for businesses.

CHAPTER SIX
The Regional Evolution of Exhibit Builders and Convention Centers in America

In 1974, Fredrich Hayek won the Noble Prize in Economics. He was one of the few economists who predicted the market crash in 1929. He later was recognized for seeing the concept of trade shows as a valuable way to grow the US economy.

"The real role of a trade show? The sharing and coordination of knowledge and information without anyone being in charge. Industry marketplaces process more information than could possibly be mastered by a mastermind working with a computer. They demonstrate how decentralized, unorganized individuals and individual decision-makers who collect seeds of thought can outperform a central planner. The magic of trade shows is what unfolds thereafter.

…...Friedrich Hayek: The Use of Knowledge in Society, 1945

Post-World Fairs, industry trade fairs really began to grow in the early 1900's. In these early days, show contractor companies helped to organize/manage parades and events. They then expanded to manage and organize the trade show floor for industry conferences. Industry associations would contract a conference space from a hotel or an events building, usually in a major city. For industry trade shows, the association would hire a show contractor to organize and manage the exhibit hall portion of the event. The show contractor then offered the organizer a basic exhibit package for each exhibitor. The basic exhibit space included a draped backwall, an ID sign, floor tiles, a draped table, and chairs. In time, the exhibitors wanted to display their company with a little more flair to create a stronger image. The basic exhibit package offered was not enough. Exhibitors wanted a better image, so this is when exhibit companies came to be formed throughout the nation, city by city. Other exhibit specialty service companies followed shortly thereafter for graphics, furniture, flooring, floral, portables, exhibit systems, shipping, and I&D.

There is no ranking order for the city locations listed below who began to provide exhibit design/build services. They each evolved in similar fashions, filling a void that show contractors did not adequately provide the exhibitors at the time. The concept of industry conferences with a trade show component began to unfold in each major city.

The shows started as regional and expanded to be national with modern highways, air, and train travel to business city locations. New York, Chicago, and Los Angeles led the way as economic hubs and conducted national trade shows. During this time, there were also many regional shows that were a driving distance away to attract industry attendees within 200 miles. The ease and availability of air travel, taxis, and hotels changed all that in time.

Each of the regional convention centers, show contractors, and the exhibit houses evolved in a similar manner. The exhibitors from different industries believed in the power of face-to-face sales and preferred to coordinate their displays with an exhibit house in their area to customize their image. Outlined below are how the convention centers and the exhibit houses unfolded in each region to meet the needs of the exhibitors.

> Note: Although the industry as a whole is huge, the companies that provide design and production services for exhibitors are generally not big companies. The size of the average exhibit house in 2017 was $7 million, per the EDPA Economic Survey. Many are smaller, and quite a few are much larger. Overall, the typical exhibit house is a boutique business, with the employees of these small companies developing a passion for what they do. On the flip side, the convention centers built in each city were billion-dollar investments funded by the cities and by no means an emotional decision to make. If you build it, they will come, but it does not always work.

New York City

Of all the cities in America, New York City and Chicago led the way to accommodate the concept of trade show exhibiting as an effective means to introduce new products and attract new sales. Door-to-door **traveling salesmen** were popular in the early 1900's, but it was an extremely time-consuming job to travel and knock on doors for sales. As industries created associations, they arranged conventions to bring people and companies from their industry together to introduce new ideas and sell their products at a four-day event in a single location. Much more efficient than selling door-to-door. Trade shows caught on quickly in the big cities with ease of transportation, hotels, and a large enclosed convention space in a desirable location to attract industry attendees.

Many events started in hotels, but with the growth of shows, they proved to be too small. New York City played a big role in encouraging and conducting industry trade show events when it built the **Grand Central Palace**. The original structure was a six-story structure built in 1893 between 43rd and 44th Streets. It was demolished during the construction of the Grand Central Terminal, and a new 13-story structure was constructed. The Palace served as New York's main exposition hall from 1911 until 1953. One of its largest events was the **NY Auto Show.** The building was demolished in 1964. Throughout its

history, the Grand Central Palace has hosted auto, boat, flower, and many other trade shows. During its later years, New York City lost opportunities to host several large expositions due to the inadequate facilities at the Palace, the city's only convention center.

The city of New York was very responsive to merchants who saw value in conducting business transactions at trade shows and raised $26 million to build a new convention center. Money was raised by the Bridge and Tunnel Authority from toll revenues. The **New York Coliseum** opened in 1956. It was promoted as the largest exhibit space in the world. The exhibition space did not contain any windows; its exterior was instead sheathed in plain white stone. The space had three separate entrances and could host up to six shows at the same time. Nine elevators and five escalators were installed in this part of the building. Upon the Coliseum's opening, trailers of exhibit freight have to be loaded onto an elevator to be delivered to the different floors. As it was on the waterfront, there were some unusual unions involved, such as the Stevedores. All unions played a strong role in trade show

labor. This became a sore point for many show organizers in later years, with other city centers being built with fewer union regulations.

In its 30-year life, hundreds of events were held at the Coliseum, with shows dedicated to yachts, futuristic cars, watches, typewriters, photography, jewelry, and flowers. The New York Coliseum's last show featured 800 vendors of men's sportswear. By the late 1990s, it was clear that the New York Coliseum had fallen out of favor as a desired show site. Groups of homeless people regularly slept in its doorways. The New York business community continued to believe in the power of trade shows to grow the city economy and made plans to construct a new convention center, the **Jacob Javits Center.**

By late 1981, the upcoming new convention center had booked 171 conventions for shows between mid-1984 and late 1986. The problems with the center's construction started in 1982, when it was revealed that there were difficulties in manufacturing the custom parts for the Convention Center's structure. In March 1983, officials stated that the Convention Center was facing cost overruns and that the center's opening date had been postponed to at least 1985. In order to reduce the delay, workers were ordered to speed up construction. The delay was "disastrous" for the city, since the delays left the city vulnerable to lawsuits from the hosts of the 141 conventions that were scheduled to be held through the end of 1985. By April 1984, the opening date had been delayed further to mid-1986. In 1995, an Independent Review Board charged that construction jobs at the center had come under Mafia control. From the day the center opened in 1986, the union leaders gave the work mainly to people with mob connections, to relatives and friends of organized crime figures and to friends of union officers, the panel said.

During all this time, trade shows were growing in popularity throughout the states and new convention facilities were being built or expanded in other American cities. Another negative about the original Javits for show organizers was that there were no hotels near Javits Center. This led some convention planners to decide against holding their events there. Chicago was now the leading location for top trade shows in the USA.

In spite of all of its setbacks, Javits is pushing forward today. The Jacob K. Javits Convention Center sits squarely in the center of Manhattan's newest and most dynamic neighborhood. Having just completed a dramatic $2 billion transformation, it is ready again to welcome you. From the beginning, when the first New York Auto Show opened in November 1900 at the original Madison Square Garden, the annual exhibition of automobiles in New York has been a hallmark of the auto industry and will be held again at Javits in 2024. Javits Center is scheduled to host many international shows in 2024–25. Beauty Show, Apparel Show, Vision Expo, Furniture Show, Fancy Foods Show, Cannabis Expo, and the Toy Fair. The "Big Apple" will slowly win back trade shows for the city of New York! The city is still an attraction.

New York Exhibit Suppliers-

New York has been one of the most populous *states* in the country, and its gross economic product exceeds that of all but a handful of countries throughout the world. We often think only of New York City when we say New York, but the state includes a variety of productive cities well known for specialty industries. These cities encouraged many exhibit companies to start up to assist top corporations in growing through trade show marketing. Aside from NYC, several industries were strong in key NY cities. **Buffalo:** heavy machinery; **Syracuse:** metals; **Albany:** paper; **Binghamton:** home of IBM; and **Rochester:** strong in optical companies and home of Eastman Kodak, Eastman School of Music, and Vacuum Oil Co. (now Mobil Oil). With strong manufacturing, one-third of New York State is unionized. All this industry diversity is where the early exhibit companies grew by assisting local companies with trade shows throughout the USA.

Sidebar- Frank Baum, who wrote The Wizard of Oz, worked as a NY window decorator. He viewed the president of the US as the wizard, and the Emerald City was fashioned after the splendor of the Chicago World's Fair. The glamour of the city did have an influence on the movie! Kansas and other cities were a train ride away.

The Major East Coast Convention Centers

The **Philadelphia Convention Hall and Civic Center,** was a convention center complex located in the heart of Philadelphia. It developed out of a series of buildings dedicated to expanding trade, which began with the National Export Exhibition in 1899. Convention Hall was torn down in 2005 after more than a decade without a regular tenant. By the 1980s, state leaders had a plan for a new convention center in the heart of the center city. It was decided that the former train shed of the Reading Terminal would be the site of the new center and it opened in 1993. Playing Monopoly at its best. When it opened,

most of the events held in the Civic Center,

including trade shows and the annual Philadelphia Flower Show, moved to the new facility. **The Pennsylvania Convention Center** has four main halls, smaller meeting rooms, and the Grand Hall, which occupies much of the train shed of the former Reading Railroad terminal. The center hosts the Philadelphia Auto Show in early February and the Philadelphia Flower Show in early March, as well as numerous nonrecurring conferences and conventions. In December 2006, the Convention Center approved a $700 million plan to expand the Convention Center, bringing the amount of convention space to approximately one million square feet. The expansion was completed in March 2011. The Pennsylvania Convention Center's proven to be an excellent site for a medium-sized event with easy access to hotels and attractions in the center of town.

Boston-

Boston has two convention facilities in the heart of the city: the John Hynes Convention Center and the Boston Convention & Exposition Center.

The **John B. Hynes Veterans Memorial Convention Center** came first, was constructed in 1965, and was originally known as the War Memorial Auditorium. The building was part of a city plan known as *The New Boston*, which led to the demolition of blighted areas of downtown Boston. The goal of the project was to modernize the city, increase business opportunities, and attract shoppers back into downtown from the suburbs. *New Boston* was promulgated by Mayor John B. Hynes, and the convention center was renamed in his honor. Many national trade shows were held here in the 1970s and 1980s.

Boston Convention & Exposition Center: The push to invest in a new convention center in Boston came in the late 1990s, when the semi-annual Macworld Conference and Expo, previously held in Boston each summer, moved to the Javits. It was believed that this move was in part because no single Boston venue could contain the entire show. The center has been controversial because it is located in the South Boston Seaport, which is some distance from the main concentration of hotels in Boston. However, several new hotels have been planned or built near the convention center.

The new convention center opened in June 2004.

That summer, Macworld returned to Boston as the BCEC's first trade show, but the show's reduced size, due in part to a lack of participation by Apple, relegated its 2005 meeting (its last) to the smaller Hynes Convention Center in Boston's Back Bay.

The Westin Boston Waterfront hotel opened next door to the BCEC in June 2006. In 2007, the convention center saw over 1.6 million attendees book over 1 million hotel room nights. This equated to an economic impact of over $890 million for the city of Boston.

In 2012, the large Biotechnology Industry Organization conference said it would not return as scheduled in 2018 without more capacity. In April 2020, the Convention Center was set up as a 1,000-bed alternate care site for COVID-19 patients, which also eliminated demand for conferences. In 2022, Governor Charlie Baker proposed selling the Hynes Convention Center and investing the proceeds in the BCEC.

The BCEC has attracted many shows back to Boston and will continue to do so with the city's historical interest and a beautiful bayfront to attract visitors to attend a trade show in Boston.

** Courtesy of the Massachusetts Convention Authority

Washington Convention Center

Construction on this original center began in 1980, and it opened in 1982. At 800,000 square feet, it was the fourth-largest facility in the United States at the time. However, during the 1980s and 1990s, numerous larger and more modern facilities were constructed around the country, and by 1997, the Washington Convention Center had become the 30th largest facility. The Center was replaced by the new Walter E. Washington Convention Center; the old convention center was then demolished.

The new **Walter E. Washington Convention Center** is a 2.3-million-square-foot convention center located in Washington, D.C. It was completed in 2003. The center is noted for its extensive permanent collection of contemporary art, the largest of any convention center in the United States and one of the largest public art collections in Washington, D.C. In 2006, the **Council of the District of Columbia** approved legislation naming the then-Washington Convention Center in honor of the city's first home rule mayor, the late Walter E. Washington. In 2008, the WCSA Board of Directors agreed to expand the newly built convention center by 75,000 square feet. Many medium to small shows are held there each year, with the center hosting several inaugural presidential balls. Since 2014, the National Book Festival has been held at the center.

In 2011, ground was broken to build the 14-story Washington Marriott Marquis "convention center headquarters hotel" with more than

100,000 square feet of meeting room space. This adds greatly to the appeal of selecting the GWCC for any industry event in Washington, DC, along with the appeal of the city attractions within walking distance. Washington Times-CityCenter, DC.

Some of the early exhibit companies who started to service trade shows on east coast:

Hale Expo Services: Hale got its start in 1901 during the Pan American Exposition held in Buffalo, NY. The Pan American Exposition was a world-class World Fair that introduced the world to commercial AC electricity. Realizing a need for decorative support, the organizers of The Pan American Exposition turned to a local florist

named George D. Hale. Using his talents,

George decorated many of the venues that were created during the Pan American Exposition. This is how Hale came into existence. He expanded his services and began decorating with lattice work, festooning, bunting and flags to create a more festive atmosphere for any event. Through his meticulous attention to detail, many national leaders and captains of industry who were in attendance took note of George's work. After the exposition, George began receiving requests to provide his services in other cities such as Pittsburgh, Chicago, Detroit and Kansas City. Well-known aerospace defense contractors and auto manufacturing companies were based in Buffalo, NY, in the 1940s. Companies like Curtis Wright, Bell Aircraft and American Car and Foundry Company called on Hale to decorate their assembly facilities creating a patriotic atmosphere and producing enthusiasm amongst their workers. In the 50's and 60's, George Hale's sons took over, and Hale Expo went on as a show contractor and a designer and builder of trade show exhibits.

Another early exhibit company was **Hadley Exhibits.** They started with display windows before the 1920's and expanded to do trade show exhibits and museum displays. Norman Hadley was a respected painter and attended Albright Art School, then began his marketing career. In 1932, he purchased International Displays and named it Hadley Advertising and Displays. He designed and built exhibits for East Coast corporations that were used at East Coast trade shows. In 1948, he moved and renamed the company Hadley Exhibits. In 1959, a well-known exhibit designer named David Johnson teamed up with Norman as his partner. In time, the sons of Norm and David took over the company and incorporated it. David Johnson then purchased the company, and his son Ted took over as CEO. The company is still in business today, with all employees expressing a deep respect for the Hadley name.

An early exhibit company in Philadelphia was the **Art Guild.** They grew greatly through acquisitions. The Art Guild was founded in the early 1920s by a pharmacist named Morris Beck. He began by creating signs and displays for his pharmacy. His early business grew primarily as a sign shop doing window displays and elaborate movie marquis displays in Philadelphia. Signage became more three-dimensional over time. In 1925, Art Guild and other local shops grew exponentially as a result of the 1926 Sesquicentennial International Exposition, which was hosted in Philadelphia to commemorate the 150th anniversary of the signing of the Declaration of Independence. The creation of exhibits for this event transformed the Art Guild from a sign shop into an exhibit company. Post-exhibition, Art Guild retained many of the companies they worked with to do trade shows for them. In 1976, **Doug Zegel** joined the firm to help with sales and marketing and the company increased revenue growth year over year through the expansion of existing clients, new client acquisitions, and the acquisition of a number of other exhibit firms: Beital Displays and Syma Systems from Trenton, NJ; National Display, Pennsauken, NJ; Eastern Display, Pawtucket, RI; Renaissance Display, Belmawr, NJ; Display Arts, Wilmington, Delaware; Display Presentations, Long Island, NY; and Lynch Exhibits, Pennsauken, NJ. . John Ricciuti retired in 2001, and ownership was passed to Doug Zegel and Om Machhar until Doug sold his interest to the Machhar family and retired in 2017. Today, Art Guild headquarters are in West Deptford, NJ, and it operates facilities in NJ, DE, NY, NC, GA, NV, and Illinois. The lesson here is growth through acquisitions.

Three other successful exhibit companies on the east coast were **Lynch, Impact Display,** and **Sparks Exhibits** in New Jersey. Don Sparks took over his grandfather's exhibit business, which was started in 1919. Don Sparks supported the growth of the exhibit industry and became president of EDPA in 1983. **Sparks** went on to become a national exhibit company. who purchased 3D Exhibits from Chicago and was later purchased by Freeman, another family-owned company. **Lynch Display** started in 1926 as a storefront signage company and expanded to do trade show exhibits and museums. Lynch reached a pinnacle of growth only to go bankrupt in 2017. **Impact Display** (Dick Johnson) provided system exhibit solutions as one of America's first Octanorm distributors. In 2015, they sold to a Canadian company, Aura

XM, and became **Impact XM,** now a custom exhibit designer and manufacturer in several US locations.

Over the years, many exhibit companies in the USA have roots as honored family businesses. Successful companies like Freeman, Derse, and GP Johnson each started with an owner who shared their passion with their families and fellow employees. Over the years, the 'other' employees have considered themselves a part of the family as well. There are a number of exhibit companies today that are, or have been, father-grandfather, father-son, or fatherdaughter relationships that carry on the spirit of their father's vision.

Some of the notable exhibit design and build companies on the east coast:

NEW JERSEY:

Lynch Exhibits, Pennsauken, NJ, Trade Shows, Museums

Sparks Exhibits, Pennsauken NJ, Trade Shows

Charles Maltbie and Associates, Mount Laurel, NJ, Trade Shows and Museums

Beitel Displays, Trenton NJ, Trade Show Exhibits, Lottery Equipment

Dimensional Displays, Runnemede, NJ, Trade Shows, Museums

Art Guild, Inc. West Deptford, NJ, Trade Shows, Museums (D. Zegel EDPA president, 1993)

Mercon Industries, Pennsauken, NJ, Trade Shows, Millwork

Showtime Paulsboro NJ, Trade Shows, Events

Impact Exhibits, Princeton NJ, Trade Shows

Walode Displays, NJ (later became MC2)

PENNSYLVANIA:

Riley Gander and Showalter, Emaus, PA, Trade Shows

GRS&W, Pittsburgh PA, Trade Shows (later became Giltspur)

Berm Studios, Yeadon PA, Trade Shows (Berman's served as EDPA presidents in 1971 and 1989).

Visual Communication, Aston, PA

NEW YORK:

Jack Morton Productions, NYC, New York, Trade Shows

Ivel Display, NYC Trade Shows (later became Exhibitgroup)

Design Build, Long Island: Harold Averick was EDPA president in 1960.

Consultants & Designers, NYC (later created Exhibitgroup)

Cal Island, NYC Trade Shows

Kingsley Display, NYC Trade Shows

Structural Exhibits, NYC

Gilbert Displays, Long Island, NY

MASSACHUSETTS:

Sacks Exhibits

DELAWARE:

Display Arts Studios, Wilmington, DE, Trade Shows, Museums

VIRGINIA: Design and Production, Alexandria VA, Trade Shows and Museums (Jay Barnwell serves as EDPA President, 1994)

Washington, DC: Hargrove, Washington, DC, Trade Shows.

Convention Centers & Exhibit Suppliers in The Cities of the Midwest- U.S.A.

The start of convention centers in Chicago began early and changed often before the construction of McCormick Place

Participating exhibitors nationwide wanted more than the show contractor offered in their basic exhibit space package. Exhibitors wanted a stronger way to express their image and to attract visitor attention to their exhibit space.

Chicago-

From 1860 to 1982, there were three different Chicago Coliseums built for events and trade fairs. Each stood at a different period. The third Coliseum (1879–1971) hosted a few trade shows, six political

conventions, and many music concerts. When the Chicago Stadium was built in 1929, it took its place along with the Interstate Expo Building. Today, the Stadium is home to the Chicago Black Hawks and the Chicago Bulls.

After the Chicago fire of 1871 and before the Chicago World's Fair of 1893, Chicago built the **Interstate Exposition Building** on the lakefront of Chicago. This was one of the first purpose- built structures dedicated to trade fairs. The concept took off like a rocket, then faded with the planning of the 1893 Chicago World's Fair. It was demolished in 1892. The spirit

THE EXPOSITION.

Ninth Annual Display of the Fine and Industrial Arts.

Many New Exhibitors, with Novel Wares and Attractions.

Decided Improvement in the General Appearance of the Show.

The Art Gallery, Its Paintings, Engravings, Etchings, and Decorative Designs.

THE CHICAGO TRIBUNE: SEPTEMBER 1. 1879.

GRAND

INAUGURATION

OF THE

INTER-STATE

INDUSTRIAL

EXPOSITION

OF CHICAGO.

of Chicago was always strong when it came to trade and industrial initiatives. The concept for this building and the two Chicago World Fairs established Chicago as a city for the advancement of commerce and trade. In the 1930s, Chicago was the hub of the livestock industry. The blue-collar neighborhoods were changing as Kansas City took over the processing of livestock.

Union tradesmen were abundant and looking for new ways to survive. The 1933 Chicago World Fair was a huge success, drawing attention to Chicago as a trade center. The Fair employed many for a while. In 1934, the **International Amphitheater** was built and held events, so union

workers now had new jobs. Chicago business leaders helped expand and refine the exhibition industry with the completion of its International Amphitheater. The Amphitheater was constructed adjacent to the famous Union Stock Yards (meatpacking district), primarily to host the International Livestock Exposition. Being a large indoor arena, it was among the first such exhibition centers to have "air conditioning" and other unique architectural features. The Amphitheater quickly established Chicago as the "convention capital of the world," hosting some of the world's largest conventions and exhibitions over the coming decades. The Amphitheater maintained this prominent position until McCormick Place was built and became the leading convention venue in the city (and beyond).

Before the **first McCormick Place**, shows and events were held at the International Amphitheater, Navy Pier and Hilton Hotel, and the Palmer House. All labor was managed by unions, who ruled with an iron hand. Show contractor companies were created to set up and manage the exhibit space and assist exhibitors at trade shows.

Participating exhibitors wanted more than the show contractor offered in their basic exhibit space package. Exhibitors wanted a stronger way to express their image and to attract attention to their exhibit space.

The Early Exhibit Supplier Companies-

Some of the early show contractor companies were United Expo, Andrews-Bartlett, Fern, Brede, Poirot Exposition, and GES.

The original McCormick Place burned to the ground the night before the 1967 Houseware Show. Rebuilt in 1971, it then took on a leadership role as the nation's top trade show city, attracting a variety of the biggest industry trade fairs and events in America.

Prior to the boom in the late 1960s, several exhibit companies started up to pre-build exhibits for shows and events held at the Amphitheater or in hotels. In the early days, exhibits were often built on-site with union labor. Chicago formed Poirot Exposition to supply carpenter labor for the installations. They also provided rental carpet, floor tiles, furniture, and freight movement. They soon were assigned to manage the show floor for an entire show. Exhibit installation needs changed quickly when the exhibits were now fabricated in advance. The exhibits were shipped to the site in a crate to protect the contents when unloaded from the trucks by teamsters. Pre-built exhibits saved hours of labor on the show floor and the exhibit parts were now simply assembled on site. Exhibit weight was not yet an issue.

The first Chicago exhibit companies to do this included Czarnowski (1947), Luellen & Best (now LAB) (1954), Kitzing (1952), MG Display (1959), RAE Systems (1960), Abco Display, Escort Display, Exhibits Inc. (1964), and Award Exhibits (1965). Many of these first exhibit service companies were owned by carpenters and/or designers. Their companies were located in multi-story buildings in the city, with fabrication, painting, warehouse, and

design on different floors. Few invested in decorating their office lobby. This trend came later. In the 1980's, exhibit companies began to move to the suburbs with a single floor of working space. This second wave of companies were truly entrepreneurs who had a new vision for assisting exhibitors. In time, many employees of these first companies broke away to start their own companies to improve on the services offered. One such company was **RAE Systems.** When they closed, new companies were started from RAE-Dimension Craft, Premiere Exhibits, Dimension Works, and Design Agency Fritkin-Jones. Other successful companies thereafter were Exhibits Inc., Stevens Exhibits, MG Display, CB Display, Contempo (a spin-off of Dimension Works), Matrix, McCormick Display (owned by Don Svehla's father), and General Exhibits, which specialized in museum exhibits.

James Casell/Exhibits Inc
1974 Musuem Display for
the Dept of Energy

In 1971, Exhibitgroup was created. It became one of the first exhibit companies to create a national network of exhibit companies to serve their customers nationwide. Note that the concept of a national network was also brewing in the same way with a competitor named Giltspur. Others followed.

As each company evolved, merged, or went bankrupt, the new owners created new ways of doing things and expanded services for their clients. Many of the first exhibit companies in Chicago are still in business due to their willingness to adapt to the changing exhibit environment. After 1995, other exhibit company spin offs formed to create new companies in Chicago, like 3D Exhibits, Folio, Matrix, and a few national exhibit companies, like Derse, which opened a division in Chicago to be near the church at McCormick Place. Many exhibit

companies in Chicago were successful for two reasons. One, being located in a city with many corporations headquartered nearby and who exhibited nationwide. Secondly, McCormick Place now hosts many of the top U.S. trade shows. Be near your customer, or be near the center where your customer exhibited, was the formula to attract business. With many annual shows in Chicago, exhibit companies offered storage for exhibits between shows. This added profit.

During the 1980's, McCormick lost a number of shows when building expansions started by adding the North, South, and West Halls. A major show loss was the CES Show going to Vegas. The first CES Show was held at the Chicago Hilton Hotel. All freight was unloaded in the street and carried in with a dolly—no forklifts.

Note that the major show contractors in Chicago at the time were Poirot, United Expo, Rieber Friel, Andrews Bartlett, and Greyhound. GES then bought out many of them. Working closely with the show contractor with rules and unions at any show was a requirement for an exhibit supplier to succeed and to ensure a smooth experience for their customers at show sites. Union labor rules grew stricter over time.

A Chicago union rule change in the 1990s eliminated the legality of exclusive set-up labor at McCormick. This improved business opportunities for independent I&D companies (Note that CB Displays was one of the first companies to provide I&D services for other exhibit companies). With this change came the creation of a new association, EACA (Exhibit Appointed Contractor Association). This new association spun off of EDPA for Exhibit Service Contractors to speak with one voice. While a few exhibit houses provided their own I&D labor crews, other exhibit houses began to contract with I&D companies and sent a supervisor to direct the crew. This was done to provide a personal service for their exhibiting customers rather than using the show contractor labor pool. Exhibitors were now shielded from on-site union labor confrontations with a personal guard dog to make the installation experience positive. Customers really liked this new personal service and were willing to pay extra for a hassle-free experience at show sites nationwide. This new level of added service fueled loyalty between the exhibitor and the exhibit houses.

In addition to independent I&D companies, other independent service companies began to form in Chicago. These new companies offered exclusive auxiliary exhibit services, like carpeting, raised floors, furniture, graphics, fabric signs, florals, system components, portable exhibits, A-V, ceiling trusses, and shipping. They each grew to be successful businesses in and of themselves, nation-wide.

> Note that the creation of these new exhibit supplier specialty companies began in the early 1990's in each major trade show city nationwide.

Through the years, Chicago has led the way in the trade show industry. To this day, Chicago has more exhibit design, fabrication and show service companies than anywhere else in the USA. Today, Chicago shares America's largest trade shows with Orlando and Las Vegas.

Exhibitgroup was created in 1971 by Charlie Zimmerman, who owned a company in New York called Consultant & Designers. They bought Ivel Exhibits in NY, then Award and 3D Exhibits in Chicago, then Product Presentation in Cincinnati, and then Presentation Exhibits in Los Angeles. Leo McDonald, who led the Chicago division, was made president of the group, and later Exhibitgroup was bought by the Greyhound Corporation, which also bought GES. Greyhound then asked Leo McDonald and Tony Vastardis (the CFO) to explore other companies to purchase and add to the Group. They then bought Mobius (owned by Hertz) and Barry Bush, Cecil McCowen, and Carl Bokland to create Exhibitgroup San Francisco. Later, Greyhound bought the Stuart-Sauter company, which provided contractor services in SF. This was the start of both EG/SF and GES in SF. Greyhound Exhibitgroup then bought Matrix (Dick Foot) in Atlanta and Display Contractors and David Gibson Co. in Dallas. These seven locations were the start of Exhibitgroup before they purchased Giltspur to create Exhibitgroup-Giltspur, an 18-city network of companies. In 1997, Viad Corporation purchased Greyhound Dial and kept both GES and Exhibitgroup/Giltspur. They were later folded together to create the new GES as one company, now headquartered in Las Vegas.

Convention Centers & Exhibit Suppliers in The Cities of the Midwest- U.S.A.

Detroit- Info provided by Derek Gentile- EEI Global /past president EDPA

Prior to 1965, Detroit had few exhibit houses, with GP Johnson being one of the first. GPJ was founded in 1914 by its namesake, George P. Johnson, in Detroit, Michigan, as a flag-making and sail-repair establishment. Initially, it established itself as an event management firm for the auto industry in the Detroit area. The company's early years were heavily rooted in working with the automobile industry and managing trade shows and events. In 1956, GPJ assisted in producing the first International Auto Show in New York. This was the company's first venture outside of the Detroit area with automotive events. Later in 1961, the firm introduced the spinning turntable for presenting cars, which would later become an auto show standard. In

In 1980, Robert Vallee was appointed account executive and was assigned to work with American Honda, one of the first foreign carmakers that the company had worked with. In 1985, JPJ opened an office in Los Angeles and won new business with Toyota and Nissan.

In 1899, William E. Metzger (the first auto dealership) helped organize the Detroit Auto Show, only the second of its kind after the 1898 Paris Auto Show. The auto show was held in Detroit in 1907 at Beller's Beer Garden at Riverside Park and since then annually except 1941–1953. During the show's first decades of existence, it portrayed only a regional focus. In 1957, international carmakers exhibited for the first time.

The Detroit-based exhibit industry was largely built around servicing the automotive industry. In 1965, Cobo Hall opened, and the Motor City had three primary exhibit design and fabrication companies centered around what is often referred to as the Detroit "Big 3" automotive companies. These original equipment manufacturers

(OEM) companies were some of the largest in the country, if not the world, had significant marketing budgets, and demanded some of the highest service levels the exhibit industry could provide. Display & Exhibit Company (D&E) was the agency of record for Ford Motor Company, George P. Johnson Company (GPJ). handled Chrysler Corporation, and H.B. Stubbs (Stubbs) handled General Motors Corporation. The Big 3 doled out big money for the major auto shows, the annual dealer announcement meeting, and various industry events. There were a handful of smaller companies that supported automotive supplies and a few non-automotive businesses, but the lion share of the exhibit business was supported by these three companies.

D&E, GPJ, and Stubbs maintained dominance on the auto show floor from the 1960s to the 1980s. They enjoyed the successful growth of auto shows in major markets like Detroit, Chicago, Las Angeles, and New York. At the same time, the United States was growing rapidly, and additional auto shows became important in dozens of mid-sized markets like Dallas, Houston, Miami, San Francisco, Minneapolis, Atlanta, and Denver. These exhibit companies grew to become some of the largest exhibit companies in the nation, given the high level of demand the automotive industry placed on them.

The North American International Auto Show (NAIAS, aka Detroit Auto Show) had a 25-year run as the premier global automotive industry show, which provided tremendous opportunity and placed even greater demands on the exhibit companies that serviced the show.

Sophisticated, complex, multistory structures were produced and included every conceivable type of engagement and interactive technology. At the height of the show, it would take over three months for the installation; the show ran for fourteen days, followed by fourteen days or more of dismantling!

The Big 3 automakers mandated that all their suppliers be unionized to do business with them. Therefore, Detroit-based exhibit companies were Union Shops and signatory with the carpenter's union as well as the teamsters and the sign and pictorial (painters) unions. All the design, engineering, and fabrication were completely self-performed in-house. The companies had robust carpentry shops, metal and aluminum fabricating departments, paint departments, sign shops that relied on screen printing and hand lettering, and even sewing departments to produce drapes and table skirts. Everything was produced in-house. The displays and exhibits were crated and shipped to each auto show around the country. Installation and dismantling were supported by a traveling supervisor with support from local union labor companies based on jurisdictions set by the local market and/or venue.

In the early 1980s, D&E experienced a management shakeup that resulted in the eventual closing of the company. Two new players emerged from the wind-down of D&E. Exhibit Works, Inc. (currently EWI Worldwide) was founded in 1979, and Exhibit Productions, Inc. (currently EEI Global) was formed in 1981. Both companies quickly absorbed the business of D&E. Exhibitgroup Chicago joined in the fun and gained ground on some of the General Motors business. Around the same time, many of the Asian and European automotive OEMs began marketing in the USA, which provided tremendous opportunity for the traditional automotive exhibit companies in Detroit. Toyota, Hyundai, and BMW, to name a few. GPJ, EWI, and EEI Global have all respectfully capitalized on these foreign OEMs for several decades.

Prior to 2000, you could characterize the Detroit automotive exhibit market as "an island." The automotive clients were on the island, along with a short list of Detroit-based exhibit houses. The relationship between the automotive OEM marketing departments and the exhibit houses was extremely close. Competitive bids were made within this close circle of suppliers. It was difficult for any new supplier to get "on" the island, which was great for the Detroit-based exhibit houses. The bad news was that it was difficult to get "off" the island as well. The Detroit-based exhibit houses had a hard time diversifying outside of automotive.

Since 2000, the competitive landscape has changed. The NAIAS attracted OEMs from around the world to exhibit in Detroit. International exhibition providers were contracted by European OEMs to help service NAIAS. The traditional Big 3 no longer mandated that suppliers must be unions and opened their doors to non-union competitors. Not only did the landscape of exhibit companies change, but the methods for designing and producing exhibits did as well. Exhibit companies were forced to find lower-cost solutions, and more and more of the content needed to be outsourced. As the industry became more global, so did the methods and resources for material and service suppliers. The Detroit-based exhibit companies expanded and transformed into agencies. They expanded their footprint and/or built extensive networks of key supplier partners to remain competitive. Companies such as Display International, Hoynck, and Imagination assumed the role of lead design and build partners for many of the automotive OEMs.

The Detroit exhibit market is considerably different today. GPJ, EWI, and EEI Global have remained key players in the market. All three companies have diversified customer bases beyond automotive and maintain offices outside of Detroit. Czarnowski now has a significant presence in Detroit and serves several automotive OEMs. Numerous other national exhibit houses and agencies have representation in Detroit. Sadly, H.B. Stubbs closed shop shortly after the '09 recession.

Employees from each of the Detroit-based exhibit companies have traded back and forth between the companies for years. There are similarities in how the companies are structured, but the cultures are very different, and competition between them remains fierce.

The exhibit design and build demands in Detroit still require much of the same custom high-end solutions, global execution, and multi-channel integration that they have had for years. However, there is a significant increase in the utilization of the latest digital engagements, including live streaming and virtual broadcasts. All of which the Detroit-based exhibit agencies are excellent at providing. Detroit exhibit companies have led the way with their in-shop fabrication capabilities due to the high demands from the leading US automakers. These unique internal resources are now utilized by many exhibitors outside of the automotive industry.

Side Story on Cobo Hall

Built by the city and opened in 1960, the convention center, first known as **Cobo Hall**, was named after the former mayor, who died in office of a heart attack in 1957. The name of the 723,000-square-foot facility, which annually ranked as a top 10 convention center in the Midwest, came under fire for policies Albert E. Cobo enacted as mayor of Detroit in the 1950s. Cobo Hall had been named for an individual who was responsible for policies that moved large numbers of African-Americans out of their homes and out of their businesses and who had no place to go in the name of urban renewal. Calls to purge Cobo's name from the facility arose as movements across the country began to remove from public spaces the names and statues of historic leaders whose actions do not meet today's politically correct standards. Now, some 60 years later, Cobo reminds the people of Detroit of an era that they seek to keep in the past. The center's name was changed in 2019 to **TCF** (TCF-Financial). Shortly thereafter, TCF Bank (TCF Financial Corp.) merged with Huntington Bancshares. The property was remodeled in 2020 and is now called **Huntington Place**. Huntington Place is 2,400,000 square- feet (220,000 m^2) in size and has 723,000 square feet (67,200 m^2) of exhibition space, with 623,000 square feet (57,900 m^2).

Some of the roots of Detroit's urban decline lie in the way the city was planned in the first half of the twentieth century. The unbroken arc of automotive factories that ran along the Detroit Terminal Railroad (DTR) in the 1910s essentially blocked the downtown from spreading outward into the neighborhoods. Much of this has been drastically improved today.

Today, Detroit continues to be called "The Motor City" and is also recognized for the unique Motown sound in music. Other than trade shows, The Detroit Lions almost added a third attraction in 2024. Maybe next year!

Convention Centers & Exhibit Suppliers in The Cities of the Midwest- U.S.A.

Milwaukee, Minneapolis, Indianapolis, Ft Wayne, Cincinnati, Cleveland

Many of the show contractor companies in the US were at the forefront to assist the many industry associations to organize their industry gatherings. Decorator companies like Brede, Fern, Shepard, Freeman, and Manncraft led the way to work with industry associations to manage their industry events that included a trade show. They assisted in coordinating the entire event, including exhibitor display materials. In time, there was a demand from exhibitors to create a 'better image', beyond the basic display materials provided by the show contractors. With this desire to have a better image, exhibit houses were formed to create custom-designed exhibits. Some of the first to design and produce a 'classier exhibit' for exhibitors were exhibit houses formed in the Midwest and in the East Coast.

Cleveland & Cincinnati, Ohio-

By the 1940's, it had become increasingly obvious that, with the post-war boom in manufacturing and greater ease of travel, an emerging strategy for companies looking to expand was to exhibit at an industry trade show. Exhibit houses were created to accommodate this need to effectively present your company. For the Midwest, **Ohio Displays** was one of the first US exhibit design and build companies. A Cleveland-based company since 1919. They were originally known as the Ohio Sign Company, whose clientele primarily requested the design and fabrication of window displays, outdoor signage, and some interior retail environments. The Ohio Sign Company evolved into Ohio Displays and is now focused on the design and production of exhibits, becoming one of the first display companies in the country. Another local company still with us today was **Rogers Co.** in Mentor, OH, which started in 1945. Another notable exhibit company was **Exhibit**

Concepts in Dayton (1978). The Ohio Valley was instrumental in the formation of many exhibit industry organizations, such as IEA (to TSEA), IAEM, and EDPA.

In the late 1950s, Cleveland prided itself on being an international convention city, competing with New York and Chicago. Cleveland was centrally located with train access and good roads for easy access. With the opening of the NY Coliseum in 1956 Cleveland felt it was losing convention business due to the small size of **Public Auditorium.** The city of Cleveland then proposed to build a new convention center, but voters twice rejected initiatives to fund it. They finally approved a bond levy to build a new center in 1963, seven years later. Construction was plagued with all kinds of issues and finally opened in 1964. The new center had many negative issues and was not attracting shows. Events were now going to New York and Chicago. The center underwent major renovations in 1983 and 1987. By that time, competition from other convention centers in other cities had put Cleveland on the back burner as a location for show organizers to consider. The convention center was demolished in 2011 and rebuilt larger at the same location, completed in 2013, and renamed **Huntington Convention.**

In the 1950s, Cleveland was a thriving economic center. One of the city's architectural marvels was the Arcade of Cleveland. Very similar in design to the Great Exposition Palace in 1851 discussed in Chapter One.

One of the largest exhibit centers in the USA today is the IX Center in Cleveland, which is now used for many consumer shows and is hardly a consideration for major trade shows due to its location. Two other popular convention centers in Ohio are the

Palmer Rolls Out Sales Room

Bartlett Palmer, right, president of the Palmer Instruments, Inc., Cincinnati, and George Benkenstein, secretary of Product Presentation, Inc., also of Cincinnati, inspect a "salesroom on wheels," designed by Product Presentation for Mr. Palmer's firm. Inside the trailer, wall displays show Palmer instruments, which indicate and record temperatures and pressures.

Columbus Convention Center and the **Duke Energy Center** in Cincinnati.   In Cincinnati, **Product Presentation** started in the 1950s', later becoming Exhibitgroup, which then became Phoenix Presentations, a spin-off of Exhibitgroup started by Ray Steiner. Cincinnati was also home to **Positive Productions**, which later became **Display Sales.** Each of these exhibit companies had a client base of Fortune 500 companies that were mainly local but who exhibited throughout the US. Another company of note was **Adex** in Cinncinati (1978). In Canton, Ohio, was **Communication Exhibits**, which is doing well after 47 years. It was started by Dick McLaughlin and is now led by his son, Scott McLaughlin, and it is still going strong.

Convention Centers & Exhibit Suppliers in The Cities of the Midwest- U.S.A.

Milwaukee *Input provided by Bill Haney- Derse*

Badger Exposition was a leading show contractor in the Milwaukee area and provided early exhibiting services for trade shows in the area. Early shows were conducted at the MECCA, The Fairgrounds, or in hotels. The Milwaukee Convention Center today is the **Baird Center.** It is now under reconstruction and will double in size by late 2024. This expo center offers the best of amenities for any small to medium sized

conference in the US.

Exhibit companies in Milwaukee started in a similar fashion to those in other US cities, filling a void that show contractor companies could not fill for exhibitors. Exhibitors did not want the basic exhibit space amenities offered by the show contractor. They wanted a cool exhibit to showcase their image. Exhibitors contracted with decorators to fabricate a custom-looking exhibit. Many exhibits were built on site, and many were pre-built and shipped to show for installation. The early exhibit providers were widow decorators, float designers, and sign painters. The first exhibit companies in Milwaukee assisted the strong corporations from the area with exhibit needs at trade shows throughout the US. One of the first was **Derse Exhibits**. Derse was founded in 1948 by James F. Derse as

a sign-painting business in the back of his mother's garage. In 1955, Derse began to sell rotating signs in Milwaukee, quickly selling 62 rotating signs in the area. In 1956, Derse painted the prominent Miller Brewing logo on a city wall and on many outdoor billboards for Citco and Mrs. Karl's Bakery, the largest sign in the city. In time, Derse began producing the highway signs for the state of Wisconsin in Racine, WI, which became the first offsite division of Derse and later became

Derse Chicago. There were many Fortune 500 companies located in Milwaukee. One of which was Derse's first large exhibit client, Cutler Hammer, who remains a client to this day. In 1989, Jim Derse sold the company to its current owners, Bill Haney and Bill McNamara. Over the years, Derse has added multiple full-service offices in key U.S. cities. Double-digit growth continued into the 21st century, and their services expanded to include the customer experience, international, and client marketing services beyond the exhibit. Today, Derse is a leading national company with multiple locations. In 2022, Bill Haney passed the flag of leadership to his son Brett. Although started by Jim Derse, Derse Exhibits remains a family-run business.

Other early exhibit houses in Milwaukee were Hartwig Exhibits, KMK, Lother, Exhibit Tree, and later MG Exhibits. Many of the Milwaukee exhibit company owners worked very closely with EDPA or served as EDPA presidents. EDPA national headquarters were located in Milwaukee for over 20 years.

Convention Centers & Exhibit Suppliers in The Cities of the Midwest- U.S.A.

Indiana- info provided by D.Cantor-Hamilton/ J.Frisby-ExhibitHouse/ Debbie Parrot-HighMark

In 1847, Indianapolis was established as a manufacturing hub and a transportation center for freight and passenger service. With an expanding network of roads, Indianapolis is connected to other major cities. Originally named the **Indiana Convention-Exposition Center,** the venue opened in 1969. The original venue included one ballroom, three exhibition halls, and 23 meeting rooms encompassing 160,000

square feet. The exhibit companies in this area worked with many national corporations as well as local corporations that exhibited throughout the USA.

Like other midwest exhibit companies, the start of the trade show exhibit house in Indianapolis began with a signage and decorating company. In 1947, Renzie Hamilton founded **Hamilton Display Manufacturing Company.** Their base of business was local manufacturing and healthcare. companies for trade shows in the US. In the 1960's, Hamilton Displays was widely known as the "King of Floats" for building most of the floats for the Indianapolis 500 Festival Parade, as well as the Indiana University Big Ten float at the 1968 Tournament of Roses Parade. In 1990, Dan Cantor and Joel Coleman purchased

Hamilton Displays from Renzie's brother, Kenneth Hamilton. They then expanded with the acquisition of Dimensional Designs, their largest competitor and a company with over 15 years of industry experience with a full-time focus on trade shows, exhibits, museums, and events.

In the coming years, three other exhibit companies also entered the Indianapolis marketplace to offer exhibit design services. There were **Coppinger Exhibits** and then **The Exhibit House.** Started by Larry Minnick in 1980, it was later purchased by Jeff Hoffman, Ben Ipema, and Jerry Frisby to carry it forward.

An exhibit company outside of Indianapolis was in **Ft. Wayne, IN,** that started in 1946 as Customcraft, which later became ICON Int'l., and then **HighMark.** Custom-built exhibits using vacuum forming, which was quite innovative at the time, In 1979. Mick Parrott acquired Customcraft and changed the name to ICON. Mick created a modular exhibit with aluminum extrusions he called ExZact. He went on to create a modular double-deck system with engineer Tim Searle. He patented the connectors and named the two-story exhibit Expo Deck. In the 1990s, Mick created a separate company to promote his new exhibit system and called it Highmark.

HighMark was set up to sell exclusively to exhibit companies and not to end-user exhibitors directly. HighMark was then sold to Group Delphi

in 2009, which was bought by Sparks and then by Freeman. No longer a good fit for their business model. Mick's daughter, Debbie Parrott, then bought back HighMark in 2016 to continue their business model of not selling to end-user exhibitors so as to respect the important relationships they had started with many exhibit houses nationally. This was quite an innovative move to keep sales and relationships exclusively with the industry family of exhibit design builders throughout the US. This exclusive buyer strategy is now very similar to that of many of the other exhibit systems companies, portable exhibit companies, furniture companies, flooring companies, A-V companies, and I&D companies in the USA today.

Another early company in the surrounding area was **Deckel & Moneypenny** in Louisville, KY. Bruce Deckel and Gary Moneypenny were coworkers at Louisville Sign Company and decided to focus on exhibits after the Kentucky Exposition Center opened in 1956. At the time, this new facility was one of the largest in the country, so Bruce and Gary realized that it could be more lucrative to make exhibits than only the signs for an exhibit. They are very successful to this day, with 98% of their work for shows outside of the region. Note that there were many exhibit houses in US cities that did not have a convention center close by.

Convention Centers & Exhibit Suppliers in

The Cities of the Midwest- U.S.A.

Minneapolis/St Paul (info provided by Mark Bendickson)

Today, the **Minneapolis Convention Center** is a great venue for medium-sized conventions with plenty of meeting rooms. It also hosts many public shows and events. Dealing with weather issues in Minneapolis is not a concern with the Minneapolis Skyway System, which connects all major buildings and the convention center with covered walkways.

The Twin cities played a strong role to jumping-starting exhibit companies in the industry. Like in other cities, the decorator/show contractor companies lead the way for exhibit companies to follow. One of the leaders was **Brede Expo, which** who started in 1898 by an immigrant Norwegian sign painter named Hans Brede. He rented furniture and carpets from his home for exhibitors and grew to extend his show contractor services. Later purchased by Bill Casey, then sold to GES. Brede was one of the first major casualties of the 2020 covid mania in the US.

In 1925, one of the first exhibit houses in Minneapolis was **Stephens Display**, which later became Display Arts. Their specialty was window dressing, model building, and stage props. They then evolved into trade show exhibits.

It was not until the 1960's that the early exhibit houses began to be dedicated solely to trade show exhibits. Some of the first were Rutherford Display, Custom Display, and DD&D (Dimensional Display & Design), founded by Don Bendickson and Don Bucher. Bendickson came from the Emporium Department Store in St. Paul as a window decorator. He was also very instrumental in the development of EDPA in the 1960s. Other exhibit companies then formed during this period: Haas Display, Display Masters, Artec Display, and Display Arts.

Display House?

Interesting how many exhibit companies in the US used the word "Display" or "Exhibits" in their name. Not so much today. The buzz word now is 'experiential'.

In 1980, **Heritage Communication** (from Des Moines) was formed, purchasing Custom Display and DD&D to create a network of companies. Note that Heritage, Giltspur, and Exhibitgroup were the first companies to really create multi-city locations under a single company name. Heritage went on to purchase Brede St. Louis and Industrial Design & Display (Dutch Antonaisse) in Dallas.

Heritage was later sold to an investor on the east coast and added Atlanta, Chicago, SF, and Las Vegas to their group. When Heritage downsized in 2004, new companies were created: Shocraft, Chandler Exhibits, Vertex Exhibits/Lincoln Studios, and CenterPoint Marketing.

The Start of the Portable Exhibit Concept

Two Minneapolis companies that changed the landscape of the exhibit industry were **Featherlite Exhibits**, started by Leroy Nelson in 1973, and **Skyline Exhibits**, started by Gordon Savoie in 1979. Gordon was working for Rupp Industries when he designed a half-dome structure to provide shelter for workers as they installed outdoor HVAC units. While showcasing the product at a trade show, a neighboring exhibitor joked that if the tent was turned on its side, it could be used as a display. Savoie didn't take the remark lightly and turned that portable shelter into one of the earliest pop-up displays, which launched Skyline in 1980. At that time, the industry did not take portable exhibits seriously. It was thought that nothing could replace the look and feel of a sturdy wood or metal-built exhibit. It took a while, but exhibitors were seeking a cheaper solution when exhibiting at smaller shows, let alone the rising costs for drayage and labor to install. Many other portable exhibit companies were then created in the US to start a new trend. Most then became very successful through dealerships. Skyline Display is today one of the largest exhibit companies in the USA, providing custom exhibits, installation, and full marketing services beyond exhibits.

Why Pay Others if we can do it Ourselves?

In the 1980s, several US corporations who exhibited at many trade shows began to manage their exhibits internally. Some have purchased an exhibit company to exclusively manage their exhibit properties. **CES** in Minneapolis was formed by 3M Corp. CES would bill 3M Corp. for labor and materials, using the 3M exhibit inventory. This concept was copied by several other corporations that exhibited a lot in the USA.

In the 1990s, many new exhibit companies were formed in the Twin Cities. Nygard Dimensions, Haas Display, Vertex Exhibits, and Star Exhibits were formed. **Star Exhibits** was created by six former employees of Display Masters, a startup trend that was followed by many other national exhibit companies that worked for large exhibit companies and lost their entrepreneurial spirit, which encouraged new companies to start up and maintain the entrepreneurial spirit that many small companies thrived on. Star Exhibits went on to acquire Featherlite Display. Display Masters was then acquired by GES in 1996.

To this day, Twin City exhibit suppliers continue to play a strong role in the exhibits industry, as well as with exhibit industry associations like EDPA. Many of these local companies support Bemidji State University, one of the only colleges in the USA that offers an undergraduate degree in exhibit design. Note that the only other college to offer such a degree is FIT in NYC, which offers a master's degree in exhibit design. This degree includes retail, museum, and marketing center exhibit design training as well as trade show exhibit design. Each of these specialty groups are considered an exhibit design. Minnesota companies have played a leading role in supporting education within the exhibit industry. Bemidji State University and Exhibitor Magazine are both headquartered in Minnesota.

Convention Centers & Exhibit Suppliers in the U.S.A.- SOUTH

Dallas - 1965- 2010 Major input by Ray Rogowicz

After World War II, Dallas experienced rapid growth and development, becoming a hub for transportation, industry, and commerce. The

railroad's arrival in the late 1800s helped cement Dallas's position as a major trading center, and the city continued to grow throughout the 20th century, becoming a leader in industries such as oil, banking, and technology. Dallas has long been known as a business hub with a thriving economy. The city is home to a number of Fortune 500 companies. One of the reasons why Dallas is such an attractive business center is its favorable tax policies. Texas has no personal or corporate income tax, making it an ideal location for businesses looking to reduce their tax burden. During the 1960s, Dallas became a desirable city for trade show conventions.

As the popularity of trade fairs grew in New York, Chicago, and Cleveland, the concept then grew in other major US cities, starting with the show contractor/decorator. companies providing the basic services for the show organizers and the exhibitors. For Dallas, Freeman Decorating expanded from Des Moises in 1927 to Dallas in 1950 to serve the area as well as other US cities. Freeman has grown to be a diversified leader in the entire American trade show industry. The Freeman journey from Des Moines is a story in and of itself. (See

Chapter 10: Change Makers). Freeman has grown to be a respected leader in the entire industry, beyond being only a show contractor.

Some of the first exhibit design and fabrication houses...

In Dallas, 1965

Monty Montgomery Display-Monty Montgomery

Display Contractors: Mark Roberts

Freeman Displays: Buck Freeman

In Fort Worth,

Bob Powell Display: Bob Powell

Charlie Mann Displays

Art Fair Displays: Art Fairchild

In 1972, Monty Montgomery sold to Gene Rogowicz and Dutch Antonisse to form Industrial & Merchandising Displays (I&M Displays), later sold to Target Communications, who became Heritage Displays. Display Contractors then sold to ExhibitGroup to become Greyhound ExhibitGroup Dallas/Ft Worth. They then purchased David H. Gibson to be a part of ExhibitGroup/Giltspur. Many Dallas exhibit companies applied their exhibit design skills to real estate developers to fabricate marketing center displays and scale models for building development sites.

In the 1970s, many convention centers were built in Texas: the Dallas Convention Center, Dallas Market Hall, Dallas World Trade Center, Houston Astro Hall, Austin Center, and San Antonio Convention Center. With new shows coming to Texas, the exhibit business now prospers. In the early 80's, many of the top shows in Chicago were now moving to Dallas: Home Builders, Home Center, FMI, IFT, RSNA, NSDA, and many medical shows, to name a few. During this time, McCormick Place was working to expand, building the new North,

South, and West wings to win back the business. Venue expansions were also happening in Atlanta, LA, SF, New Orleans, and Las Vegas. These expansions took a few years, so other cities prospered in the meantime, like Dallas.

With many new shows now coming to Dallas, I&D labor was in high demand. The local exhibit house companies would provide I&D labor for other exhibit companies nationwide. Exhibit companies from around the country would send a supervisor for an installation in Dallas, done

with local carpenters. Due to the shortage of I&D labor, local Dallas firefighters were used for set-up labor. They were great workers with a lot of common sense. The problem was that they were not available for the teardown. After this boom period, many Dallas shows returned to Chicago and other cities with newly renovated venues.

Dallas venues did not expand and then fell off the popular venue list.

In spite of this, Dallas remains a lucrative location for exhibit builders, with Freeman Decorating headquartered in town. For Dallas exhibit companies, added exhibit building business came from shows in the Houston Astro Center, real estate marketing centers, and from strong regional corporations that exhibited nationally.

With the expansion of convention centers in other major cities, Dallas was losing some of the big shows it previously had. (Boy, we heard this story before). The sentiment from the organizers was, we love Dallas, but we don't like your convention center. You lack adequate breakout spaces." Add to this the competition from neighboring cities like the like the Fort Worth Convention Center and the Irving and Austin Convention Centers. Winning back major trade shows from the shows that left was a challenging task. Competition for major trade show events to be held in your city can be fierce, but the economic impact that conventions bring to a city can be huge. Agreeing to invest in a new center is not always a welcome idea for a city, in spite of the potential impact on the city and the state economy. In 2022, the Dallas City Council voted to demolish and expand the existing **Kay Bailey Convention Center.** The expansion would double its present size and connect it to adjacent business districts and hotels. The new center is expected to be completed by 2028.

Dallas has always been known to think big. This new center will bring many shows back to Dallas, as long as the power of trade show marketing remains popular and they deliver results for the exhibiting companies and associations that invest in them. Time will tell if convention center expansions throughout the USA will continue as aggressively as in the past.

Convention Centers & Exhibit Suppliers in the U.S.A. -SOUTH

Atlanta- 1960- 2020- Info from Gary Stewart & Robert Laarhoven

In the late nineteenth century, fairs and expositions were an important way for cities to attract visitors and investors who, in an era before radio and television, were eager to see new technological marvels on display. As discussed in PART ONE of this book, in the years following the Civil War (1861–65), Atlanta's leaders hosted a series of three "Cotton Expositions" that were important to the city's recovery and economic development. These expositions helped Atlanta stake its

claim as the center of the New South and helped relieve regional sectionalism that may have been lingering after the Civil War. Expositions provided Atlanta civic leaders and companies with a showcase to lure visitors, who were urged to come and do business in the region. In 1881, 1885, and 1895, Atlanta was the host city for three **Cotton States Expositions**. Primarily, the Cotton Expositions were established to promote Atlanta's rebuilding from the Civil War, promote its industrial

capabilities and accomplishments, and lure northern investment into the city and region. The most ambitious of the city's cotton expositions was staged in 1895. The Cotton States and International Exposition's goal was to foster trade between southern states and South American nations, as well as to show the products and facilities of this south region to the rest of the nation and to Europe. It was here that the Charles Jenkins motion picture projector was featured, leading the way to TV broadcasting. The expo buildings were divided by industries, showcasing the latest technology in transportation, manufacturing, mining, agriculture, and other fields. Amusements such as the "Phoenix Wheel" and an early introduction of motion pictures were set up as part of a midway to attract visitors. Other attractions included the Liberty Bell and celebrities like Buffalo Bill and the composer John Phillip Sousa, who wrote "King Cotton March" specifically for the occasion. On opening day, Booker T. Washington delivered his famous "Atlanta Compromise" speech. The Cotton States Exposition successfully showcased Atlanta as a business center and attracted investment to the city. After the exposition, the grounds were purchased by the City of Atlanta and became Piedmont Park and the Atlanta Botanical Garden.

The Trade Show Industry in Atlanta-

The Right Time for a New U.S. Convention Center

Like many of the top convention cities in the USA, the trade show

exhibit design companies evolved from the show contractor companies that started in the region. For Atlanta, Shepard Exposition Services started in 1905 to service local events like parades, World Fairs, and early trade shows at hotels. Shepard expanded its service reach to assist industry associations with trade show management beyond Atlanta and is now located in twelve US cities. Shepard Expo Services managed the first shows at the **Georgia World Congress:** The Bobbin Show and the Poultry Show. In the beginning, the show contractors in the US helped organize and manage the trade show events. They provided basic exhibit booth spaces with optional furniture and graphics. The exhibitors at trade shows now wanted a more sophisticated exhibit design look to enhance their image. Many exhibit companies were formed in Atlanta to design and fabricate creative and appealing exhibits directly for the exhibitors.

Note that in later years, most all show contractors in the US also stepped into the business of designing and building exhibits for individual exhibitors, as well as their core strength of managing an entire trade show. This trend for show contractors to design and fabricate exhibits really did not kick into high gear until 2000. So before then, the show contractor was not considered competition, other than for shell schemes.

The **Atlanta Civic Center** was built in 1967 and was used as a convention center. The state of Georgia took it over in 1976 and then invested to build the **Georgia World Congress Center.** It was a state-owned convention center. State ownership of a venue proved to be successful and served as a model for other states. This new center was originally built at 350,000 square feet and expanded several times in 1985, 1992, and 2002. It now offers 1.5 million square feet as one of the largest convention facilities in America.

The 1990s were the heyday of trade show activities in Atlanta. The Atlanta Dome (now Mercedes-Benz Stadium) added further attractions for events in Atlanta. Many shows were attracted to Atlanta during the construction expansions at McCormick Place in Chicago and the Moscone in San Francisco in the 1990s.

When Atlanta was awarded the site of the Olympic Games in 1996, many of the regular trade shows Atlanta has attracted were forced to change locations and then never returned. This also happened in 2008, when a tornado badly damaged GWGC. From this, many shows elected to go to the Morial Convention Center in New Orleans and the Orlando Convention Center. The Olympic Games generated $5 billion for the city, but Atlanta lost more over the next three years when many trade shows elected to go elsewhere and slowed down their continued growth. During this same time period, convention center expansions were underway in Orlando and Las Vegas, which are now the leading trade show sites in America. In spite of all this, Atlanta holds strong as a premier venue location.

Exhibit Design & Fabrication Companies- Atlanta

Some of the early exhibit design companies in Atlanta were **Murphy & Orr,** a second-generation cabinet shop that built bank interiors and museums. They then started to do exhibit design for Bell South, which became part of AT&T.

Robert K. Price Co. is a firm that did smaller exhibits and did work on the Georgia Welcome Centers. **Custom Creations** was started by Dick Foote and Bug Haney. They went out of business in 1977. **Design South** was started by Gary Stewart, who picked up some of the Construction business to jump-start Design South. SummDesign did work for Design South as a job shop.

Dick Foote started **Matrix**, which was then purchased by Greyhound Exhibitgroup to become **Exhibitgroup Atlanta.**

When GWCC opened in 1976, several new exhibit companies entered the market in Atlanta.

C. Henning Studios / Cassandra Henning acquired the Coca-Cola account for exhibits and then sold it to **Czarnowski Atlanta.** A dominant player to this day. **Sugar Creek** was owned by Guy Langston, and Geoffrey Winslow was a partner. Winslow then started his own company, **Design Productions,** and sold it to Display Corporation of America. He then started a new company named **Ideas Inc.**, which later became **Folio Exhibits.** Ideas became a high-end boutique exhibit house, attracting big brands like Nike and Sony as well as exhibitors in the.com industry and cable industry. The Folio Group (investors out of Boston) bought up five companies in the US to create Folio. Like many companies that bought up companies to create a single big one, their ability to manage and blend the different company cultures was not one of their strong points. The company dissolved in two years.

Laarhoven Display/ Robert Laarhoven moved his exhibit company from NJ to Atlanta in 1985 as Laarhoven Display and also became partners with Geoffrey Winslow to start Ideas, but sold his interest to focus only on Laarhoven Display.

Robert then began to promote a Belgian exhibit system called DeltaMatrix. He rebranded his company as e4Design to promote DeltaMatrix in the US. The owner in Belgium then sold DeltaMatrix. Robert Laarhoven and e4Design partner Lance Wacholz then partnered with the owners of Delta Matrix in Belgium to create **beMatrix USA**, a new exhibit system in the USA that is now used extensively with many exhibit design companies. Other companies that surfaced during the 1975–2000 time period were Derse Atlanta, Exhibitus, Exponents Atlanta, Team One Exhibits, Blue Sky, and Mc2 (now a part of the MCH Group in Basel, Switzerland).

Beyond the exhibit design companies in Atlanta, other exhibit supplier companies surfaced strongly in Atlanta to serve the nation. Octanorm, beMatrix, I&D (now nth Degree), Momentum, Renaissance, Skyline, and Brumark were all exhibit supplier companies and not exhibit designers or builders. Dave Walens started with a portable exhibit company in Atlanta and then expanded to start a successful flooring company called **Brumark**. He then created a company he named

Exploring, which combined Brumark for flooring, exploring with graphics, and ID3 GROUP which does unique exhibit fabrication beyond traditional exhibit fabrication methods. This was a new, innovative move within the industry.

1975–1985: The majority of clients served by the exhibit companies in Atlanta were companies outside of the Atlanta area and for shows beyond the GWCC.

Today, the exhibit houses in Atlanta and the Georgia Wold Congress continue to remain strong, but the late 80's and late 90's were their hay days of growth and popularity.

Trend Changes- During the early 80's in the USA most exhibits were fabricated from wood, including 10 x 10 and 10' x 20' exhibits. Portable and system exhibits then changed the demand for custom-built exhibits. The majority of exhibit house clients were men. In the late 80's and into the 90's, 75% of the exhibit house customers were now female with the title of exhibits manager. This is when the role of AM's was created at most exhibit houses in America. For the Fortune 500 companies, purchasing agents now get involved in deciding who to contract with for exhibit services. This forced many previous long-term relationships between exhibit houses and the client contact to end. In the 80's and 90's, most new project presentations were done in person with hand-colored renderings or a model; now they are done in CAD. Designers no longer needed to be gifted artists, but CAD designers. T-squares and magic marker designs are now replaced with life-like CAD renderings. Today, new exhibit presentations are done via the internet using Zoom, in many cases never meeting the client in person except on the show site for set-up. Many AEs today do travel to the show site during installation, as this may be the only time they meet with the client in person. A new world of communication!

New Orleans-

The **Ernest N. Morial Convention Center** is located on the Mississippi River in downtown New Orleans. It is named after former Mayor of New Orleans Ernest Nathan Morial. The first portion of the building was constructed as part of the 1984 Louisiana World Exposition, a financial disaster. A series of building additions were added in subsequent decades, expanding the center further upriver in a straight line. If you were attending an event in Hall J and your taxi dropped you off at Hall B, you would then walk over a half mile to your destination. Morial provides the largest single exhibit space under one roof in the country. The center gained added popularity when McCormick, World Congress, Javits, and Orlando were all expanding and the 1984 World Expo created positive attention. A window of opportunities opened during this period.

The center started in 1978 and opened for conventions in 1985. It was the fifth-largest facility of its kind in the United States, and it hosted many of the largest conventions in the country. 2005 was the second-busiest year. This is no longer the case due to Hurricane Katrina, which

hit in 2005. It then converted the center into the largest care center and hospital for the next 3 months. The Convention Center finished a complete renovation of the facility in November 2006. Like other convention centers that are forced to cancel availability for whatever reasons (McCormick, Georgia World Congress, Moscone, Javits), when trade shows change their regular venue locations, many shows do not return. Katrina stopped shows in New Orleans for four years. With their renovation and marketing, many top shows are now reconsidering holding their events in New Orleans. Like Las Vegas and Orlando, New Orleans has an emotional attraction. Everyone is simply excited to be in one of the world's most storied and culturally rich destinations. Traditional jazz music enlivens the soul, the cuisine is incomparable, and the city's charm captivates. Never underestimate the power of a city's attractions when selecting a location for a trade show. People decide to attend a trade show for three reasons: industry knowledge from sessions and exhibit show floor, networking with peers, and the emotional attraction to a city.

New Orleans Economy and Exhibit Houses

New Orleans has a diverse economy with the main sectors being energy, advanced manufacturing, international trade, healthcare and tourism. New Orleans is a major grain port both in the United States and worldwide; exports include raw and processed agricultural products, fabricated metals, chemicals, textiles, oils, petroleum and petroleum products, tobacco, and paperboard. Tourism and conventions account for 45% of New Orleans' economic impact. Both Las Vegas and Orlando do not have an industrial economic base to attract exhibit houses to set up facilities. Their attraction to do so in later years was the number of trade shows held annually to serve their customers. Most suppliers started with warehouses and then exhibit fabrication. Exhibit design companies in New Orleans did not start up until 1985. Czarnowski was one of the first to set up shop in New Orleans. Other exhibit houses slowly followed, like Cardinal Expo and Beaumont & Co. Through Katrina, the show contractor companies remained in place awaiting the comeback. Show organizers today are now again selecting New Orleans as a venue location for their events due to its festive attractions.

Convention Centers & Exhibit Suppliers- WEST

San Francisco: Info provided by Dave Hardbarger and Frank Grossman

The City by the Bay Played a Major Role to Attract Visitors to Attend Major Trade Shows

Each exhibit company in the USA seems to have followed a similar historical path. They got started as tent makers, sign painters, parade floats and widow decorators. They then evolved to work with show contractors who were managing a trade show. For San Francisco, two World Fairs (the Pacific Int'l Expo-1915 and the Golden Gate Fair-

1939) served to pave the way as an entrée to the show contractor and exhibit design / builder businesses in later years One of the early exhibit suppliers in San Francisco was the **Stewart Sauder Company** in 1935. They specialized in large tents for events. They provided most of the tents for the 1939 World Fair on Treasure Island, SF. After the Fair they started a show contractor service company for events and early trade shows at the Cow Palace, Brooks Hall, and the Masonic Auditorium. In 1971, Stewart Sauter was purchased by RCA, and in 1974, Greyhound was purchased to form GES-SF and Exhibitgroup SF.

The original Moscone Convention Center Hall opened in 1981 on the site of what is now known as Moscone South. The Moscone Center is named after he murdered mayor-George Moscone. Moscone initially opposed the development of the south market area when he served on the SF Board of Supervisors in the 1960s. He felt it would displace elderly and poor residents of the area. As mayor, Moscone convened a special committee of proponents and opponents of a convention center. Hearings were held throughout SF seeking citizen input. A compromise was reached which was supported by Moscone. He put the matter on the ballot in November 1976 and it passed overwhelmingly. The original Moscone Convention Center Hall opened in 1981 on the site of what is now known as Moscone South. It was not until 1981 that Moscone Center was open for business. Since then, it expand twice to add Moscone North and West buildings. It's popularity was at its highest during the late 90's. Designing an exhibit for a show at Moscone South could be tricky with the arched ceiling supports that may cross into your exhibit space if not aware.

One of the big trade shows in Northern California was the **Semicon Show** which started in 1971 at the San Mateo Country Fairground. The Santa Clara Convention Center opened in 1985.

The Exhibit Houses-

In 1965, there were three well-known exhibit companies to design and build trade show exhibits:

Novell Art, Palmer Displays (in Berkley), and AD Gordon (in Oakland).

By the early 80's, the major design/fabricators were Exhibitgroup SF (in S. San Francisco), Giltspur (in Burlingame), Bluepeter, Formetrics, and Exhibit Place (both in San Jose).

An economic recession in the early 90's led to a softening of the exhibit business. Formetrics was purchased by Color & Design from Portland, and Contempo Exhibits took over Exhibit Place. In 1995, Exhibitgroup acquired Giltspur and merged the two in Fremont, CA. Exhibitgroup then acquired Color & Design to also join them in Fremont. During this ruffled period, Pinnacle Exhibits were also formed.

In the late 90's the popularity of portable exhibits flourished so new exhibit companies were formed in the Bay Area—Skyline, Blazer, and ProExhibits each surfaced to success.

Through the 80's and early 2000, Moscone Hall attracted many top trade shows from around the country. Moscone expanded twice to attract more business. Many of the top high-tech and computer shows were now held at Moscone, as well as medical shows. The demand for conferences and cool exhibits skyrocketed.

The Bay Area exhibit companies in the 90's were recognized nationally for providing creative design, as fabrication was viewed as a given. They produced exhibits for exhibitors at shows in Los Angeles, Las Vegas (Comdex), Dallas, and Chicago (Computer Conference). As new companies grew in the **Silicon Valley**, Bay Area exhibit houses were running full steam to design and build exhibits for hi-tech companies. The exhibit companies also attracted I&D business for events at Moscone from other exhibit companies throughout the US. The 90's was a period of transition when it came to how exhibits were now designed and fabricated. Bay Area exhibit design led the way. System exhibit components, fabric components, hanging signs, new graphics technology, and AV components started a new trend in exhibit design nationwide. Many creative exhibit solutions unfolded without the need to build an exhibit from scratch in house. Exhibit design was now using components bought on the outside and assembled in the shop, requiring less wood construction, lower cost, and lighter in weight.

With convention center expansions in the US, the dot-com bust, the 2008 financial meltdown, and covid mania, many of the new Bay Area exhibit companies like Sparks, Group Delphi, and Exhibitgroup/Giltspur had their businesses slow down. They then merged, or now cease to exist. It was a good run for many and still a dynamic area for exhibit design.

> ### *The Silicone Valley Story:*
>
> ### *Paving the way for new Trade Shows*
>
> Many new high-tech products that were developed in the Silicon Valley were first introduced at a trade show. Stanford University played a major role in the development of the culture of collaboration among high-tech companies in Northern California. A powerful sense of regional solidarity shaped the outlook of inventors and engineers in California, contrasting markedly from the insular and competitive environment of engineering firms on the east coast. From the 1890s, Stanford University's leaders saw its mission as service to the American West and shaped the school. At the same time, the perceived exploitation of the West at the hands of eastern interests fueled attempts to build self-sufficient local industries. Thus, regionalism helped align Stanford's interests with those of the area's high-tech firms. Frederick Terman, as Stanford's dean of the school of engineering, encouraged faculty and graduates to start their own companies. In 1951, Terman spearheaded the formation of Stanford Industrial Park. Terman nurtured companies like Hewlett-Packard, Varian Associates, Eastman Kodak, General Electric, Lockheed Corporation, and other high-tech firms until what would become Silicon Valley.
>
> In 1951, to address the financial demands of Stanford's growth requirements and to provide local employment opportunities for graduating students, Frederick Terman proposed leasing Stanford's lands for use as an office park named the Stanford Industrial Park.

Terman invited only high-technology companies. The first tenant was Varian Associates, founded by Stanford alumni in the 1930s to build military radar components. Hewlett-Packard became one of the major success stories. Founded in 1939 in Packard's garage by Stanford graduates Bill Hewlett and David Packard, Hewlett-Packard moved its offices into the Stanford Research Park shortly after 1953. In 1954, Stanford originated the Honors Cooperative Program to allow full-time employees of the companies to pursue graduate degrees from the university on a part-time basis. The initial companies signed an agreement to pay double the tuition for each student in order to cover the costs. In 1956, William Shockley, the co-inventor of the first working transistor, started Shockley Semiconductor Laboratory. Unlike many other researchers who used germanium as the semiconductor material, Shockley believed that silicon was the better material for making transistors. Both Frederick Terman and William Shockley are often called "the fathers of the Silicon Valley".

Woman in the Business of Trade Shows

In the late 80's, throughout the United States, there began to be an influx of woman exhibit managers at major corporations. This trend created the role of AM's (Account Managers) at most US exhibit companies, who were also women. The AM worked closely with the AE and a team of support staff to manage their client show program throughout the country. Relationships mattered. Today, women in the exhibit industry play a significant role in the methods and success of trade show marketing. This was not the case in the 60s and 70s.

West Coast - Los Angeles, San Diego, Seattle, Portland, Denver

Los Angeles

The **Los Angeles Convention Center** broke ground in 1969 and opened in 1971. Two sites used then for convention and trade shows were the Shrine Auditorium and the Pan-Pacific Auditorium. The business community wanted a convention center to compete with other major U.S. cities, and various sites were considered. The new convention center opened in 1971 and expanded in 1981, 1993 and 1997. The northeast portion of the center was demolished in 1997 to make way for the Staples Center. In 1983, a tornado ripped through the center, closing it for two years. Many regular shows then went elsewhere. It has since survived and come back to life.

Some of the early exhibit houses in Los Angeles were Exhibitgroup (Chuck LaRocco), Giltspur, Universal Exhibits, Exhibitree (Dave Black), Grondorf Field Black, The Exhibit Place (Rich Swartz/Jerry Jones), Abex Exhibits (Robbie Blumenfeld), and Exponents (Bruce Baker/Steve Rossman)—one of the first companies with a custom modular system in 1979. Other reliable companies today include Insight Exhibits, Display International, Laguna Displays, ASV Experiential and Freeman.

Anaheim

The **Anaheim Convention Center** was one of the largest exhibition facilities on the West Coast. It was located across from the Disneyland and two major hotels. A convenient setting with the attraction of Disneyland. Built in 1967, the Anaheim Center has undergone six major expansions (1974, 1982, 1990, 1993, 1999–2000, 2016–2017).

The **NAMM Show** has been running at the Anaheim Center since 1977, except for a three-year break in 1998–2000 while the Convention

Center underwent major renovations, and in 2021 due to the Covid 19. In 2008, news reports indicated that NAMM's long-term lease with the Anaheim Convention Center authority would end in 2010, and NAMM was applying pressure to the City of Anaheim to further expand and improve the convention center. The NAMM Show did ultimately occur in the convention center in 2011 and the subsequent years.

Another large convention held at the center is the *Medical Design and Manufacturing Show*, held shortly after Winter NAMM. Disney's inaugural D23 Expo, a biennial convention for Disney fans, was held at the Anaheim Convention Center in 2009. The convention center has hosted all subsequent D23 Expos since.

San Diego

San Diego has the best climate of any city in the United States. The original design of the **San Diego Convention Center** aimed to capitalize on this with open-air pavilions. By the time San Diego's Convention Center was set for construction, pretty much every major city in the United States already had their own. Architect Arthur Erickson drew inspiration from the adjacent waterfront. Throughout the composition of the structure, elements clearly pay homage to sails, masts, and waves. The facility first opened its doors on November 24, 1989, and since that day it has welcomed over 20 million guests and generated over $26 billion in regional impact. The demand to book an event was so high that the need for more space was soon apparent. In

1998, City voters approved a proposition to expand the Convention Center by a 62 percent vote.

The **1st Comic Con** at the San Diego Convention Center was in 1991. Many top shows have been held there over the years. The center's best-known feature is the Sails Pavilion. Known for incredible panoramic views of San Diego Bay and five-star service, the San Diego Convention Center is a meeting planner's dream. For starters, the building is in a vibrant downtown setting within a mile and a half of more than 11,000 first-class hotel rooms, including four headquarter hotels, and 10 minutes from the airport. A great location for a medium-sized trade show

Denver-

Denver Convention Center

In 1908, the Denver Municipal Auditorium opened and hosted the Democratic National Convention. It was the second largest convention center in the nation, after Madison Square Garden in New York. In 1969, Currigan Exhibition Hall opens with 100,000

squares. feet. of meeting space and a bridge connecting it to meeting rooms in the Auditorium Arena. The new Denver Convention Center opened in June 1990, the first event being the NBA draft for the Denver Nuggets. The convention center was expanded in 2004 and again in 2023 to include several meeting rooms, two ballrooms, and an indoor amphitheater. The building holds the Guinness World Record for the largest beer tasting ever held on the planet—the annual Great American Beer Festival. In 2014, it was voted as one of the top 10 centers in America.

In 2017, the Gaylord Hotel opened a huge meeting and convention facility near the airport. For many smaller meetings and trade shows, this proved to be an excellent location, with a United Airlines hub in Denver for nonstop flights as well as international, making it a convenient location.

Denver Exhibit Houses-

Denver, Colorado is home for Condit Exhibits, but they work around the globe. Condit has been a Colorado company for over 75 years. Founded by Bill Condit in 1945 as "Condit Advertising Art" with only $88, the Denver facility employed just two people in a windowless attic office. Condit was the first graphic arts and graphic design studio in Denver. Bill and his advertising team initially specialized in airbrush painting. Condit headquarters bounced all around Denver as the company grew and evolved—first as an ad agency, then a cabinet maker, and eventually morphing into the exhibit design and fabricator. One of Condit's first booths was for Martin Marietta. This project was also their first modular exhibit. Condit designed and managed Coor's Beer for many years. Today they have a full facility in Chicago to extend their reach.

Over the years other exhibit houses set up in Denver. Companies like Czarnowski, IGE Group/Gino Pellegrini, and PG Exhibits/Jim McGrath. The top Colorado companies enjoyed having a local exhibit house to service their exhibiting needs.

Seattle-

Since opening the original **Seattle Convention Center** in 1988, the location has attracted many trade shows to be held there. There are now two Seattle Convention Center locations one block apart from each other. Essentially, it's a bet that a bigger convention center will bring more hotel guests, who, in turn, will pay more hotel tax, which will then be used to pay back the cost of building the bigger convention center. The new facility will be used as an addition to—not a replacement for — the existing convention center, known as the Arch, which hangs over Pike Street, just a block away. Officials hope the new building can help revitalize downtown, which hasn't seen office workers fully return since the pandemic and has seen retail vacancies soar. Another location is the Bell Harbor International Conference, which opened in 1996 with The World Trade Center across the street. This historical harbor location is a great spot for a medium-sized conference and trade shows. Seattle has invested greatly to attract trade shows and business conferences to Seattle.

The business of trade shows did not start in Seattle until after the **1962 World's Fair** at the Seattle Center. Shows were held at the Coliseum & Exhibition Hall at the Seattle Center. The Kingdom was then built shortly after. One of the first exhibit companies to start up in 1968 was the David Strong Design Group. Another early exhibit company was Berg & Associates, who later became AIMEX and became the major exhibit house in Seattle. Other exhibit design houses were PPI (Promotion Products Inc. and Color & Design), Seattle Exhibits, and Orca Exhibits. Many are no longer in business. Seattle is a strong business city with some top corporations. The new convention center will attract new shows and exhibit design to Seattle, especially for shows that return yearly.

Portland

The Oregon Convention Center in Portland opened in 1990. The Oregon Convention Center serves as a catalyst for Oregon's economy. In addition to the thousands of jobs supported by the facility, consumer spending totals more than $500 million each year as a result of the convention center's business. It was the first convention center to receive the highest platinum rating in the U.S. Green Building Council's LEED certification program. Portland has made remarkable progress to lead convention centers across the United States in achieving LEED certification and reducing carbon footprints. The Oregon Convention Center is on the rise to be a popular destination going forward.

Portland Exhibit Houses-

Portland had a few very successful exhibit houses—PPI/Promotion Products and Color & Design—who are no more. With each merger came a new company to open. There are two successful companies in Portland today. Classic Exhibits, started in 1993, specializes in custom hybrid exhibits and rentals. They have a network of distributors around the country and are very reliable. The other is Pinnacle Exhibits, founded in 1998 by Chris Olberding, an ex-Color & Design employee. They have since been acquired and expanded with four US locations, each providing more than just exhibits.

Today's Two top Convention Center Cities in the USA

What was the Fuel that brought these two Cities to be the Top Attractions?

Orlando & Las Vegas

The popularity of trade show marketing in today's two top convention center cities did not begin to be embraced until much later than in other US cities. Both Orlando and Las Vegas did not initially view trade shows as a number one way to attract visitors to their cities. After all, they had entertainment, gambling, and Micky Mouse to fill this need. The decision from the city officials in Orlando and Las Vegas to invest in a convention center took a lot of convincing. They were not really anxious to invest the major dollars required to do so. Their investments to date have now paid off greatly in spades!

Three of the major incentives for an industry association to select a city for their show are availability of exhibit floor space, ability to house attendees, and an attractive location. Chicago has provided this for years and became the number one city, but years later Chicago then dropped to number three. Today, for every exhibitor who participates in eight trade shows a year, half are in one of the three cities above. The largest of trade shows are really limited with their choice of city locations if they want to accommodate the exhibiting space needed and the attendees need for hotels and meeting rooms. Both Orlando and Las Vegas do this and provide added emotional attractions for visitors to choose to attend. If your intention to attend a trade show in the USA is strictly business, there are many excellent centers in the USA to plan your event. The added attractions of New Orleans, San Diego, San Antonio, and Anaheim provide a strong emotional incentive, but these cities cannot always accommodate the space needed for a top trade show. These two cities check all the boxes when it comes to filling a location need.

Orlando-

The **Orange County Convention and Civic Center** (OCCCC) was born out of a 1977 law passed by Florida's State Legislature to permit counties to collect a "Tourist Development Tax" on top of regular sales tax on hotel room stays. In April 1978, the voters of Orange County

approved a 2% Tourist Development Tax (the limit set by the state) to build a convention and civic center. That August, the Orange County Board of County Commissioners (BCC) approved a location for the OCCCC on International Drive. The original building (the "West Concourse") housed an 11,300-seat arena from 1983 to 1992. It hosted concerts by top entertainment artists. Its use declined after the Orlando Arena opened in 1989. The arena closed in 1992 and was renovated and converted into the main exhibition hall in 1996. Orange County Convention Center continued to expand for the next 20 years. The OCCC now consists of two buildings joined together by a covered pedestrian bridge. The West Building, opening in four phases from

February 1983 (with an initial 150,000 sq ft of exhibition space) and in 1996, is located on the south side of International Drive. The North/South Building, located on the north side of International Drive, was completed in 2003. Phase V of expansion started in August 2000 after a large convention organizer, Reed Exhibitions, agreed to move 42 conventions to Orlando into the new phase. It opened one month ahead of schedule in September 2003. Today, the first four phases are referred to as the "West Building" and Phase V is referred to as the "North/South Building." This rapid growth, at a time many other US cities were doing the same, skyrocketed Orlando to be one of the three top convention destinations in the USA. OCCC is now the second-largest convention facility in the United States. Aside from Disney World, each year the OCCC attracts more than 230 events to the center. As a result, roughly 1.4 million attendees contribute approximately $2.4 billion to the area's economy each year.

Orlando Exhibit Builders-

Exhibit design and fabrication companies did not start in Orlando until the early 90's. Many of the larger exhibit houses started with a storage warehouse and then expanded to provide design and fabrication for the growing number of trade shows held in Orlando. Some of the leading exhibit companies include Czarnowski, Color Craft, The Exhibit Builder, Absolute Exhibits, and Pure Exhibits.

Las Vegas-

In the 1950s, the city and county community leaders decided they needed a convention center. Their goal was to increase hotel occupancy in the off-tourist season. The story goes that they decided to build it one block east of the Strip on the site of the Las Vegas Park Speedway. This was a failed horse and auto race track from the early 1950s. They then built a 6,300-seat silver-domed rotunda with a 90,000-square-foot exhibition hall.

While Chicago had grown to be the number one convention city in the USA, Las Vegas was still growing. In actuality, the Las Vegas Convention Center was built before McCormick Place. Las Vegas Convention Center opened in 1959 with 90,000 sq ft and hosted more entertainment events than trade shows. McCormick opened a year later in 1960 and took off like a rocket, attracting many top trade shows. Las Vegas did attract shows during this period, but not the big shows just yet due to space available.

It was not until 1993 that the Las Vegas Convention and Visitors Authority (LVCVA) purchased the defunct Landmark hotel-casino, which was across from the convention center. LVCVA demolished the resort in 1995 to develop additional parking on the site for convention guests and expanded the center in 1998 to increase the space to 1.9 million sq ft. This was the start of real growth. While it functioned, COMDEX was the most attended trade show in the United States, with over 200,000 attendees on several occasions. In 2000, early planning began for another expansion of the center. The new $150 million South Hall was finished in 2001. It would now consist of 1.3 million sq ft. Since then, LVCC has expanded twice.

Today, the Las Vegas Convention Center is one of the busiest facilities

in the world—a 4.6 million-square-foot facility with 2.9 million square feet of exhibit space and 225 meeting rooms, and located within a short distance to 150,000 hotel rooms. McCormick Place is the only other facility in the US that is larger but not as busy. Today, the Las Vegas Convention Center is the most popular convention center in the US.

Sheldon Adelson was a Las Vegas trade show industry super star. He became one of the richest men in the world. In the late 1970s, Adelson developed the **COMDEX** trade shows for the computer industry, beginning in 1979. It was one of the largest computer trade shows in the world through much of the 1980s and 1990s. In 1995, Adelson sold the Interface Group Show Division, including the COMDEX shows, to SoftBank Group of Japan. In 1988, Adelson purchased the Sands Hotel and Casino in Las Vegas. The next year, he built the **Sands Expo and Convention Center**, then the only privately owned and operated convention center in the U.S. In 1991, while honeymooning in Venice with his second wife, Miriam, Adelson came up with the idea for a mega-resort hotel. He razed the Sands and spent $1.5 billion to construct The Venetian, a Venice-themed resort hotel and casino in 1999. Sheldon Adelson went on to invest in many other hotels and centers throughout the world. One of the most famous was the Marina Bay Sands in Singapore, which included a convention center attached. It is said to be the most expensive building in the world! Adelson brought an added popularity for trade shows held in Las Vegas.

CES, World Concrete, Magic, Hardware Show, Home Builders, Restaurant Show, NAR-Realators, SEMA Show, Con Expo, NAHB, Int'l Builders Show, SHOT Show, Int'l Pool & Spa, CosMoProf, G2E, Pizza Expo, and a non-trade show event. the NFR (the Super Bowl of Rodeos). There are at least 4-5 trade shows going on each week in Las Vegas at the same time throughout the year.

Las Vegas Exhibit Houses: In the beginning, the show contractor companies started up strong in Las Vegas to support the growing trade show activity beginning to expand in Las Vegas. Mancraft and Las Vegas Convention Service were the early show contractors. GES then purchased Mancraft in 1969 and LVCS in 1973. Exhibit houses did not start strong until the mid-80's. **CB Display** was one of the first with

Exhibitgroup Las Vegas, now called **Spiro,** a part of the GES family. **Structure Exhibits** opened in early 2000, and then many others followed. Exhibit service companies like A-Plus Expo, Color Craft, Expo Group, Beaumont & Co., Circle Exhibits, Steelhead, SAK Design, Absolute Exhibits, Design Factory, Impact XM, Int'l All Space from the UAE, and several other of the exhibit companies with a national network of facilities all pitched a tent in Las Vegas to manage the exhibit programs for their clients who all had several shows in Las Vegas. In addition, many companies that offered ancillary services like flooring, furniture, AV, lighting, and florals followed to set up shop in Las Vegas. For a city that had few exhibit supplier companies in the 80's, it now has suppliers representing each of the leading exhibit design companies in the USA with a facility to offer local services. Note that the two leading show contractors and exhibit design companies in the US are GES (Spiro) in Las Vegas and Freeman in Dallas.

All roads lead to Las Vegas. Of the top ten convention centers in America, Las Vegas has three. Between the Sands Expo Center, Mandalay Bay, and the Las Vegas Convention Center, there are about 75 major trade shows every year and approximately 24,000 conventions and meetings of all sizes in Las Vegas. Because of this activity, exhibit houses had opened to accommodate storage and refurbishing needs between shows and to save on shipping costs. These exhibit houses also began to be built new when needed. Being close to the church had major advantages for exhibit suppliers!

Why Orlando and Las Vegas took the lead… The popularity of Orlando and Las Vegas in the convention business did not expand until the late 80's. The other major convention centers in US cities have been in the trade show business since the 70's. The decision for a trade show attendee to attend any show in the past was mostly for business. Orlando and Las Vegas both provided an added incentive. So why did Orlando and Las Vegas enter the convention business so late? The answer is that they did not need the added incentives to attract visitors to their cities. Micky Mouse and gambling served them well when it came to tourism revenues. In time, tax incentives and a realization that convention business provided some real added benefits to their economies and hotel occupancy rate. Today there is no doubt why Las Vegas and Orlando are considered the number one and two destinations for business meetings and conventions. Trade Shows mean Business, but never underestimate the secondary emotional attractions for deciding to attend, or not attend, any event.

CHAPTER SEVEN

Evolution of Exhibit Design & Methods at Trade Shows

Trade Show Exhibiting

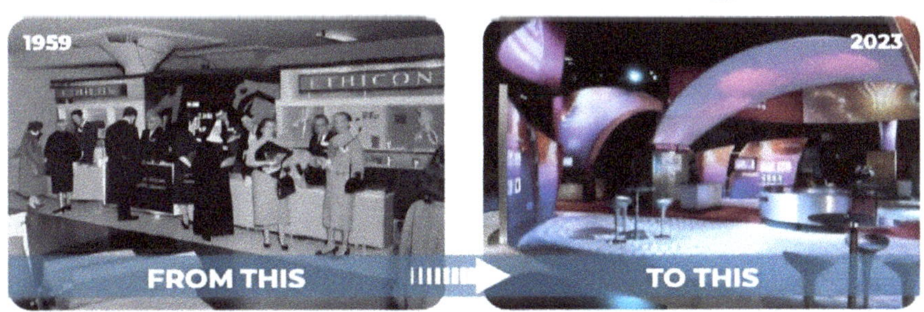

Intro by Kevin Sweeney- Exhibit Marketing Veteran

In the bustling landscape of marketing, trade shows stand as bastions of innovation, where businesses unveil their latest marvels, engage with customers, and forge lasting connections. Through the annals of time, trade show exhibits have morphed from mere displays showing products to immersive brand experiences, reflecting the evolving dynamics of experiential marketing. Let's embark on a journey through this transformation, unraveling the layers of evolution that have shaped the look of trade shows.

The Evolution: From Display of Wares to Demonstration of Product

Traditionally, rows of booths adorned with products, ready for eager attendees to explore, characterized trade shows. Yet, as attendees' expectations soared, a shift towards interactive engagement became imperative. Thus emerged the transition from static displays to live product demonstrations. Companies recognized the allure of allowing attendees to experience products firsthand. Today's trade shows have evolved into interactive hubs where visitors can touch, feel, and immerse themselves in products, creating personal engagements that linger in the memory long after the event concludes.

Attraction to Storytelling: Weaving Narratives into Brand Experiences

Amidst escalating competition within trade shows, attracting and retaining attendees became a formidable challenge. Mere flashy displays and giveaways fell short in capturing attention. Recognizing the power of narratives, brands turned to storytelling as a potent tool for forging an emotional connection. Compelling stories became the lifeblood of experiential marketing, captivating the imagination of attendees and transporting them into the brand's narrative realm. Whether recounting the inception of a product, the journey of its creators, or its impact on customers' lives, storytelling became the heartbeat of trade show engagements.

Elevating Experiences: From Brand Experience to Brand Immersion

With the dawn of the digital age and the cacophony of sensory stimuli, brands realized the imperative of elevating trade show experiences further. Thus emerged the concept of brand immersion—a holistic approach transcending mere demonstrations or narratives. It's about crafting environments that engage all the senses, leaving an indelible mark on attendees. From virtual reality escapades to interactive installations, brands blurred the lines between the physical and digital realms. Attendees ceased to be passive observers; they became integral parts of the brand narrative, actively willing to participate in immersive experiences that resonated deeply.

Exhibit Design Through the Decades- 1960-2023
By Larry Kulchawik

Over the past 60 years, the trade show industry has changed its path and methods each decade, due in part to available technology, materials, and a desire to make exhibits more eye-catching, and a welcoming stage to feature a product or service. A secondary goal objective in exhibting was to control the costs of doing so.

Starting with the Persian street vendors to the World Fairs, the concept of trade shows evolved. Unlike a World Fair, trade shows evolved to be industry-specific. They became an effective way to introduce a new product to a known audience within a specific industry. Many trade shows started with their industry association. In the beginning, the event organizer would select a venue and then hire a show contractor to prepare the show floor and manage the event. The contractors would also assist exhibitors with their displays. Over time, exhibitors wanted more than the basic exhibit choices offered by the contractor, so exhibitors began to hire outside exhibit designers to build their stands for added pizzaz. Many exhibitors would ship in lumber, build a stand on site, paint, apply hand-painted graphics, and add live plants. Exhibitors wanted a stronger image at shows, so exhibit design companies began to form.

Many of the early exhibit design companies were owned by carpenters, sign painters, or decorators, each with an entrepreneurial spirit. They designed, built, and crated a prefabricated exhibit and shipped it to the show to be installed by a carpenter crew. Wolla! The exhibit houses were born and were now in high demand in the USA!

There were trade shows in the early 1900's, but they came to a halt with World War II. The concept of industry trade shows picked up really strong after the war years and rapidly grew with a thriving economy. Each time there was a world conflict, an economic downturn, or a pandemic, the style and methods of exhibiting changed. How exhibits were designed and built evolved to suit the times, available materials, and the space allowed. Technology and materials played a key role in influencing the methods for exhibit design each decade. The exhibit structure created an effective company image to introduce and promote products and services. At the early shows, men and women dressed formally. Companies wanted an attractive-looking exhibit to display their products, and wanted their representatives to do the same.

> The start of EDPA…In the early 60's, there were now many exhibit companies in business. The Exhibit Designers & Producers Association for exhibit design firms was formed for display houses to share exhibiting and business knowledge nationwide. EDPA was formed in 1956 with Norm Hadley serving as the first president from Hadley Display in Buffalo, NY.

Face-to-face exhibiting delivered results. Along the way, Convention Centers, show contractors, show organizers, industry associations, and exhibit design and service companies altered their methods each decade to create greater value for the exhibitors and attendees. During this period, the trade show industry in the USA created their own way of organizing a trade show event. The use of show contractors, material handling, exhibiting design rules, union labor, and exhibit materials created the American model of show management. These methods were much different than the trade show practices in the rest of the world.

Below is a snapshot showing the evolution of the **exhibit design and services** segment of the trade show industry after WWII. It shares how trade shows readjusted each decade—and how they grew to include new secondary supplier businesses that were created along the way. All through this time, air travel, hotels, and the expansion of convention centers played a role in making it easy to attend and growing in popularity nationwide.

1960-1970 Industry Expansions through Trade Fairs:

During this period, most trade shows were held in a coliseum or in hotels. Exhibit houses were beginning to grow, and most exhibits were fabricated from wood and crated for shipment. Weight was not a factor then. Most were 20'-30'x 8high in-line designs and used backlit transparencies for graphics, lighted with ball lights. The floor was covered in vinyl tiles. Wood paneling, slat walls, and painted box-framed panels were popular backwalls. The exhibitors were mainly men, and all attendees dressed in suits. There were few women who attended,

except at this nurse show in Washington, DC. This changed quickly over time. Two popular trade show cities in the 70's were Chicago and New York, with other cities beginning to create new facilities.

Exhibit space cost per sq ft was $4.74 on average.

1970-1980- Industry Convention Parties:

During shows, everyone dressed in suits, smoked, and drank more than usual. Networking at its best. The exhibits continued to be fabricated from wood and were crated for shipment to protect contents when unloaded at show site. Graphics were produced with silk screening. Light boxes for graphics, ball lights, slide projectors, and TVs were the main reason to order electric. The European aluminum systems were slowly entering the market as a frame to support a wall panel. Wood was still the preferred method to fabricate an exhibit. Technology was unfolding. The digital camera, vinyl letters, Sintra, aluminum systems, the Walkman, floppy disc, the cell phone, Betamax, and the Mac computer were all new tools to now consider.

1980-1990- The Go-Go Years! Trade shows were picking up steam in popularity and were viewed by many as an industry party. Show, The Housewares how, the Hardware Show, and CES were the places to be to make contacts, hire reps, and show your products. McCormick Place was a leading location. Venues were now being built exclusively for trade shows throughout the USA. McCormick was a leading location, with Atlanta, San Francisco, and Dallas venues quickly growing. New York was dropping off, and Las Vegas and Orlando were still preparing for the future. Many new shows and industries began to unfold: National Computer Conference/NY, Semicon/SF, Comdex/LV, SCTE Cable Expo, and ICSC/LV.

With so many more shows and larger booth spaces, exhibit houses were now managing their customers exhibit programs and not just a single show. Larger exhibit spaces, exhibit design ideas quickly evolved. Exhibit space was now on average $12.20 sq ft.

New materials to design an exhibit created a wide variety of creative solutions. Materials like tambour, slatwall, sintra, aluminum systems, velcro, fabric, vinyl graphics, fabric, and Zolatone paint gave exhibit designers new ideas. Exhibitors purchased larger exhibit spaces, so islands and peninsula spaces became more popular. Exhibitors wanted to be seen and wanted a 'cool-looking exhibit' to attract attention, and were willing to pay for it. Exhibit builders now purchased display components on the outside, creating an explosion of new companies that specialized in providing a single exhibit service. New companies were formed to exclusively provide carpet, graphics, furniture, shipping, lighting, fabric, AV, light boxes, systems, double deckers, and I&D services. Show contractor site restrictions were slowly being lifted in many of the top cities. The centers that did not adjust their rules would lose shows.

Exhibit builders were no longer carpenters but assemblers of components. For each installation, exhibit houses would send a supervisor for the set-up, using an independent I&D labor company. Exhibit houses now arrange all the exhibit services for their clients to extend their services. Loyal partnerships were created between the exhibit manager and the exhibit company team, but this changed with time.

1990-2000- The Years of Technology: New shows and venues continued to grow. With the rising popularity of trade show marketing came the rising costs of exhibiting. The cost to rent space on the show floor and the cost to build a classy exhibit began to rise. The on-site costs for material handling and the cost for labor were two major cost drivers. The words 'drayage' and 'labor unions' were

becoming dirty words. *Doing more with less* was the battle cry from exhibitors. As a result, exhibit designers pushed to create solutions to make exhibits lighter and to reduce the labor cost to install. From this driving desire came portable exhibits, aluminum system exhibits, fabric exhibits, light weight monitors, and I&D companies. All exhibit houses now use these new exhibit components to mix into their designs. This period was also the start of another trend—fabric hanging signs.

During this time period came the stronger use of computers and cell phones. All exhibit companies now discarded their T-squares, magic markers, and table saws and converted to using CAD design and CNC machines. This new technology was not quickly embraced by builders due to cost, but all eventually did so to reduce the time needed to meet deadlines.

CAD technicians began to replace carpenters. Exhibit components were purchased on the outside and the assembly of exhibit parts was the new skill needed. All production teams now included project and account managers.

2000-2010- Trade Shows Mean Business!

The power of trade shows remained strong until 9/11, and economic downturns forced the CFOs of companies to work with their sales and marketing managers. The purchasing agent now got involved to work with the exhibits manager. There were more shows for companies to consider, so budgeting to get the greatest return were decisions made beyond the exhibits manager. Big shows got bigger, and the trade show investment was not getting cheaper. The exhibitors at smaller shows used portables and set them up themselves. For the larger shows, exhibit materials in general were lighter but now incorporated overhead lighting trusses, fabric signs and canopies, and monitors for a stronger image. The labor costs here shifted from using exhibit walls to

overhead truss lighting for sizzle. This was the start of the visitor experience approach to exhibit design and the start of measuring the value of each prospect. Companies were formed to assist show organizers and exhibitors to measure results. Exhibitor CFO's wanted justification for their trade show investments. Las Vegas and Orlando now became the top venue locations for shows. They increased their floor space availability, saved on costs, and were located in appealing locations for a stronger emotional experience. Trade shows were still viewed as a powerful marketing tool, but the investment needed to be justified. Trade Shows Mean Business was the battle cry.

2010–2020 * Experiential * Technology * International

Exhibit design/builder companies are now becoming 3D marketing agencies. Exhibit design needed to create an image and to deliver an experience for visitors to remember you by. Design included attractions

from live presentations, engagement tactics, and quality video stimulation. "No one walks away without knowing our value, says Exhibits Managers". New companies with dedicated specialties (lead management, live presentations, exhibitor engagement) were formed and partnered with exhibit houses. Exhibit companies now began to merge with other exhibit companies. The show contractor companies also began to merge and expand, now offering AV services and custom exhibits. Since many corporations were expanding their reach globally, exhibit companies also began to provide global services. All exhibit houses now offered rentals, portables, systems, and international exhibit services. Each exhibit house established international partners and quickly learned the different ways of exhibiting to participate internationally.

2020-2024- Rediscovering the Human Element: The covid years forced all companies to uncover new ways of

communicating. The exhibitors and the exhibit companies that survived those two years experimented with digital ways to market. The virtual trade show was one way to create an opportunity for attendees to participate without physically being there. But what this lacked was the power of the human element; it lacked emotion. People buy from people they trust. Trade shows are not like shopping on the internet. Face-to-face marketing creates human interaction that serves to enhance a decision to buy. But for many, the attraction to attend are the educational sessions. The power of trade shows has made an amazing comeback from 2020. People did want to get out and engage with real people again. Exhibit design now incorporates digital ways to visit with

a potential customer at your booth space who is not physically there. International visitors could now visit exhibitors at the event without being there. Attracting attendees to visit your booth space was now achieved through both in-person engagement as well as digital engagement. Both works, but one is more powerful than the other. Is it no wonder why the top two U.S. convention cities today are in attractive locations? Trade shows do mean business, but don't underestimate the power of the event location to encourage attendees to experience their personal desires as well as achieve their business goals. Business can be a pleasure. Locations matter!

Exhibit Fabrication Methods

Unique materials that opened up new ways for exhibit design

In the beginning, many exhibits were built and decorated on site. Plywood, lumber, and fabric would be shipped to site, and a designer and a carpenter would build the display directly in the booth space. The backwall was hand painted with hand lettering applied for the company name and product specialty features. Lights may or may not have been used. The floor was tile. A display table may be built covered with fabric material. Green plants were added to liven it up and to hide any flaws. At the end of a show, they would simply discard, thus the term *build and burn*.

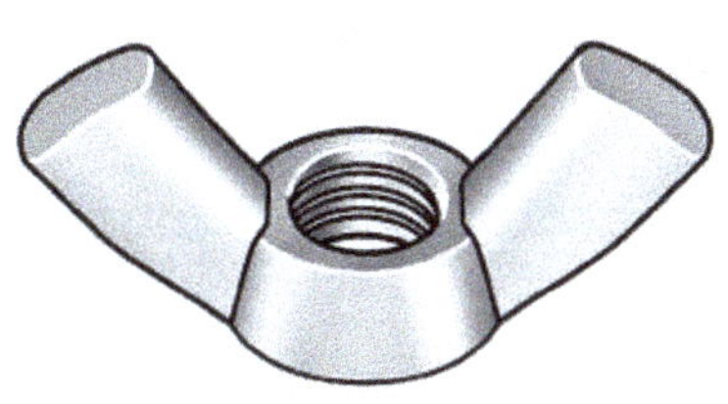

In the 70's, exhibits were now designed to be used over again at different shows throughout the year. Some were now available as rentals. The durability of the exhibit materials used was important. Wall shelves had to support product weight and wall hanging light box graphics.

Drayage weight was not yet an issue. Durability mattered, especially during shipment. In time, exhibit weight did become an issue in light of increased drayage fees at show sites.

A review about the evolution of Portables, Exhibit Systems, and Fabric in exhibit design is shared in the 'Change Makers' Chapter. These three material changes had a significant impact on the direction of exhibit design.

Here are a few of the materials that came on the market and changed how exhibits were built:

Plexiglas: Trained as a pharmacist, Otto Röhm first studied Pharmacy and then Chemistry in Munich. In 1901, he earned his PhD with a dissertation on "Polymerization products of acrylic acid." Six years later, he and Otto Haas founded the Röhm & Haas company. Röhm was a true pioneer in the field of plastics, developing a large number of acrylate and methacrylate compounds. But the greatest invention by Röhm and his staff was the invention of PLEXIGLAS® in 1933. The exhibit industry loved it!

Masonite (also called pressboard) is a type of engineered hardboard made of steam cooked and pressure-molded wood fibers in a process patented by William H. Mason. In 1924, Masonite was patented in Laurel, Mississippi, by William H. Mason, who was a friend and protégé of Thomas Edison. In 1929, the company initiated mass production of its product. In the 1940s and 1950s, Masonite was used for applications including doors, roofing, walls, desktops, and trade show exhibits.

Sintra® was introduced to North America in 1980. Sintra® is a lightweight yet rigid board of moderately expanded closed-cell polyvinyl chloride (PVC) extruded in a sheet with a low gloss matte finish. The edges are the same color as the face and available in different thicknesses. An excellent material to mount photos or for cut-out letters. Also works well as a wall insert when building with an aluminum system.

Silk Screening came from China during the Song Dynasty (960 AD). Their technique used a finely woven mesh and block stencils to

transfer shapes onto different materials. Screen printing soon spread throughout the world. It then grew in popularity around Europe and in the USA.

In the early 1900s, squeegees were formed and used as a way of pulling ink through the screen mesh. Roy Beck and Charles Peter are credited with revolutionizing the commercial screen-printing industry by their introduction of photo-imaged stencils to screen printing. This proved to be a better solution for signage and company logos than the need for hand sign painters.

Cut-out Letters: Note that many exhibits used hand-made cut-out letters for an exhibit header. In time, computers were able to provide letters cut from vinyl. Gerber vinyl cutting machines were purchased by exhibit companies for quick and easy solutions for exhibit graphics. The sign and graphics industry is then completely reinventing itself for the future. With the rise of digital printing and demand for versatility, sign and graphics companies needed to invest in advanced digital solutions in order to succeed. Not only did technology enable signage professionals to save time and money, but it also made the end result more impactful.

Vinyl Letters: In 1956, a chemist from 3M developed a pressure-sensitive vinyl film. This enabled the use of vinyl letters to fabricate attractive signs and graphics. Two years later, an easy-to-peel, silicone release liner was developed; this has remained a mainstay in protecting vinyl film's adhesive backing. Vinyl lettering replaces some oil screening and most all hand lettering artists. In time, knife companies like Gerber developed software to design and prepare vinyl letter compositions in most any color. Gerber OMEGA software and others became quickly popular to create lettering applications for exhibit designers. In time, the technology for color imaging improved greatly for large color images to be printed and applied to any number of substrates like plastic, sintra, and fabric. This got the portable exhibit and fabric sign businesses flying high. Most exhibit suppliers did not do large graphics in house. Graphics technology became progress times two for the exhibit design industry!

Fiberglass: Fiberglass, known as glass-reinforced plastic (GRP), is a composite material made from extremely fine fibers of glass. These glass fibers are typically woven into a fabric-like mat or used as a reinforcement material in a plastic resin matrix. The resulting composite material combines the strength and durability of glass with the flexibility and moldability of plastic. In the 1930s, a chance discovery in Toledo, Ohio, changed the trajectory of fiberglass history. Dale Kleist, a researcher at Owens-Illinois, accidentally created a shower of fine glass fibers while attempting to weld glass blocks. Recognizing the potential of this accidental discovery, engineers refined the process of producing glass fibers efficiently and inexpensively, patenting it in 1933. Because exhibits are generally one of a kind, the use of fiberglass as a building material is not a cost-efficient solution unless display shapes are produced in quantity. The cost to engineer a mold can be very expensive. In the early 1970s, a number of exhibit companies designed and produced display shapes for use in exhibit design. Some companies created standard display counters, display shapes, and furniture for exhibit design companies to incorporate into a single display. A few companies like Exhibit group and Giltspur created exclusive exhibit back walls and offered them as rental exhibits. Exhibit group created Fiberwall, and Giltspur created the Metric Module. This was a worthy solution for a large company with many clients and divisions throughout the USA. Today there are many companies that fabricate display shapes of fiberglass and sell to exhibit design companies. Another use of fiberglass in the exhibit industry was to fabricate shipping containers for portable exhibits or electronic equipment. Great solution!

Slatwall: In 1964, Harold E. Graham hand-built a prototype for slatwall and filed for US Patent #US3235218A. His idea was to display items efficiently and effectively on a wall without needing a permeant fixture attached to the wall. Graham had a hard time enforcing his patent because, with superior machinery, larger companies could rapidly reproduce his invention with slight variations (thus, the many names slatwall now has). With the boom in production, slatwall became common in many retail stores and for trade shows through the 70's and 80's. Slatwall customization was exploited early on. Different slatwall styles of wood and other materials became new features of regular slatwall. Custom colors and patterns created enormous possibilities. Plastic and metal inserts were also added to reinforce and strengthen the slatwall. Slatwall continues to be one of the most popular store fixtures because it is easy to install and strong enough to display all types of merchandise.

LED Lighting:

The days of ball lights, incandescent lighting, fluorescent lighting, and track lights changed drastically in 2000. LED lighting applications became the replacement. Companies like DS&L and the efforts of EDPA past president **Rob Cohen** helped to lead the way to promote alternative applications for exhibit lighting. Safety became an issue when the incandescent clamp on lights used for portables would drop to touch the backwall. Many burned velcro-covered back panels!

Velcro officially known as Velcro IP Holdings LLC, is a British privately held company. It is the original manufacturer of hook and loop fasteners. Swiss electrical engineer George de Mestral invented the first touch fastener when, in 1941, he went for a walk in the Alps and wondered why burdock seeds clung to his woolen socks and coat, and also his dog Milka. He discovered it could be turned into something useful. He patented it in 1955 and developed a way to manufacture it until its commercial introduction in the late 1950s.

The fastener consisted of two components: a lineal fabric strip with tiny hooks that could 'mate' with another fabric strip with smaller loops, attaching temporarily until pulled apart. The fabric wall material was initially made of cotton, which proved impractical; the fastener and fabric material were eventually constructed with nylon and polyester. What a great material for exhibit producers. And then came duct tape!

Flat Screen Monitors and Video Wall: The first LED screen was invented in 1962 by Nick Holonyak Jr., an American engineer. However, it was only in the 1990s that LED screens started to be used in stage design. The first large-scale LED video wall was used by rock band U2. New technology was further incorporated into exhibit design big time in 2000. Lightweight flat-screen monitors were a welcome replacement from heavy traditional TVs. Monitors could now be easily attached to a backwall. And then came video walls. Lightweight and

could fill an entire backwall of an exhibit with a moving visual. The impact of this visual experience was extremely effective. Note that the installation of this new technology requires specialized labor beyond the union electricians. The age of theater and visual impact had arrived to deliver a true experience!

In conclusion, the evolution of trade shows and experiential marketing heralds a journey of innovation and adaptation. What once commenced as a modest display of products has blossomed into an intricate tapestry of material for brand immersion. Today's trade shows transcend mere showcases; they epitomize unforgettable experiences that resonate with attendees long after the curtains fall. As we navigate this ever-evolving terrain, one certainty prevails: the future of trade shows and experiential marketing is characterized by innovation, adaptability, and an unwavering commitment to delivering unparalleled value to attendees and brands alike.

> They always say time changes things, but you actually have to change them yourself. . .   Andy Warhol

Over the decades, design trends evolved and were influenced by available technology along with designer impressions who uncover desirable styles. Be it architecture, clothing design, hair styles, auto design, or exhibit design, styles change to appeal to the masses. Clever design is then copied to start new design trends that then become a standard. Exhibit design was no different. Style and impressions matter.

The creative thinkers within the exhibit industry are the "Change Makers" who consistently influence the look of exhibits, and the many event changes that have unfolded in the Trade Show industry. The invisible Industry has always been open to embrace new ideas for greater event success. Everchanging thinking keeps the selling environment a vibrant experience.

Trade Show Exhibits Reflected the Design Flavor of the Time

Auto design was often driven by consumer feedback.
Trend boards were created from user research
to develop a new car design each year.
Exhibit design is rarely duplicated to a tee.
The look of an exhibit strives to be viewed as' one of a kind.'
There is no single best look, or solution, for exhibit design.

" If you think you can do a thing,
Or think you can't do a thing,
You're right" …Henry Ford"

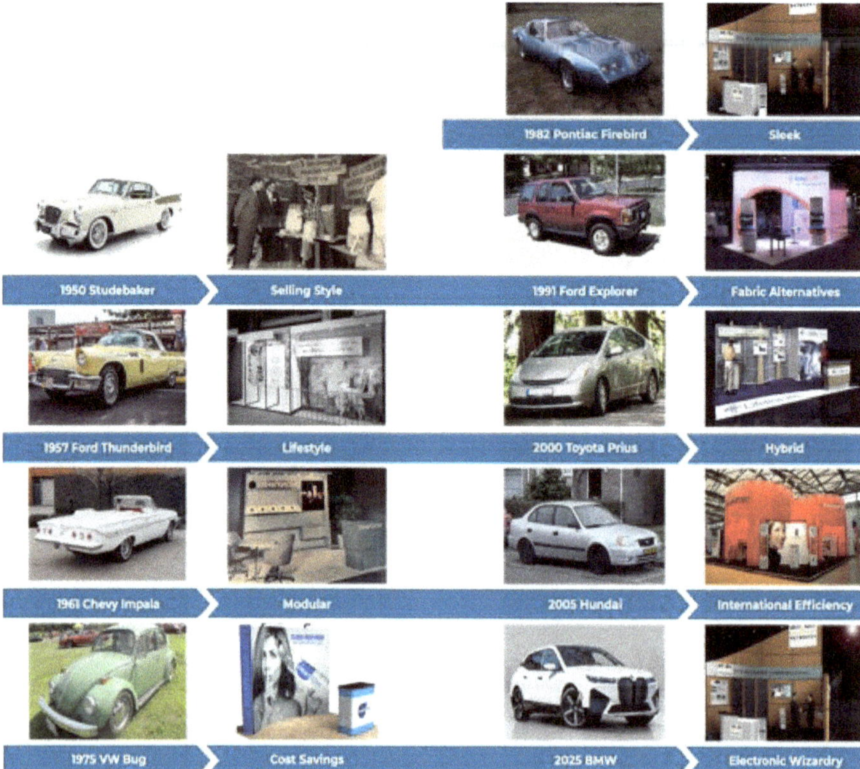

CHAPTER EIGHT

The Birth of Exhibit Installation Companies in the USA

Before the growth spurt of trade shows, exhibiting companies would contract directly with the show contractor to provide labor to install an exhibit. Many exhibitors would ask their exhibit design house to arrange this for them. A few exhibit houses began to provide an installation supervisor, and some provided in-house carpenter labor to install the exhibit. This began a new trend for I&D.

This rapid growth in exhibit marketing then created its own set of challenges for general contractors, unions, and the few fledgling specialty trade show labor companies as well as the exhibitors. With the maturation of the industry, the installation and dismantle of exhibits—sometimes referred to as "labor services", "show labor," or "I&D" (an acronym for "installation and dismantle")—was no exception to the segmentation that was taking place within the industry. Until now, there was no single (or set) approach to booth setup or installation. The "install" (or setup) may have been handled by any one of the possible entities: exhibitors themselves, general venue staff, general contractors, or in-house venue teams, depending on a variety of factors. Exhibitors often struggled with limited labor options and logistical constraints, which often led to inefficiencies and inconsistent outcomes.

As the industry grew and exhibits became larger and more complex, a variety of unions were involved in providing labor and services for trade shows and events around the country, such as decorators, carpenters, teamsters, theatrical stage workers, electrical workers, stagehands, dock workers, riggers, plumbers, and so on. The larger general contractors often negotiated "collective bargaining agreements"

(CBA's) with the various unions, which governed the pay rates, work hours, jurisdictions and many other factors in each city and venue. Many states were "right to work" states, meaning that anyone could "work" (provide labor) and were not required to be a union member in order to work there. Venues in those states provided more flexibility in how labor was handled. In the unionized states, only *union members* could work in the venue, regardless of the company they worked for. All of these factors combined into what seemed like a very complicated maze for many. Exhibitors often felt they had no *choice* or *control* over rates, hours, and arbitrary rules, which caused ongoing frustration.

Meanwhile, a broader, dramatic shift was happening in the trade show industry due to the confluence of several important factors:

- the rapid growth in the number of trade shows
- an increase in the number and larger size of convention centers
- the geographical expansion westward—enveloping many more cities across the country.

The major exhibitors took larger, prime spots in the halls, with more complex exhibits. These exhibits required taller ladders, more equipment, more manpower, and certainly more skilled laborers to match the complexity of these larger exhibits. The number of exhibitors was increasing to the point that they sometimes expanded from a single hall into multiple halls, or even into tents outside of the building in some cases. As a result, there was an onslaught of trucks delivering freight, more crates and materials on the show floor, and many more people working to set up the exhibits. More people were needed in more venues across the country.

The larger shows, with more exhibit spaces, drew more attendees, which meant more flights, hotel rooms, restaurants, local transport, crowded show halls, and so on. This shift created some tremendous opportunities for many and strains for most, creating a competition over resources for everyone.

As the geographical expansion continued across the country, the west developed differently, as it was happening at a different point in the history of the industry. Los Angeles and San Francisco were getting established, and San Diego and Las Vegas were coming on strong with expanded facilities. As a result, Las Vegas grew to create tremendous competition for McCormick Place's prominence in the convention industry. Las Vegas is a right to work state, so there are union and nonunion EAC's working in the convention venues there. Its work rules allowed for more flexibility and challenged traditional separation in labor jurisdictions, which were deeply entrenched in Chicago and the union-dominated cities of the East. Work rules, labor rates, hotel capacity, nightlife, exotics and the expanded convention center created an attractive draw when it came to bringing larger events to Las Vegas.

The Age of Specialization

Throughout this era of massive growth and expansion came specialized companies to serve niche areas at shows. Their aim was to provide higher quality and to enhance efficiency. Service companies for carpeting, furniture, AV, floral and I&D labor were created to upgrade the offerings from the show contractor.

"Independent" labor contractors began to emerge—as a way to specialize—as the trade show industry evolved. They were being referred to as "independent" to differentiate them from the "general contractors" who were hired by the show organizer to provide general services for the show, as well as to individual exhibitors. These contractors began to emerge in the industry in a couple of ways: some were an extension of an exhibit house, offering this specialty labor service; others were just independent labor management companies.

The Start of the Concept-

Noble Displays was a display house established in 1953 by New York designer Louis Barry, who got his start installing window decorations in New York department stores.17-year-old industry labor icon Andy

Codamo also got his start at Noble as a window dresser. He became the General Manager of the "exhibit service arm" (or labor services) of Noble Displays, known as Sho-Aids. Codamo later purchased Sho-Aids from Barry and moved it to Philadelphia in 1965.

Sho-Aids focused primarily on the medical and pharmaceutical industry, pioneering the concept of dedicated labor teams traveling to different cities with the client's exhibit. The beauty of this novel approach was that the team *knew* the exhibit as well as the client's needs. There was great efficiency and benefit in this unique approach, but at a price. Prior to this, exhibits would be set up by different people in each city, which had many disadvantages and challenges. Sho-Aids also pioneered the development of regional storage planning, one-bill invoicing, detailed post-show recaps, and more. All of this was unique, and certainly *not* what exhibitors were getting from the general contractors. It's possible that Sho-Aids was the first "national" (independent) contractor to offer exhibitors a choice in labor and service across the country. Codamo is credited with pioneering several innovative approaches in the labor services arena and helping to establish trade show installation and dismantle (I&D) as a profession, some of the reasons why he was later inducted into the EACA Hall of Fame. Sho-Aids was the industry's first developmental "tree" with employees branching out starting their own companies – in turn developing new branches and even new trees. Professional, CSI, EIS, Preferred, LES and the largest one I&D all stem from Sho-Aids.

CB Display Services was started in Chicago in 1969 by **Ann and Carl Birsa**, providing exhibit design and production services. In 1976, their son **Dennis Birsa**, along with colleague **Paul Willet,** opened an office in Las Vegas, becoming the *first* independent labor contractor in the city. According to Birsa, "From the onset, we provided labor services as an extension service arm of exhibit designers and producers." [16] CB was certainly one of the first exhibit houses to provide installation and dismantle labor as an additional level of service for their clients.

Howard Oshman got his start with Sho-Aids in 1968, installing displays in New York City. In 1972, Howard and Marilyn Oshman opened Professional Exhibitors 'Services in Connecticut, providing show floor help in the northeast. Mike McGuckin worked for them in NY and in Atlantic City, moved to Preferred, then started ACES in 2000. Les Bunge opened the Chicago office for Professional in 1979, then opened offices in DC and California (1986). Les founded Laser Exhibitor Services in 1991. Les had a different business model – one with licensing agreements for local owner-operators. They currently have seventeen locations in the US and Canada. Professional moved their headquarters to Florida in the early eighties and closed their doors in 2012.

Danny Molinaro and Steve Cahill once worked for Sho-Aids but left in 1972 to start their own labor company (also in Philadelphia) known as Convention Services Inc., making them one of the first independent labor contractors in the country. As the company grew and expanded over the years, it also became a general contractor, and the name was eventually changed to CSI Worldwide, as it stands today.

Several people first worked at CSI, and then moved on to start other companies: Pat Alacqua, Tony Amodeo, and Jack McEntee left in 1979 to start I&D; Joe Nuzzi left in 1984 to start EIS; Bert Taglianetti left the same year to start Preferred. Many different I&D companies began to unfold with a greater need for personalized services to install exhibits.

In the mid-seventies, the first four I&D businesses offering independent installation services in multiple cities (excluding the general contractors) were **Sho-Aids, CB Display Services (CB), Professional, and Convention Services Inc (CSI).** Initially, the independent labor contractors operated regionally, serving local exhibitors and events. However, as the industry expanded, these contractors grew into national and international entities, catering to exhibitors across different markets and venues. Several of the larger exhibit houses, such as Exhibit Group/Giltspur, started to also provide

I&D labor services to better serve their clients in the 1970s and 80s. Other exhibit houses seeking to enhance their value to their clients took another route. They started partnering with independent labor companies for shows in each city.

Several other notable individuals had their start in the industry at CSI. **Jack McEntee** began his career as a teacher in New Jersey. Eager to earn a better income than he had as a teacher, he joined Convention Services Inc. (CSI) in 1974, learning the business from Danny Molinaro and Steve Cahill. During his five-year tenure there, McEntee learned the business and had direct interaction with clients. At CSI, McEntee also had the opportunity to work with Pat Alacqua and Tony Amadeo. Each of them recognized the huge potential of this burgeoning industry. These three were forward-thinking and entrepreneurial. They decided they would create a way to better meet the needs and expectations that exhibitors had when doing trade shows across the USA.

In 1979, Jack McEntee, Pat Alaqua, and Tony Amodeo left CSI and founded their own independent labor company: Installation & Dismantle. They picked Atlanta as a base of operations because of the upcoming trade show schedule, among other factors. The GWCC had just opened in Atlanta several years before, and the labor outlook was tremendous. Installation & Dismantle (quickly shortened the name to "I&D Inc."—and later changed to "I&D Group" around 1991) started as a small storefront operation in a strip mall in Clarkston, GA, a suburb on the east side of Atlanta. Alacqua sold his Camaro (car) to provide funding to purchase ladders, which they would need to have on the show floor.

Armed with big dreams in hand, their "main driver" according to Alacqua, was to find ways to provide the *best* level of service for trade show clients, which translated into "personalized" service. That's what they were really all about. They intended to offer exhibitors a *choice* of *who* to work with—in stark contrast to the general contractors, who wanted to be the *only choice*. Sure, there were several other independent labor companies who provided a choice also, but I&D had plans to offer a level of service more distinctive than anyone had seen before in the industry, which they ultimately did!

According to McEntee, "It was common for the general contractors to send exhibitors maybe 'half' of the laborers they were promised—and there was nothing the exhibitor could do about it. But he thought, what if there was an exhibitor-appointed company that contracted with labor unions for help and then offered more competitive pricing and more efficiency? The GCs didn't realize it then, but they were setting us up to succeed."

McEntee concentrated heavily on training from the very beginning of

the company. Over time, *training* would be one *key differentiator* for I&D. At I&D, we extended the idea of teaching to the whole company, especially after we had expanded into many cities. We conducted a three-day training session, with slideshows on the company's history. But we also tried to create a culture. We taught the structure of the exhibiting world: the industry sectors, the unions, the associations, and the organizers. It provided them a thorough grounding no one else offered."

I&D taught their labor crews how to interact with clients better—something that many union workers had little previous experience in doing. They wanted them to be able to interact with clients in a professional manner, like a restaurant server—to be professionals. They also wanted their team members to have a broader understanding of how the industry works—to give them *perspective*. Branding on the show floor was also important. They wanted their people to be neat, clean, and wear branded shirts on the show floor in order to enhance their professional appearance. I&D also focused on consistency in *labor quality* and high levels of *accountability* to their clients. To create this kind of culture, they started adding people that they *trusted* and who naturally embodied their same mindset. I&D added some also former students of Jack.

including many who became notable trade show industry names, such as John Zimmerman, Scott Bennett, Thomas "Tommy" Iacovone, Jim Wurm, Mike Metzger, and many, many others—literally too many to list. Being close-knit and like-minded in many ways, they truly considered one another family. They operated from the same core values, knew how to work as a team, and 'had each other's back.'

They adopted the practice of being extremely careful about who they hired. They wanted to ensure that each person would be a good "culture fit." In order to determine that fit, candidates would spend about three hours with an industrial psychologist, working through a litany of tests including DISC, IQ, and a comprehensive personality evaluation. Many potential candidates did not make it through that process.

I&D also valued the role of the exhibit houses, which probably represented 60% to 70% of their revenue stream. They assigned account managers to every exhibit house client, with the focus on building lasting relationships to service as many of their clients as possible. This was a key impetus to their rapid and ongoing growth.

For his work in pioneering the rise of the independent contractor, Jack McEntee, the self-described "little guy," was honored with the IEA Eagle Award in 1987, the Hazel Hays Award from EDPA in 2010, and the EXHIBITOR Legends Lifetime Achievement Award in 2015.

A Battle Was Brewing

By the early 1980's, the pressure was really mounting between the general contractors and the independent contractors. All the while shows continued to grow larger and more complex. Feeling threatened by this competition, the show organizers and general contractors produced more rules and regulations to govern participation in their shows. Collectively, they used the "rules and regulations" as one way to maintain control, establish parameters, and protect *their* interests. When a company signed the contract to exhibit in the show, they were agreeing to abide by the "show rules and regulations" as outlined in the show kit or show manual (aka "exhibitor manual").

One such (controversial) rule they started to implement more frequently was that the exhibitors could ***ONLY*** hire their installation and dismantle labor from the general contractor (GC) of a show. Unions were in favor of this approach but did not have exclusive control in every venue, particularly if it was in a "right to work" state. Regardless, it did not stop the GC's from trying to implement this rule across the country, using their leverage as the "official" contractor for each show.

In a typical situation, when exhibitors wanted to get labor to set up their exhibit, they generally stood in line at the GC service desk until union laborers were assigned to them. On the next day of installation, they may get an entirely different group of workers, who, of course, were unfamiliar with their exhibit. The exhibitors despised this situation, which over time grew into a high degree of dissatisfaction amongst the exhibitors towards the general contractors.

I&D developed the concept of a "lead man." The idea was that if they could at least provide one "lead man" who would be consistent on the install as well as the dismantle, that would greatly increase the comfort level of the exhibitors. Some began referring to this as "same man up and same man down," which became a huge hit and ultimately an industry standard.

The general contractors also were not very good at recognizing and servicing the needs of the *individual* exhibitors. Their "main" clients were the show organizers who contracted them to provide the general services for the show. One could argue that the show organizer was viewed as *their* priority, not individual exhibitors. Customer service was lacking, to put it mildly. Many of these union workers were not

accustomed to interacting with marketing professionals such as exhibit managers or event planners who were responsible for their respective exhibit programs. The general attitude held by union membership was that they were there to do a "job"—and do it according to their union rules—regardless of how the exhibitor may have felt about it. Suffice it to say that these union workers, up to this time, were not given much training on customer *service*, customer *interaction*, or the importance of customer *satisfaction*. They were trained on their job skills but not on how to interact with clients. In other comparable settings, such as on a construction site, the bosses were the ones who interacted with customers, not the laborers. But here, it was likely that the laborers would be interacting directly with the clients during installation. One could easily see friction between the white-collar people and the blue-collar people in the microcosm of the show floor. As some observed, the exhibitors could likely get the get the "don't bother me! Can't you see I'm on a break right now?" type of response if they asked a question at the wrong time.

Jurisdictions were always a big concern—making determinations about *who* had the ability to do each specific type of activity on the show floor: electrical, rigging, carpentry, decorating, freight handling, equipment installation, and so on. The rules were slightly different for every venue and show. Many saw the rules as arbitrary. The rules also changed frequently, making it very challenging for exhibitors to understand and keep up with. In unionized show halls, the exhibitors were restricted from doing most things—even "plugging in" an electrical cord into a socket! A union electrician had to provide that service with a minimum time requirement and corresponding hourly rate—that is, once the appropriate form had been submitted.

The landscape of the show floor was governed by the general contractors, unions, show organizers, and venues; they were the ones who *made* and *enforced* the rules. The rules, regulations, stipulations, and mandates surrounding all of the show floor activities were quite *rigid* and *inflexible*, keeping tensions high between the GC's and the independents—and with the exhibitors. There were regular disputes over labor rights, fair competition, and service quality, which often led to tensions, strikes, and legal battles.

Knowing When to Pick Your Battles

Many of the major players in the industry lost sight of the fact that it was the *exhibitors,* after all, who were funding the whole operation of a trade show. The exhibitors were being forced to pay high rates for services that they felt were not fair. They had no *say*—and no *control*— over what they were getting, especially if they were being forced to use the general contractor.

From the perspective of the independent labor contractors and the exhibitors, this looked like a *monopoly.* There were about five or six general contractors ("the majors") who controlled everything at their respective shows across the USA, the prominent ones being: Andrews, Barlett & Associates; Freeman Decorating; Greyhound Exhibition Services; United Exposition Services; and Shepard Decorating. The "generals" were hindering the "independents" from having the ability to do their work—and were hurting the exhibitors in the process.

Even though there were "perceived issues" surrounding fair competition, most shows were "open" shows, meaning that others could work in them besides the general contractor. According to Jim Wurm, Executive Director of EACA and former employee of I&D, the only requirement for independent contractors gaining access to the show floor at the majority of events was that show management had to receive a letter on the exhibitor's letterhead that they had hired an "independent contractor" to install their booth. This is prior to the use of the term "Exhibitor Appointed Contractor" (or EAC moniker) and predated the idea of a *notification form* in the show kit.

The organizers originally created a 90-day deadline because the GCs told them they needed that much time to preplan their labor call, according to Wurm. They later learned differently. But the GCs had set this expectation because they recognized that the independent labor community was growing fast, particularly among exhibitors who had large spaces with custom and more complex display structures.

According to McEntee, "You have to understand the corner we were painted into. Our first show, for example, was in Atlanta for the Independent Telephone Association (USITA), which met three times per year around the country. We were getting maybe 10 to 15 jobs at USITA and shows like it. That sounds pretty good, but they were all 10-by-10-foot and 20-by-20-foot booths. The GCs didn't mind us having these 'table scraps, because the truth is, these jobs had tiny profit margins. And the really good carpenters only worked on the larger projects because they could rack up the hours on those jobs. We couldn't seem to break through that invisible barrier".

The number of "little guy" (independent contractor) companies had grown by this time and included companies such as CSI, Sho-Aids, I&D, Professional, Czarnowski, Giltspur, and others. They were all trying to "break through" that invisible barrier, causing the world of trade show labor in the early 1980's to become an actual battlefield at times. By about 1983, the combined labor calls for the "independents" sometimes exceeded those of the GC for some shows. Still, independent labor contractors had to battle at almost every show for the right to service their clients. Some independent labor contractors were met by GC union members with baseball bats in hand, blocking the EAC's from entering the venues.

According to their contracts with the show organizers, the general contractors (GCs) handled everything on the show floor—labor for installation and dismantle, drayage, aisle carpet, signage, vacuuming, registration, and so on, as they were hired by the show organizers. Within the framework of these agreements, there were certain services that the GC would provide to the organizer at very low, or no costs, in exchange for being appointed the "official" contractor of the show. So, as one might imagine, there are no "free lunches." The costs for those services would need to be 'covered' in some other way, such as material handling or labor services. The growing competition by the independent contractors was impacting the expected revenue streams of the GC's. So, they were looking for ways to prevent the erosion of revenue from labor and ways to increase other revenue streams, such as material handling (aka "drayage").

Every city, every show, and every venue had their own unique challenges to deal with in relation to labor services. The industry power centers (unions, show organizers, general contractors, venues) all felt threatened in some way by the increasing number of independent labor contractors. So, they devised plans—sometimes collectively, sometimes individually—to slow things down and encumber the ability of the independent contractors to continue to succeed. Among their notable approaches were:

Creating show rules that independent contractors had to "buy" their labor from the *GC*.

Creating show rules that independent contractors had to "buy" their labor from the *venue.*

Creating show rules that prevented independent contractors from bringing gang boxes, ladders, and check-in desks to the floor.

Labor unions siding with the GCs on particular issues, such as mandating that all labor be purchased from the GC.

There are many examples of troubling situations that arose over a number of years. In the words of Jim Wurm, "Jack McEntee didn't take any of those affronts lying down." To some, Jack in particular was seen as a kind of troublemaker, as he was visible, vocal, and stood strongly against what he saw as *tyrannical* and *unethical* business practices by show organizers, unions, and general contractors. To others, he was a hero and an inspiration.

The Fight Was ON!

Things finally came to a head in 1983 with the Offshore Technology Conference (OTC) at the Astrodome in Houston, Texas. It was perhaps the largest trade show (in square footage) in the USA at that time, with as many as 2,500 exhibitors. All of the independent contractors were planning to have substantial work at the show with their various clients in the oil and gas industry. But Doug Ducate, manager of the OTC show, had something else in mind. He declared the show would be "closed" to outside contractors. He ruled that if exhibitors wanted labor, they had to get it through Freeman (the GC)—end of story!

Several smaller, independent contractors filed lawsuits against the OTC organizer in an effort to get the right to work in the show. I&D decided to join the fight by bringing in their own antitrust expert, Curt Frisbie of Gardere & Wynne LLC, based in Dallas, Texas. With this move, it became more of a collective action lawsuit against Freeman Decorating and the show organizer, with I&D taking the lead. Alacqua spent nearly a year living in Dallas, trying to manage the legal battle—working with the lawyers, the unions, and coordinating with other independent contractors. In addition to the huge expense for a small company like I&D, they faced great risks going into this battle and kept their leadership tied up in meetings and traveling.

I&D, along with the other independents in this action, claimed that the organizer and Freeman Decorating (the GC) were engaging in **anticompetitive (antitrust) practices**, with the focus being that no *one* company (i.e., Freeman) should hold a monopoly on labor. In other words, the exhibitors should have a right to choose who they want to work with for their installation and dismantle—after all, this is a free market economy.

During the course of the trial, I&D's legal team coached them about also working within the "court of public opinion." They grew to appreciate the roles that associations and other entities in the industry could play in this situation. McEntee, Alacqua, Wurm, and others worked continuously to shed light on this issue by engaging heavily with other independents, the associations, and exhibitors—rallying their support. In particular, they helped the exhibitors understand that if they wanted to maintain their right to choose", they would have to get out there and fight for it. They wanted the exhibitors to understand that *they* had the power; they just needed to *exercise* it.

After about a year, the judge issued a "deferred verdict", which, in simple terms, meant they couldn't satisfy all the conditions necessary to prove an antirust charge. Despite the acknowledgement of the illegal activities that occurred, it was insufficient. The judge indicated that if they were unable to work in *one* show, the independents could work in *other* shows. They weren't being shut out of working in *all* shows. In effect, there was no monopoly in the eyes of the law. He ruled, therefore, that the defense did not need to plead their case. The lawsuit was over, and the I&D work force of the industry had lost the legal battle.

Billionaire Sheldon ("Shelly") Adelson was also involved in this complex struggle, being a show organizer himself. He owned the mega show **COMDEX**, which started in 1979 and grew into one of the largest trade shows in history. He exercised his influence across the industry as a major show organizer in support of the right for exhibitors to choose their labor contractor. His influence helped give the issue additional exposure during this time.

But the trial itself had really caused this issue to go public. The issues had garnered tremendous attention across the industry. It was being discussed among many of the associations (i.e., EDPA, SEMA, TSEA, etc.) and in the industry publications. Shortly after the verdict was announced, *Tradeshow Week*, widely read by show organizers, framed the case in an article, described as an "idea whose time had come"— and that there was no good basis for the status quo. The article recommended that show organizers should get ahead of the curve and allow companies like I&D to have an equal footing with GCs.

In 1983, the Trade Show Exhibitors Association (TSEA) held a panel discussion at their annual TS^2 Conference. The panel discussed the deadline provision that organizers should require for the exhibitors to declare their intention to utilize independent contractors. It varied widely at this time, but quite a number of shows had a 90-day deadline to request an appointed I&D contractor. The independent contractors wanted a much *shorter* deadline, such as 30 days, as many exhibitors were not thinking this far in advance to do on time. During this panel discussion at TS^2, according to Jim Wurm, "A show manager in the audience said he'd never received a complaint from an independent contractor that his 90-day rule was unreasonable. As the session was winding down and about to end, Wurm shouted out, 'I work for I&D, and I think it's unreasonable!!' Probably not the best way to bring that to his attention, but it started a conversation that created momentum to come up with a more reasonable timeframe."

Even though the legal battle had ended, it was clear that the "trial" in the court of public opinion was not over yet. In particular, more individuals and organizations were accepting the validity of the independent contractors. The show organizers started thinking that they would have to win lawsuits for every show where labor was being challenged. So, they saw the writing on the wall and opened up to the concept of EAC's, and then things began to change. There's something about the American character that loves the underdogs, and EAC's were clearly the 'little guy' in this particular fight." [21]

Charles Pappas wrote in EXHIBITOR Magazine that "McEntee fought Freeman to a standstill—only to emerge victorious when trade show organizers decided they would rather spend their time producing shows than defending lawsuits. So, despite losing the battle, the independents still won the war!

Slowly Stabilizing After the War

Even though public opinion was changing and momentum was building in favor of the independent contractors, many issues certainly had not disappeared and still needed to be resolved. In January of 1984, the new phrase *"Exhibitor-Appointed Contractor"* (later abbreviated as **"EAC"**) originated at a meeting in Dallas between Don Stacy, Don Walter, Paul Willet, Jim Wurm, and others. The term would eventually *stick*—and redefine the category of independent labor contractors going forward.

Around this time, **Ray Pekowski** (Sr) was credited with coining the term *"General Services Contractor"* or "GSC**"**, which is often used interchangeably with *General Contractor (GC),* which had already been in use for many years.

In June of 1984 at the National Cable Show in Las Vegas, I&D coordinated a "walk-off" the show floor by all independent laborers when the show organizer (National Cable Television Association—NCTA) tried to force them to "run" all of their labor payroll through the General Contractor (GC). In other words, to "purchase" all of their laborers through the general contractor—much like what Ducate implemented at the OTC show in Houston the year before. After an hour or so of the walk-off, show management dropped their demands.

It would not be accurate to say that show organizers were suddenly all "okay" with the increasing presence of the EACs. Some remaining issues just *had* to be resolved. Show management leaders became increasingly aware of and concerned with the growing number of independent contractors that were on *their* show floor. A meeting was called in January of 1985 by NAEM ("National Association of Exposition Managers"—the precursor to IAEE: "International Association of Exhibitions & Events") in Dallas to discuss and try to resolve these issues. Jim Wurm, along with another independent labor contractor, Don Stacy of Stacy Exhibit Services, and Don Walter of NAEM chaired the meeting, which was also attended by representatives from both Freeman and GES.

Perhaps addressing the easiest thing first, Don Walter started the meeting with concern over the terminology, suggesting that the independents be referred to as "Exhibitor Appointed Contractors" going forward. Neither Stacy nor Wurm objected.

The next topic was around the concept that the GCs give their shows (or the show organizers, to be more specific) a lot of "free stuff", Both Stacy and Wurm countered that it might appear free, but there's no such thing. Walter indicated that he understood what was happening, but that show management did get some services heavily discounted. He wanted to know if the EACs would be willing to pay a *nominal fee* to gain access to the showfloor, which would essentially mimic what the GCs were doing for the organizers. According to Wurm, "This is the first time I can recollect that the words "EAC Fee were ever uttered. It included another idea that to assist show management with their risk management concerns as the venue lessee and to ensure that the EAC was legitimate that the show would like to collect a *Certificate of Insurance* as well".

Wurm recalls that Don Stacy was sharp as a tack on this point. He said, "first of all, I'm happy to provide you with my *proof of insurance,* as we already do that to show our service as a courtesy. And on your other ask, sure, I'll pay a nominal fee if you put *my* order form in the show kit". Apparently, that ended the conversation about the EACs paying a fee, but the seed concept of an EAC fee had been planted in the minds of the show organizers and GCs. Within a couple of years, EAC Fees started showing up as a requirement in some show manuals, along with the *3rd Party Authorization Form* and a charge card for "at show" purchases.

In January 1985, **Tom Cassell** started Convention All Services (CAS), a labor management company in Chicago, focused on trade show labor. Later, Cassell and Joe Mondelli formed an organization called the Independent Contractors Association (later renamed the Illinois Exhibitor Appointed Contractors Association) in Chicago, with the intent to be an organization that worked with all industry stakeholders to increase exhibitor participation in trade shows by increasing the service and value at events across the country. Initiatives were undertaken to remove barriers to participation, whether it was about arcane rules, unjustifiable costs, or ineffective customer service. Tom went on to be hired by McCormick Place to work with show management for shows at McCormick. His role was to act as a mediator when labor and show regulations are challenged by exhibitors, service contractors, or labor unions.

Another EAC emerged in 1987 with the founding of Willwork by **Bill Nixon**, giving exhibitors and other EACs from around the country a labor choice in Boston. Bill Nixon had very strong relationships with the unions in Boston, which was essential for being able to effectively work there, as the unions to this day have a tight grip. I&D did not have good success in Boston themselves in the beginning. So, they forged a partnership with Willwork and worked together for more than a dozen years. Willwork had their own clients and projects going, but from the perspective of labor training, Nixon added "hands-on training" with I&D and invited reps from display houses to his Willwork University.

Ralph Ianuzzi, Jr. promoted the concept of the "EAC Fee. Ianuzzi was the organizer of the PC Expo in New York City. He was an early show management champion of the fee. He charged a $25 fee per EAC credential at his show. He also led a session at a NAEM meeting in Washington, DC, in December 1986 on that very topic. He promoted the notion that he turned every cost center on his budget into a profit center. He rationalized that the worker credentials cost him money and that the presence of EACs on the show floor increased his costs. Wurm attended the session and asked Ianuzzi how that was possible. Wurm said, "Every show has a specific and finite number of workers on the show floor; if an EAC is present, then it means they have replaced GC personnel who otherwise would be doing the work. The EAC presence doesn't increase the *headcount*; it just changes the *employer*. And, by the way, do you charge the GC for *their* credentials?" Ianuzzi didn't reply and changed the subject!

Despite the objective arguments raised by Wurm, every show manager in the room heard about the EAC fee concept, and many started to implement it on their own shows. By the mid to late 1990s, it was getting "out of hand", according to Wurm. "One of the driving forces behind the formation of the EACA (Exhibit Appointed Contractors Association) in the late '90s was the emergence of the EAC fee", said Wurm. "The EACA saw the exhibitor appointed contractor (EAC) fee as an impediment to an exhibitor's choice for selecting their own I&D contractor. The fee, as much as $500, was essentially a *surcharge* on the exhibitor's I&D service charges and penalized them for hiring anyone but the general contractor."

In 1998, **Jim Wurm** was approached by the Illinois EACA to launch a national association for the EACs, taking on the role of Executive Director. The first organizational meeting was held in Chicago in May 1998. The first Board meeting of the EACA was held in San Francisco that summer at TS^2.

During the years, under Wurm's direction, EACA experienced rapid growth on a national scale. The association's collaborative approach and commitment to excellence propelled its expansion and influence within the industry—and answered the call to raise the level of service on the show floor. The EACA worked directly with exhibitor-appointed contractors to improve the client experience, establish best practices and improve communication between contractors, associations, customers and organized labor. The action of EACA has had a tremendous impact on the industry and brought a new level of professionalism to the I&D trades. The EACA recently celebrated its 25th anniversary.

After a time, and with the pressure of the EACA, a 30-day deadline for submitting an EAC letter to the organizer became the standard, dropping from the previous 90-day deadline. The EACA educated those show managers that GCs, like EACs, placed their labor calls (with the union members) several *days* before move-in, not several *months*.

One of the largest exhibits at the Super Show in Atlanta belonged to LA Gear, a rising brand in sportswear marketing. The booth wasn't simply a booth. It was a *region* of the GWCC that flowed into corridors, lobbies, and other spaces. There were 50 tractor trailer loads of exhibit properties, stages, lighting, and equipment. Mike Miller, a seasoned industry veteran, was the project foreman on this project for L.A. Gear. Miller managed the labor call for 175 people, with shifts working 24 hours a day for at least two weeks. This was truly a choreography—an orchestration that clearly demonstrated the demands that independent exhibit installation companies were now required to handle. High-profile projects like L.A. Gear demonstrated that I&D companies across the USA had now mastered the ability to plan for a large-scale exhibit installation and work in harmony with the official show contractor to handle massively large exhibits at a single show.

The Emergence of the New Industry Landscape

As time passed and the industry settled into this new landscape, EACA continued playing a vital role in relations between the various industry sectors. One other outstanding issue that still had not been resolved was the claim by organizers that the presence of EACs working in the shows cost them more money. Wurm stated, "we didn't just want to push back; we wanted to create a sensible alternative." In 2000, Tom Cassell and Jim Wurm met with Peter Edelman, the new show manager for IMTS (International Manufacturing Technology Show) and a former friendly exhibitor. The show is always held at McCormick Place in Chicago. Wurm and Cassell conceded that large shows like IMTS incurred *some* cost burdens to process EAC notifications. They indicated that since the EACA associations know all the *competent* and *credible* members of the community, they believed they could handle those administrative tasks more efficiently and effectively, thereby saving money for IMTS.

Edelman agreed to perform a time study to calculate the costs for handling all of their EAC registrations internally. They determined that their costs were $17,000 for this large biannual show. EACA offered to provide the service for 1/3 of the cost and Edelman agreed. He was the first client of the ***EACA EAC Online Registration Service***. EACA has now been providing this same service for show organizers for more than 20 years now. In addition to IMTS, they work with other major shows such as Housewares, NRA, CONEXPO-CON/AGG, RSNA, Pack Expo, NBAA and more than 40 other events.

Keeping good talent was always a challenge for I&D companies. They liked the pay and long hours, but this kind of work was considered to be a part-time job.

Another national I&D company, Willwork, said that they were determined that it wasn't sufficient to simply recruit talent; they needed to keep "good people" working. The 1990s brought unprecedented growth to the U.S. economy and the convention industry. Shows like

Comdex and CES could not sell exhibit space fast enough. The exhibits were growing in size and sophistication, with major lighting rigs, intelligent lighting, large rear-screen projectors, double-decks, enclosed conference rooms, and live presentations. The more sophisticated the exhibit, the more skilled installers were needed—ones who were trained and experienced in "setting up" these kinds of exhibit properties and did it in four days!

In the late eighties and early nineties, more than two dozen former I&D/Nth Degree employees started their own businesses, including such companies as Eagle, Momentum Management, Renaissance, Spectrum, Nuance International and Zenith. Legendary senior industry writer Charles Pappas of EXHIBITOR Magazine wrote, "Despite a jump to the exhibition industry, McEntee never wavered from his first calling as a teacher. McEntee trained and taught hundreds of employees exhibiting expertise and life lessons, nearly two dozen of whom later launched their own I&D businesses."

Today there are many quality I&D companies that do not stem from the company I&D and also offer a high level of personalized service. Companies Coastal, Elite, Sho Link, On Location, Lancaster, NuVista, Crew XP, and many others who each service exhibitors nationwide. Numerous display companies offered in house show floor installation services as well. The larger exhibit companies like Czarnowski, ExhibitGroup. Giltpsur, MC2, and others provided in house installation services. Many changed this practice in time and elected to form exclusive relationships with an I&D company to provide this personalized service as partners.

In later years, the two biggest show contractors, Freeman and GES, added exhibit design/fabrication and installation service directly to exhibitors in addition to their role as a show contractor. It is interesting to note that the concept of I&D companies started when the show contractor labor provided to install an exhibit was not personal enough and could not meet the labor demands as exhibit design became more sophisticated and time consuming to install. Today, large show contractor companies have become a formidable competitor to the best exhibit design companies in the country. Change continues to unfold.

Due to the concept of 'drayage' (material handling at show sites) in the USA, most exhibits are shipped to the trade show site crated (vs skid wrapped). This is done to protect the contents when unloading and handled by others. This is but one major difference from how shows are managed in Europe. Note that the American Model of organizing trade shows in the USA is much different than in the rest of the world. I&D companies are unique to American trade shows, offering personal installation services for exhibit houses and direct exhibitors. Few locations in the rest of the world do

trade shows this same way. The concept of Show Contractor services and Independent Contractor labor, working together, does work well in the USA. This method of service brings added success, and less stress, to both exhibitors and exhibit builders at US trade shows. The birth of independent exhibit set up labor in the USA is a unique tale worthy of its own chapter when sharing the history of trade shows in America.

The trade show skills needed to install an exhibit are uniquely different and require training, often with support from the local union.

CHAPTER NINE

CHANGE MAKERS

The People and Associations that Drove Change
from Business as Usual.

"Successful entrepreneurs are lifelong learners who are constantly looking for ways to improve and grow." Author Unknown

If you describe a person or a group as having a **catalytic effect***, you mean that they cause things to happen, or they increase the speed at which things happen.*

History has a capricious memory. Casting a spotlight on a select few ignores many others, no matter how significant their contributions are. However, it's never too late to change this! Let's uncover some of the stories behind a few figures of trade show marketing history that, in one way or another, helped shape the direction and methods of trade shows in the USA.

Trade shows provide a very strong stage for sellers to promote new products and buyers to find new products that lift the economy forward.

There are many moving parts that have contributed to the success of business meetings, events, and trade show marketing.

The components for trade show success:

- An industry organizer.
- An attractive venue.
- An organizer's ability to create multiple attractions that encourage visitors to attend. (Exhibits, Seminars, Networking, City Sites)
- A targeted audience of buyers and sellers looking to grow in their niche and share ideas.
- Industry companies willing to invest in a show space with an exhibit that works to attract attention, leading to a sale.

An industry Supported by Passionate Suppliers- All willing to Contribute

Trade shows provide results when executed correctly. Much planning and thought is what makes it really come together for the organizer and exhibitors to achieve the expected results. The cities that invested in convention facilities with dedicated hotels did so to reap the benefits of major trade conventions coming to their city. A costly investment, but a major incentive for show associations to select a city for their meeting. The convention facility, in an attractive location, does play a part in the success of a trade show. The attraction is important, but the preparation to exhibit is most critical. Here is where the results are created.

The documented success of trade show marketing is not the result of any one location, one person, one organizer, or any one tactic. Trade show success is the result of an entire team of little people behind the scenes who are somewhat 'invisible' to the visitors at any show. The exhibiting component at any event generates the greatest impact for the selling companies.

Each exhibit on a trade show floor is a live stage play set; they tell a story, deliver ideas, and get applauded if you liked their message. Each decade, exhibit design methods improved adding new ideas to achieve greater sales results at trade shows. The best ideas often came from the creative minds of the behind-the-scenes team. They got your back and love being a part of the exhibitor's success, and often go unnoticed.

It is remarkable to note the invested energy and passion that the 'behind the scene' players contribute, to do their part, and to make each exhibit a success for the exhibitors they represent. Most trade show workers have short attention spans. They embrace deadlines and are happy when the show is over, and move on to another. Where does this added passion come from? Is this not their job? It's not the money. The preparation for the event is kind of a team game for any crew of skilled stage hands. They enjoy the feeling of victory after each and every event, then on to the next. It is also interesting to note that people who discover this industry never leave it. The passion they acquire becomes contagious.

It is with that said, that we would like to give tribute to the many 'show team leaders' behind the scenes who have gone unnoticed and have quietly provided their thoughts and ideas to improved exhibiting results. The ideas from these contributors did not personally make them rich, but made the industry rich with added value for the exhibitors who invest and expect a return.

This list of people and associations is in no particular order of importance but each contributed greatly to influencing change in the industry. These changes improved the exhibiting methods and made trade show marketing a more valuable tool for all industries to grow. Bravo to the **Change Makers!**

Fred Kitzing: *Exhibits don't sell, people do.* Tribute by Chris Kappas

Every industry has pioneers. Consider contemporaries Elon Musk, Mark Zuckerberg, Reed Hastings, and Jeff Bezos and their impact on humanity. Fred Kitzing is NOT a name you likely know. But his philosophies are regarded as "best practices in trade show exhibit marketing today." Fred's ideas transformed the trade show-event industry and perpetuated the marriages of organizations like Freeman-Sparks, GPJ Project Worldwide, Nth Degree-Fern, and others.

Fred Kitzing was CEO of Kitzing, Inc., the nation's first tradeshow marketing agency in the 1980s. A rogue entrepreneur, fine artist, philosopher, designer, marketer, salesperson, innovator, and rule-breaker, Fred was our industry pioneer. He created and curated "omnichannel marketing" solutions for trade shows before the term was coined, defined, and fashionable.

A student of famous Chicago architect Louis Sullivan, Fred applied Sullivan's architectural philosophy "form follows function." The exhibits his agency designed/produced were "machines for selling." Little ornamental, or "design for design" sake. His focus was practical exhibits featuring live product presentations and trained product presentations and trained exhibit personnel to engage and qualify guests. Kitzing exhibits were NOT monuments celebrating corporate ego.

Fred's favorite motto, *"Exhibits don't sell, people do,"* was expressed as a part of an integrated trade show marketing philosophy that included pre-show promotion, live demonstrations, lead management, and an exhibit staff training session called "You Make the Difference."

Unlike other exhibit firms at the time, Fred employed marketers, script writers, actors, magicians, and more. His "curriculum" was not always embraced, but for his clients, the strategies, although unorthodox, produced results. For a wood-burning stove company, Kitzing created an exhibit that promoted: "Make more money with XYZ stoves." Fred reasoned that visitors are drawn to the personal benefits, not product features. Another Kitzing exhibit for a floor stain company promoted its scratch resistance and durability by featuring a skater rollerblading on the interior of a spinning wheel. No scratches are visible.

Fred believed exhibits were intended to be "selling machines." He thought they should be designed to attract attendees into the booth and enable the closing of sales. But in order to do that, he believed the salespeople had to be energized, passionate, and involved. At a food show in Atlanta in 1984, one of his exhibits was a large island booth for Kraft. The night before the show opened, he approached the I&D City Manager and said that in the morning he wanted to "fire up the sales staff with enthusiasm." He wanted to startle and wake them up. He wanted to discharge a gun and get everyone's attention. It was Saturday night in Atlanta, Georgia. Weapons could not be purchased (at least not legally), and it was too late (after several phone calls) to secure a starter's pistol. Having been trained to do "whatever it takes" to please a client, the leadman offered to bring a pistol loaded with blanks.

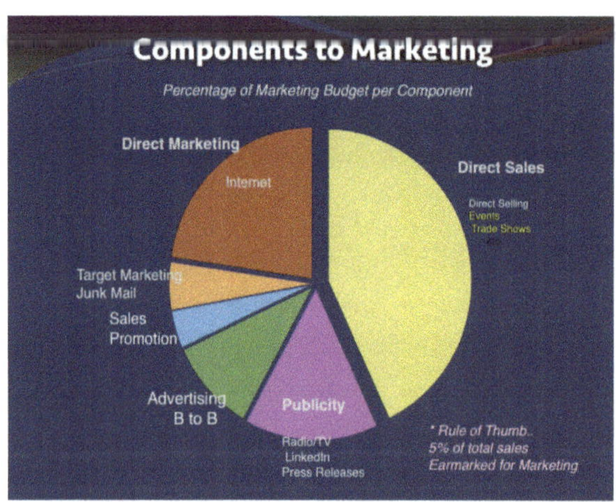

Sunday morning, with a Saturday night special in hand, Fred Kitzing startled more than just the sales staff. Fortunately, no one was arrested, and there were no serious repercussions.

After Fred passed, his wife **Llona Kitzing** continued his passion and developed a pie chart showing the dollars spent for each element in the marketing mix. Trade show marketing occupied the largest piece of the pie. Her message was to integrate all the components for overall success at a trade show. The industry took notice after Freds passing to introduce new businesses to the world of trade show marketing. Each of the people below were disciples of the Fred Kitzing philosophy.

Elaine Cohen- *Live Marketing*   Elaine was a disciple of Fred Kitzing. She was the first to start a company dedicated to writing a script, training a presenter, or hiring a professional presenter for a trade show. It was appropriately named Live Marketing. The company continues today, offering an extended list of added services.

Elaine Cohen won the EDPA Hazel Hays Award in 2005. Elaine was one of eight women in the exposition industry to be given this highest award for their contributions to the growth and success of the industry.

Allan Konapacki- *Booth Staff Training*   Dr. Allan Konapacki was a firm believer in the power of face-to-face selling. He started a company dedicated to "exhibit staff training" to help booth staff with engagement methods. He wrote several books on this subject and wrote a famous article entitled Eye Movement Tells Thought Process. Many other companies now provide booth staff engagement training at trade shows. This has now become a very important service for exhibit staffers.

Richard Erschik- *Lead Management*   Richard Erschik began his career in the 70's as an exhibit manager for a prominent company in the machine tool industry. He became chairman of the National Machine Tool Builders Association, where his committee members admittedly encountered a common pitfall with the companies they worked for—poor lead follow-up after a trade show. Trade shows were beginning to get more expensive, and corporate management began to challenge the cost to participate. What are we getting for this level of marketing investment? Richard learned much from his peers, so a few years later he started a new business called **Leads to Sales.** This was a business directed to help exhibitors, from any industry, follow a unique formula for following up on the contact leads they gathered from a trade show. Richard became one of the top speakers at the Exhibitor Show educational sessions, designed to prepare exhibit managers to earn a CTSM (Certified Trade Show Manager) certification.

During this time period, Richard became close to a fellow Chicagoan, **Allen Konapacki.** Allen was a professor and consultant specializing in trade show marketing. He spoke on the power of selling in a trade show environment and was a strong believer in education within the trade show industry. Allen and Rich were both disciples of Fred Kitzing. Richard Erschik followed Konapacki's passion to teach within the industry. Richard's career took a strategic turn when he sold his company of 22 years and dedicated his energy to teaching and sharing his knowledge with trade show managers hungry for success. Over the following years, Erschik conducted over 350 seminars, webinars, and workshops across the globe. He also collaborated with trade show organizers eager to assist their exhibitors to address the 'what' and 'why' of trade show marketing for greater success. Today, trade show marketing education and lead management services play a strong role in the justification of trade show marketing investments.

Richard Swandby- *Measuring the Value*

For over 50 years, Richard K. Swandby pioneered exhibition research in the field of trade show marketing. He brought a much-needed level of professionalism to the meetings industry by developing methods and data to quantify the value of the exhibition medium.

Up until the early 1960s, there was little data available, much less 3rd party data, that measured the value of trade shows for organizers, attendees, and exhibitors. Generally, total attendance figures were reported by the show organizer and only sometimes provided basic demographic profiles of the attendees collected in the manual registration process.

Exhibitors and potential exhibitors had little verified information to determine whether they belonged in a show and, more specifically, how much they were justified in investing relative to the overall value of the segment of the audience they wanted to reach. There was also little data to measure an exhibitor's specific performance in a show other than counting their leads, and they struggled to follow up there after. Exhibitors had very little data that offered them insights into why they did, or did not, perform as expected so they could improve and make better decisions in the future.

The trade show organizers needed this kind of data as well to give them insights to improve and grow their shows. For example: improve attendance promotion; optimize exhibit and sponsorship sales; refine show strategies; define new growth segments of attendees and exhibitors; better understand the needs of their attendees and exhibitors. For the most part, data and research generated prior to the early 1960s was done in-house by organizers of individual shows—both privately held for-profit shows and not-for-profit association or society conventions and expositions. There was no standardization of the metrics to create benchmarks of performance for comparison purposes to identify strengths and weaknesses.

In 1963, the first company to independently measure the value of trade shows and exhibits exclusively was formed. **Richard "Dick" Swandby** was the founder of **Exhibit Surveys, Inc.** He was a chemical engineer and MBA who had a strong technical background, enabling him to develop the foundation for unbiased research using widely accepted market research methods and techniques. Since its inception, Richard's company has quantified the value of more than 9,500 individual exhibits in more than 2,400 exhibitions and produced over 20 studies for the Center for Exhibit Industry Research **(CEIR).** Among his contributions are the development of many standard benchmarks of performance for exhibitors and for the show organizers, including net buying influences, audience interest factor, traffic density, exhibit efficiency, and cost-per-visitor reached.

The original target market for Swandby's research were the major industrial companies/exhibitors of the era whose marketing and exhibit managers were being questioned by their senior management about the ROI of the shows in which they exhibited. In general, exhibitors' focus was on ROI to justify their exhibit budget, but Swandby's concept for exhibitor measurement went far beyond ROI. The measurement methodology he created was also designed to quantify the potential value of a show to each client in order to optimize spending relative to the total potential value of the show, budget accordingly in the future to ensure a reasonable cost per visitor reached, and identify which exhibiting tactics were driving ROI and which fell below the norm so that performance could be optimized in the future.

Although major exhibitors were the initial target market for Exhibit Surveys' research, it didn't take long for most show organizers to recognize that there was also value to them in the research Exhibit Surveys was conducting for exhibitors, particularly the data relative to the quality and activity of the overall audience attending the show. Specific data about any one exhibitor being measured was always kept confidential, but the overall audience demographics, attendee activity at the show, and buying power of the total audience were shared with each exhibitor participating and the show organizer for their cooperation in conducting the research.

Many of the show organizers now saw the value of the research Exhibit Surveys was conducting for exhibitors and began contracting customized research on their own with Exhibit Surveys. Some organizers even partnered with their major exhibitors by funding the base cost of the research they mutually needed.

In the 1960s and early 1970s, trade shows were the predominant type of face-to-face event marketing activity available to companies. As event marketing evolved and more companies began creating their own private event activities to augment trade shows (e.g., product launch events, private customer and partner conferences, road shows, b2c experiences, and virtual events), it was also critical to research and measure these other event types to develop their total event mix strategies. Show organizers were also in need of additional types of research as they looked to grow and further substantiate the value of their shows (e.g., post-event exhibitor research, new show feasibility studies, co-location feasibility

studies, post-event sales conversion research, non-attendee and non-exhibitor research).

In 1978, the **Trade Show Bureau (TSB)** was founded and supported by a consortium of other trade show industry associations. They all promoted and supported research data to sustain the industry's growth and to ensure its stable future. Many of the early TSB reports came from summary analyses of **Exhibit Surveys'** existing research. The volume of TSB research reports produced by Exhibit Surveys to substantiate the value of the industry would not have been possible in the early years without Exhibit Surveys' existing database.

Swandby realized that the many small companies who could not afford to use Exhibit Surveys' services could at least use the basic ES tools offered free of charge to plan more effectively. Dick Swandby generously gave back to the industry to support his passion for collecting data to justify business investments made at trade show events.

Swandby retired in 2005 and was succeeded by **Jonathan "Skip" Cox** as CEO and owner of Exhibit Surveys. Skip started in the business full time in 1971 and became a partner in 1990. Exhibit Surveys then sold to Freeman in 2016, who continues Dick's passion for measurement and data for trade show marketing investments.

During his career, Swandby received the top awards for his contributions to the industry from the major exhibition industry associations—EDPA, IAEE, and TSEA. Swandby received the prestigious Hazel Hays Award, the Exhibitor Legends Award, and the Events Industry Council Hall of Leaders. His contributions have allowed the industry to rapidly grow by assisting exhibitors and associations to measure the value of their marketing investments.

George Furman- *Exhibit Sales and Ideas in the 60's & 70's*

After the new McCormick Place reopened in the 1970s, many exhibit companies in Chicago began to open. One company, prior to the fire, was R.A.E. (Rental All Exhibits), started by George and John Furman. RAE Systems was forced to close down after the McCormick fire and city snowstorm of 1967. More than 50% of their exhibits were on the show floor at the Housewares Show. Add to this, the roof on their company building collapsed during the blizzard of 1967. Many of their employees went on to start their own companies—Premier Exhibits, Design Agency, Dimension Craft, Fritkin-Jones, Contempo, and Exhibitron were formed. Many followed and improved upon the concepts that they experienced at RAE Systems. Chicago exhibit companies like Kitzing, MG, Stevens, Firks, and General Exhibits also began to flourish at this time, each focusing on a unique specialty to offer exhibitors.

George Furman Sr. at RAE Systems was quite the innovator for the exhibit industry. George started as a window dresser (Decorators Union). The union boys liked George and had him go to McCormick for a decorator job. He went on to help start the Decorators Union at McCormick Place.

RAE Systems was one of the first exhibit companies to offer custom-designed exhibits as a rental, which included shipping and installation at site. Not common then, but sure is today! He created a sales idea for his company called *"The Swinger Program"*. What it entailed was to send a salesperson to the show floor at Chicago trade shows with a Swinger Polaroid camera and take a picture of exhibits that seemed to need help. They would also pick up some literature and a business card from an exhibitor.

Upon return, RAE Systems would then prepare an unsolicited design drawing and a price for a new exhibit. To make this work, he created an assembly line of artists who drew exhibit ideas using magic markers. The first person would create the space from perspective, the second would be the architecture of the booth, the third was to add an accurate logo and tagline, and the last was to add plants and people figures for a real feel for the space. The approach was a big success, and then RAE went on to start a company in NYC offering the same. Note that he was not soliciting on the show floor as frowned upon today.

George Furman Sr. also created the concept of the **self-contained exhibit,** in parallel with Mike Grieves at **MG Display** in Chicago. The self-contained exhibit was a crate that folded open to create an exhibit and fill a 10' space. Little to no assembly was required.

These exhibits were a little heavy, but drayage was now an issue back then. To test the self-contained exhibits for wear and tear during shipping, they would push them off the loading dock, open for damage, then reinforce. The concept solved a few problems to save time at installation, but the concept did not last long when drayage rates began to increase.

To promote his business during the 1967 Democratic Convention in Chicago, George would have his bright yellow trucks stall out on the highway overpass road when politicians were arriving from Midway

Airport. His company got free TV time when the TV News covered the incoming of attending politicians.

When he left the custom exhibit business, he started a new company called **PEP (Packaged Exhibit Program)** and created the **Escort Display,** a portable exhibit.

Note that a few other companies were also starting to promote different design styles of portables. Portable exhibits were not so popular back then and were treated as a commodity. The PEP program would collect show books and get names of exhibiting companies to mail out and promote the 'portable' idea. To handle the national audience, George created a network of advertising agencies as reps. The agencies would promote, and Escort would produce and deliver. Before selling the company, Furman had over 250 agencies to rep the idea of a 'Portable Exhibit'. We all know how popular portables then became in late 1990. Promoters like George Furman changed the minds of many with innovative thinking about exhibiting agencies as reps. The agencies would promote, and Escort would produce and deliver. Before selling the company, Furman had over 250 agencies to rep the idea of a 'Portable Exhibit'. We all know how popular portables then became in late 1990. Promoters like George Furman changed the minds of many with innovative thinking about exhibiting.

Buck, Don & Carrie Freeman- *Super Game Changers*

Without a doubt, the history and contributions of **Freeman Decorating Company** can be a book all to itself. Freeman has led the way to creating industry change and has done their part with a commitment to grow the industry and its shareholders. There have been many father/son and father/daughter family leaders in the exhibit marketing industry. The entrepreneurial spirit of owners within a family business has proven to be contagious to their employees and to the supplier companies they work with. This spirit has made it special for all those lucky enough to have found their way to doing trade shows and events for a living. Buck, Don, and Carries Freeman have stood tall, contributing to positive growth within different segments of the overall industry, and are still going strong. Freeman has contributed greatly to helping the industry attain a level of professionalism among the 22 industry associations dedicated to trade show marketing and within the overall marketing mix utilized in corporate America today. Freeman has been committed to making events work for all, and especially for the exhibitors who invest big dollars expecting results.

Freeman Decorating started in Des Moines, Iowa, in 1927 by Buck Freeman. It all began with a party. While pledging a national fraternity at the University of Iowa, young **Donald S. "Buck" Freeman** discovered his passion for party decorating and parades. He saw an opportunity to use his enthusiasm for bringing people together to create meaningful experiences.

A true visionary, Buck firmly believed in creating personal relationships in an impersonal world. As Freeman grew, Buck's commitment to building these meaningful customer relationships became infused throughout the organization. This never-ending drive to meet customers' ever-changing needs better than anyone else has made them one of the world's leading event companies. Freeman was "a local and regional decorating company" when Don Freeman Jr. became president in 1972. Five years later, he was named chairman and CEO and set the company, which only had offices in Des Moines, Iowa, and Dallas, on a growth trajectory. When Don Jr. became president, there were several other service companies under the title of Freeman, so they became known as Freeman Companies, and right about the time they were hired to assist with the development of NAMM's (National Association of Music Merchants) trade shows. At the time, NAMM exhibits were held in hotel sleeping rooms, and a new set of policies were required for a professional convention type setting. Don has not only led the service industry with his creative input into the NAMM show but has been awarded as a pioneer within the medical industry as well.

"I was never really focused on being the biggest, simply being the best." ...
Buck Freeman

As **Don Freeman, Jr.** moved into the role of chairman emeritus, he agreed to an acquisition of six new locations of what was then Greyhound Exposition Services in 1981, which was the most challenging time of his tenure. The acquisition doubled Freeman's size, but bigger did not automatically translate to better. "The cultures of the companies were pretty dissimilar," cited Don Freeman. That situation has replayed itself during other growth opportunities at Freeman. When **Carrie Freeman Parsons** stepped in to assume a leadership role, she stated, "We've had a couple of acquisitions where we weren't culturally as aligned as we believed. Now, as we look at acquiring companies or hiring people, they have to be a cultural match. If you don't stay disciplined to that principle, the body will reject the organ. We want Freeman to be the No. 1 place for team members to work, say Carrie Freeman Parsons. I can't imagine working at a place where I could love the people more". That focus on building a culture, not just a company, trickles down to everyone. Freeman has extended this commitment to create a position called Chief People Officer, now held by Amy Wynn-Steffek.

In recent years, Freeman has embraced many ideas that served to change and improve the path of the industry. In 1995, Freeman offered the first online show service ordering service. All show contractor companies followed this thereafter. Regarding sustainability, Freeman was a founding member of NZCE (Net Zero Carbon Events) and a member of DID (Diversity in Design). Today sustainability and diversity are areas of major concern not only in the exposition/event industry but in the world of business. Freeman publishes a yearly impact report that shares what they have done to improve issues regarding people, principles, and the planet.

Freeman is truly a global leader in events, on a mission to redefine live for a new era. They have a data-driven approach with the industry's largest network of experts. Freeman's insights shape exhibitions, exhibits, and events that drive audiences to action. Their creation of integrated solutions has leveraged their 97-year-long legacy in trade show and event management. Freeman has been a commendable 'change maker' within the industry.

Leo McDonald- *National Network of Exhibit Companies- 60's-90's*

With the end of WWII, American prosperity was booming between 1945 and 1960, with the gross national product more than doubling, from $200 billion to more than $500 billion, fueling "The Golden Age of American Capitalism." The returning soldiers who were settling down, getting married, and starting families were the driving forcfe behind the booming economy. Companies were expanding their product offerings and were looking to effectively market their products.

Trade shows became an effective place to do so, which led to the growth of exhibit companies in America. In the 60's and 70's, exhibit companies were formed throughout the USA and were growing. The owners were entrepreneurs with backgrounds in design, carpentry, and decorating.

Leo McDonald attended school at the Chicago Art Institute and then founded Award Exhibit in Chicago in 1965. In 1970, he was introduced to Charlie Zimmerman, who owned a company in NY called **Consultants and Designers**. C&D provided technical and engineering services to Fortune 500 companies and saw trade shows as a way to expand their services. They purchased **Ivel Exhibits** in NYC and then reached out to Leo McDonald to purchase Award exhibits. Zimmerman was quite the businessman and proposed to McDonald that they create a network of exhibit companies that would appeal to exhibitors who participated in multiple shows throughout the USA. Charlie made Leo the manager to build the network. Zimmerman bought award exhibits and then 3D display also in Chicago. They then bought **Product Presentations** in Cincinnati and **Presentation Exhibits** in Los Angeles, all in the late 60's. They called this new group of companies **Exhibitgroup**, thus becoming the first national exhibit company under a single owner. A year later, the **Greyhound Corporation** saw promise in this type of service company and took a substantial stake in C&D. ExhibitGroup was the first exhibit company to be owned by a corporation on the New York Stock Exchange. Greyhound made Leo McDonald the CEO of ExhibitGroup and encouraged him to purchase other exhibit companies. Leo expanded his team by hiring **Anthony Vastardis** as Chief Financial Officer to provide the financial management expertise needed when acquiring new companies. ExhibitGroup now manages their companies like a business. Greyhound was pleased with the success of Exhibitgroup and saw the potential of being vertically integrated and expanding with show contracting for entire shows. Greyhound then purchased Mancraft, with offices in Kansas City, Miami, and New Orleans. Leo introduced Greyhound to the Las Vegas Expo, and Greyhound purchased them directly without C&D. They named this show service contractor group **GES (Greyhound Exposition Services)**. With ExhibitGroup and GES, the Greyhound Corporation now owned the largest players in the trade show industry with a network of locations. In time, Greyhound would purchase a formattable competitor-Giltspur, to create Exhibitgroup-Giltspur.

Exhibitgroup went on to acquire **Mobius** in San Francisco and later purchased **Stuart-Sauter**, a show contractor in SF, who became a part of the GES Group. The following year they acquired **Matrix Exhibits** in Atlanta, and then **Display Contractors** and the **David Gibson Co.** in Dallas. Greyhound Exhibitgroup now consisted of seven experienced exhibit companies under the name **Greyhound Exhibitgroup**. Greyhound then appointed Leo McDonald CEO of both ExhibitGroup and GES (Greyhound Exposition Services). As the GES CEO, Leo created a rapport with Don Freeman from Freeman Decorating. They agreed to share an exhibit system called GEM and a fiberglass exhibit backwall called Fiberwall to offer to exhibitors as a rental.

As head of Exhibitgroup, Leo instilled trust, respect, and cooperation between the divisions. This was a challenging task. He held the belief that each location should offer common exhibit components for rental. Each division of ExhibitGroup now offered similar exhibit rentals to avoid cross-country shipping. He developed a hard backwall exhibit called Fiberwall, offered in 10' sections, all packed into a single crate. Then he developed a backlighted 39" x 96" light box he named Lumawall, to be used alongside Fiberwall. The cost to produce large backlighted graphics helped to grow Exhibit Groups graphic capabilities for added profit. Other common rentals were counters, literature stands, monitor housing units, as well as box-framed panels and small light boxes. Each Exhibitgroup division also provided in-house I&D and supervision for each of their sister companies. This was an innovative new trend.

With more US companies now participating in multiple shows in multiple cities, the concept of renting an exhibit locally offered a cost reduction for exhibitors. A network of company locations also offered exhibitors, who owned a custom exhibit, a warehouse to store and manage their exhibit between shows and save on shipping.

Leo McDonald can be credited with forming one of the first networks of exhibit companies in the USA and one of the first exhibit houses to offer rentals to offset costs. Today, having a network of companies is a common concept that has been followed by many other exhibit houses.

Side note: Leo McDonald retired from Exhibitgroup when Greyhound was acquired by Viad Corp. Exhibitgroup continued to acquire exhibit companies nationwide, including their biggest competitor, Giltspur. Other exhibit companies began to do the same. Each merger struggled with a similar fault—their inability to manage and blend the different cultures within the companies they purchased. As a result, many of the best big company employees left to start their own companies, taking their customers with them. Two plus two always equaled three, and not five. Successful small companies all established an entrepreneurial spirit of team cooperation. A loyal culture was difficult to sustain when companies grew bigger. With mergers, processes and procedures needed to be put in place. Many of the big fish did not like being told what to do, so they left to start again.

Lee Knight- *Exhibitor Education-*

Over the years, there have been a number of publications dedicated to trade show marketing. There was **TradeShow Week** (Darlene Gudea)

and **Exhibit Builder** (Jill Brookman). Today there are two leading publications, **Exhibit City News** (Don Svehla) and **Exhibitor Magazine**. Exhibitor Magazine was created by Lee Knight. Lee started in the industry as a card trick performer working for respected companies like 3M. He was a true believer in the Fred Kitzing concept that you need to create an attraction in a trade show booth and make the attraction relevant to your product. Lee went on from being a magician to creating the first publication dedicated to exhibitors to share exhibiting success stories and tips for better results. He named the publication Exhibitor Magazine. This publication brought awareness and legitimacy to trade show marketing on all levels of involvement. The color photo examples (many photos taken by **Jamie Padgett,** another formidable contributor to the professionalism of the industry) served to share the success stories and creative tactics used by exhibitors at different trade shows. To better connect the exhibit suppliers with the end-user exhibitors, Lee created a trade show for people who did trade shows called ExhibitorLive. The event also offered educational sessions for exhibit managers or anyone interested in knowing more about successful exhibiting. Since most people working in the trade show industry did not go to school to learn about the industry, they became experts by trial and error. Lee created the **CTSM** (Certified Trade Show Marketer) certification program. He hired **Dee Silfies** to manage it. Credits are earned by attending education sessions at the ExhibitorLive event or sessions held in select US cities throughout the year. **Dee Silfies** leads this program for industry education to take a giant step in providing training and guidance for exhibit managers and exhibit suppliers in the trade show industry. Lee Knights vision and leadership have provided the industry with greater awareness and have given exhibitors the added tools to support their marketing investments.

Donald Svehla- *Publisher to provide a Voice for the Exhibit Supplier Workforce*

Don started his career in Chicago, working for his father's company, **McCormick Display**, as a carpenter and traveling supervisor doing exhibit installations in Las Vegas and Chicago. His passion and appreciation for the exhibit industry workers at the many US convention centers had influenced him to start a publication dedicated to the convention centers and to the people behind the scenes who work diligently to support the exhibitors to succeed at any trade show. He moved his operation to Las Vegas and called his publication **Exhibit City News.** Unlike Exhibitor Magazine, which focused on the exhibitors and their success at trade

First Issue

shows, ECN focused on the work forces, exhibit houses, and industry associations who work hard to ensure that the 'show must go on' for the exhibitors at any given trade show in America. After 30 years, Exhibit City News has grown to be a respected publication honoring those who support the exhibit needs of exhibitors. ECN also acknowledges the convention centers and to the good works of the industry associations. Don has worked hard to recognize the people in the trenches who go unnoticed within the $138 billion invisible industry in the USA. Dons publication has brought pride and respect to the many hard workers behind the scenes that make each trade show event a success.

Industry Associations- Believe it or not, there are over 25 different associations in the USA dedicated to serving a specific specialty niche within the $138 billion exhibition industry. Some are no longer alive. Creating an environment for knowledge sharing is one of the true legacies of the industry. The endgame is to build knowledge and connections that live on long after the events and conferences are over. If we think of our industry more as knowledge brokers than planners, buyers, or doers alone, associations then play a more strategic role with exhibitors, service companies, and associations. The associations have played a meaningful role in growing the industry.

Exhibit Industry Associations Represent All Segments of the Trade Show Marketing Industry

IAEE—International Association Exhibitions & Events

EDPA—Experiential Design and Producers Association

IFES—International Federation of Exhibition Services (world service exhibit suppliers)

ESCA (Exhibition Service Contractors Association) (The Freeman/GES Contractors, USA)

EACA (Exhibit Appointed Contractor Association): Independent I&D companies

ESA: (Convention Services Association)

SISO—Society of Independent Show Organizers

HCEA—Healthcare Exhibitor Association—Serving the needs of medical trade shows

TEA—The Exhibitors Advocate

CEIR—Center for Exhibition Industry Research

ASAE—American Society of Association Executives

MPI—Meeting Professionals Int'l (Meeting Planners)

PCMA—Professional Convention Management Association

MPI—Meeting Professionals International

GLT—Go Live Together

UFI—The Global Association of the Exposition Industry (includes all industry segments)

EIC—Events Industry Council

ILEA—International Live Events Association

IELA—International Logistics Association (Expo Freight Carriers Association)

IAVM—International Association of Venue Managers.

ACOM—Assoc for Convention Operation Management

IAAPA—Int'l Assoc of Amusement Park

Bill Mee - *Trade Show Bureau*

Bill Mee, along with Lew Johnson and Don Vaughn, founded the TSB Trade Show Bureau (now CEIR—Center for Exposition Research) in 1978. A graduate of Harvard University and Harvard Business School, William served as an executive at the Point of Purchase Advertising Institute (POPAI) and the Association of National Advertisers (ANA). Bill served as the TSB president from its beginning until he retired in 1989. He was its leader in promoting the exposition medium through research to sustain the industry's growth and to ensure its stable future.

In the early 1980s, a major shift in the allocation of marketing budget dollars spurred the growth of the trade show industry. It resulted in the increase of the number of trade shows from 4,000 to about 9,000, and the need for research to support further investments was needed.

Corporate downsizing and the corresponding reductions in marketing budgets intensified the competition for budget dollars, leading to a resurgence in interest in trade show research. It was TSB and Bill's foresight that have served to enrich public understanding not only the value of trade shows but also the significant economic impact the industry has. In 1989, IAEE (International Association of Exhibitions & Events) awarded him the Pinnacle Award in recognition of his service.

E. Jane Lorimer- *A Unified Voice to the Industry*

While exhibit houses, show contractors, and other exhibit service companies were growing, so were the exhibit industry associations that were established to specifically support them. Associations like EDPA, TSEA, ESCA, IAEE, EACA, and IEA.

In 1978, E. Jane Lorimer started her career in the trade show exhibits industry, working for Coors Beer (now Miller Coors Molson) in Denver, Co. She was the first female beer rep for Coors and later became manager of corporate trade shows for Coors. Coors management believed that their managers should be experts in their respective fields, so they supported her to receive an MBA and to be a board member of the IEA (International Exhibitors Association). This experience offered her a learning curve about the value of trade shows within the marketing mix. Deciding to leave Coors, she started a consulting business. Miller Freeman (a show organizer) was her first client. When Bill Mee decided to leave as the first president of the Trade Show Bureau, Lorimer was selected to take his place. The decision was based on her experience working as an exhibits manager for Coors, experience working with a trade show organizer, and her go-go spirit. As President of Trade Show Bureau Lorimer paved the way for many women to enter executive roles previously held by men as industry leaders.

Since the focus of the Trade Show Bureau was to assist the players in the trade show industry as a whole, Lorimer collected their concerns and data from each industry segment.

From this data, the TSB compiled their research findings and revamped the way the research was being presented so that all could understand. Lorimer spearheaded the creation of a publication containing facts, figures, and the economic impact of trade shows in the USA. This was distributed to every media outlet across the country and internationally. **Doug Ducate** took over as president after Lorimer to continue the work forward. When the Trade Show Bureau stopped, **CEIR (Center for Exposition Research)** was created to continue collecting industry data. CEIR then became a part of **IAEE** (International Association Exhibits & Events), another leading industry association that contributes greatly to the growth of the industry. Today, the invisible industry continues to grow, based in part on the research data now provided by CEIR and others to strengthen the belief for investors that trade shows work and are proven to fuel the US economy.

Carol Fojtik- *Show Management within the Mix*

Fojtik joined the industry by starting at a trade show management company owned by Martin C. Dwyer. As a show manager, she worked on such shows as "Neftagaz" in Moscow and CONEXPO, among others. When the company sold, she brought the knowledge she had gained with her to Hall-Erickson, Inc.

Fojtik worked with Hub Erickson as a show director on events such as "Automechanika in Frankfurt, Germany, serving the automotive industry. It was in 1984 that she really opened new ground for women in trade shows when she managed the U.S. Pavilion at "Automechanika" at a time when there were very few women managing trade shows overseas. Fojtik managed one of the biggest U.S. Pavilions.

Fojtik helped launch one of the trade show industry's most exciting trade shows, **"The Exhibitor Show,"** now known as

"EXHIBITORLIVE." The first show was launched in 1989 with 75 exhibitors. Under her direction, the show has grown to almost 300 exhibitors. For almost 30 years, she has led the team at ExhibitorLive to produce this successful event.

Fojtik also managed the National Mining Association; the world's largest mining equipment show called "MINEXPO" in Las Vegas. With over 1,200 exhibitors and occupying over a million net square feet of exhibit space, Fojtik again broke new ground as the first female to manage that major trade show.

Carol Fojtik has been very involved with IAEE since 1985 to share her knowledge as a show manager with exhibit industry members. She was known for her generous mentorship and has helped shape many well-known industry leaders. Across the industry, Fojtik was well known for her expertise in the management of trade shows. The indelible mark that Fojtik has made on IAEE as an organization and the overall exhibition and events industry embodies the spirit and significance of IAEE's highest honor, the Pinnacle Award, of which Carol was awarded in 2018. Carol's contribution in sharing the role of a show manager with each of the other industry segments has provided valuable insights for trade show and event marketing associations to think and act as one. Fojtik has been a true leader and pioneer in the industry.

Hubbard H. "Hub" Erickson, Jr- Hall-Erickson, Inc.

Inducted in the 1988 EIC Hall of Leaders,

A respected entrepreneur dedicated to trade show management as meaningful business. He has enhanced the industry as a founding member of the Trade Show Bureau (now CEIR—Center for Exhibition Industry Research) and past president of the National Association of Exhibition Managers (now the International Association of Exhibitions and Events).

Bob Dallmeyer-

Robert (Bob) Dallmeyer has shaped the industry not only as the founder of a consulting firm, producing hundreds of events, exhibitions, and shows, but also as an author, facilitator, educator, and exhibition Robert (Bob) Dallmeyer has shaped the industry not only as the founder of a consulting firm, producing hundreds of events, exhibitions, and shows, but also as an author, facilitator, educator, exhibition organizer, mentor, and communicator. His insights into how he views the future of the exhibitions and events industry have served him well. While serving as Chairman of the International Association of Exhibitions and Events (IAAE), he created the Future Strategies committee as well as the exhibition industry's Global Council. Bob has received numerous achievements throughout his career. He received the Trade Show Exhibitors Association's (TSEA) Chairman Award in 1980 as well as the TSEA Distinguished Service Award in 1983. In addition, Bob was honored with TSEA's Lifetime Member in 2001. Bob also received the IAEE's prestigious Pinnacle Award in recognition as a thought leader and motivator of others. He is a former director of the Center for Exhibition Industry Research (CEIR). He has served on the International Center for Exhibitor and Event Marketing (ICEEM) board of directors. In addition, Bob taught IAEE's "Certified in Exhibition Management" (CEM) certification courses in the USA, Europe, Latin America, Canada, and China.

Gene Winther - Connecting the Associations

Gene Winther began his career in 1963, preparing theater sets in northern California, and in 1968 he started a business to provide holiday decorations for the streets of Sacramento. In 1970, he launched an exhibit company called Three Sixty Designers, which later became Expon Exhibits, that focused on custom modular exhibit systems. Although Gene was an exhibit designer/builder, he was involved in several exhibit associations, giving him well-rounded knowledge about the needs within the industry beyond exhibits alone. Winther was very active with IAEE, the International Association of Exhibit Managers. He was a board member of the Trade Show Exhibitors Association and served as the chairman of the first TS2 show. In 1995, he joined EDPA and served on their board of directors, and then served as president of EDPA in 2000. He won the EDPA Ambassador Award in 2001 and was awarded the EDPA Hazel Hays Award. He went on to serve as the first chairman of the newly created EDPA Foundation. Winther's major contribution to the industry was to build harmony and a connection between the many associations that served the industry. He jump-started the EDPA Foundation, serving as their first chairman. The mission was to financially support industry education. His enthusiasm about building the EDPA brand has been much appreciated by the entire exposition industry. "I never felt that there was a day that I actually worked hard for a real living. I mean, I worked, and it was sometimes hard, but I always loved this business," said Winther. "When I got into the business, I realized that there was more to it than just building exhibits. I love connecting with new people. I love face-to-face marketing, so it was always a fun career."

Industry Associations

With 22 different associations within the exhibition industry, we have a tendency to speak to each other more than the people we all wish to help—the **exhibitors.**

While all of the industry expresses their dedication to exhibitors, there are several associations that are specifically dedicated to the exhibitor. There are also a few publications and industry associations who conduct a trade about trade shows like ExhibitorLive, IAEE-Expo! Expo! Show, and HCEA. Each are dedicated to the needs of exhibitors at any trade show. One of the first shows of this nature was the TS2 Show, managed by TSEA (Trade Show Exhibitors Asdsociation).

IAEE-International Association of Exhibitions and Events®

In 1928, **William Hunt Eisenmann**, an exhibition organizer, along with a small group of like-minded colleagues, organized the National Association of Exposition Managers (NAEM). The association did not have a headquarters, so each year the chairman would host the organization's annual meeting.

In 1955, NAEM created the **Guidelines for Display Rules & Regulations**, a compilation of guidelines and procedures intended to ensure that the exhibit floor would be fairly structured for all exhibitors. An additional benefit was to allow the industry to operate more efficiently. In the time since, Guidelines for Display Rules & Regulations have, in effect, become an industry standard—many show organizers simply include Guidelines for Display Rules & Regulations into their exhibitor contracts. A task force is appointed every 3 to 5 years to review and revise the guidelines to ensure they are kept relevant and contemporary. Most recently, language has been added to help manage the increasing number of international exhibiting companies who are accustomed to using the entire cubic content of their exhibit spaces.

Beginning in the 1950s, the industry began to grow significantly and became much more sophisticated. Service contractors became an essential ingredient for success. Without companies like Freeman, GES, Shepard, and dozens of others to assume management of logistics, most shows could not adequately manage the thousands of complex details that make for a successful exhibition.

The Guidelines for Display Rules & Regulations and the practice of hiring a show contractor to manage key exhibiting activities are what make participating in a US trade show different than most of the rest of the world. The American Model of organizing and managing trade shows has worked very well in the United States for decades.

In 1991, NAEM hired **Steven Hacker** as its CEO and President. Hacker and his staff quickly energized the association to reflect substantial issues for a rapidly growing industry. Among the initiatives that were adopted was renaming NAEM to reflect the increasing globalization of the industry. The organization was renamed the International Association for Exposition Management (IAEM). Hacker's mission was to bring greater benefits to IAEE membership. IAEM reworked its certification program, Certified in Exhibition Management® (CEM). The role of exhibition organizers grew to become a very important job. Exhibitions were opening vast sales opportunities for most companies. The cost to host organizations and for exhibitors to participate was becoming expensive. Most host organizations recognized the need for a full-time manager to monitor activities and to manage increasing costs. Organizations quickly recognized the need and benefits of educating their staff to perfect their job skills, and the CEM program began to grow rapidly. Associations of exhibition organizers in other nations took note of IAEM's success and began adopting CEM under licenses granted to them by IAEM. Successful CEM programs continue to take place today in Mexico, China, Taiwan, Thailand, Saudi Arabia, Dubai, the UAE, and Canada.

Another vital change was adopted permitting Associate Members of IAEM, largely employees of vendor companies providing support to exhibitions, full access to all IAEM benefits, including voting and holding elective office. Several Associate Members have since been elected to IAEM's Board of Directors, and several have risen to the Board's Chairman.

 In 1993 NAEM also launched an annual meeting and named it Expo! Expo! This event, along with ExhibitorLive, are the two most important trade shows that represent and promote the trade show and event marketing industries in the USA.

In 2006, IAEM once again changed its name, this time to recognize the growing presence of events other than trade shows in which buyers and sellers regularly come together. The new name is The International Association of Exhibitions and Events® (IAEE). Note that IAEE was the first industry association to have elected a woman Chair of the Board, Patricia Farias, from Mexico. IAEE is also the first exhibition industry organization association to place international directors on their board.

Another new IAEE initiative was the launch of a government affairs function that represents the industry and its members before state and federal legislatures as well as a host of federal and state agencies. This industry representation today is composed of a powerful group of advocates who lobby in Washington, DC, each year. **David DuBois**, CMP, CAE, FASAE, CTA, was selected as IAEE's President and CEO. in 2012 and continued to lead the association for the next 11 years. David was particularly effective in collaborating with all of the other industry associations to establish a coalition that presents a joint voice for the industry. DuBois led IAEE to a higher level of participation to lobby in Washington on behalf of the exhibition and events industry to be recognized for its economic impact. When DuBois retired, **Cathy Brendon** took over the reins and in 2024, **Marsha Flanagan**, M.Ed., CEM, assumed the role as the new IAEE President & CEO. Marsha has been a long-time staff member of the IAEE management team to carry on with leadership within the industry.

ESCA- *The Show Service Contractors Association*

Established in 1970, the **Exhibition Services & Contractors Association** (ESCA) serves as a unified voice for service contractors and their partners in the exhibition industry. Both Freeman and GES are the biggest in this sector, but there is a strong network of other **service contractor** companies across the United States and Canada. ESCA collaborates with its members as well as other industry organizations to build harmony in the exhibition sector and advocate on behalf of the interests of their members. The American model of organizing a trade show in the USA is different than anywhere else in the world. The initial goal of ESCA was to establish a sustainable competitive edge for member companies. This strategy aims to enhance organizational alignment for US trade shows. The mission of ESCA is designed to adapt and evolve in response to the changing needs of their members and the shifting competitive landscape of the exhibition industry. The show contractor involvement with each event relies on a spirit of cooperation to follow the established guidelines (American Model) and the show management methods that are followed throughout the USA. ESCA is the glue that works to unite the many show contractors throughout the US.

EDPA-Experiential Designers & Producers Association

Exhibit Designers Unite to serve Exhibitors

Jim Derse Sr/president of chicago chapter of EDPA

Of all the industry associations, EDPA **(Experiential Designers & Producers Association)** has been a leader dedicated to exhibit designers and producers. When EDPA started in 1956, many of the member companies resided on the east coast, with the NY Coliseum being a leading convention center. It quickly grew in the Midwest and south to become a strongly unified voice for exhibit builders across the nation. Over the decades, EDPA grew its members and their dedication to improving exhibiting

services for the exhibitors and education for exhibit designers. Most of the EDPA members were the owners of their companies. They believed in the power of face-to-face communication and

participated each year in the EDPA annual meeting with its members at the close of the trade show season.

The Chicago chapter of EDPA initiated the first scholarship award to students who have demonstrated a keen interest in exhibit design. The EDPA scholarship was given to two students from Layton Art School in Milwaukee. Layton was one of the few colleges in the country to offer an exhibit design program. "It is our hope that other colleges will soon offer exhibit design courses in the USA," says **Jim Derse,** Derse Advertising Company. Jim Derse's successor was **Bill Haney,** who made certain this would happen.

Each year, the annual EDPA meeting (now called ACCESS) uncovered new issues to deal with and to take action. They were passionate about creating a brighter future. They took action on many issues that are programs today. In 1961, EDPA president **Harold Averick** was instrumental in creating MEA (Medical Exhibitors Association) that later became HCEA. He also started the beginning of the

1991 EDPA Board (Gary Stewart, Ingrid Boyd, Ron Malliet, Skip Speerschneider, Doug Zeigal, Bruce Deckel)

EDPA Economic Survey, then later expanded with EDPA president **Dan Hartwig**. In 1974, EDPA president **Charles Manne** helped launch the IEA (International Exhibitors Association). In 1982, EDPA president **Jan Spiezney** 1991 EDPA Board (Gary

Stewart,Ingrid Boyd, Ron Malliet, Skip Speerschneider, Doug Zeigal, Bruce Deckel) supported the launch of the Trade Show Bureau with Lew Johnson. Both he and **Bob Firks** were the only EDPA presidents to also serve as presidents of the Trade Show Bureau. In 1990, **Ingrid Boyd** became the first female president of EDPA and introduced EDPA to **IFES** (International Federation of Exposition Services). As a result, EDPA then became further involved with the world of international trade shows and suppliers thanks to Ingrid's vision of the future.

In 1997, EDPA president **Larry Kulchawik,** with an EDPA team, promoted the involvement of EDPA with college-level education dedicated to trade show design. EDPA was successfully involved with exhibit design training at Bemidji State, but then extended an arm futher to start a master's degree in exhibit design with FIT/NYC. The program is now in its 16th year.

Larry also led an EDPA team of exhibit fabrication experts to work with Underwriters Laboratory to create standards for safety when building exhibits. The standard **UL2305** was never embraced by the other industry associations. It was introduced at a time when union regulations and high costs were a major issue. Exhibitors feared that this new standard would add fuel to the fire to create added costs and regulations. Good idea, but bad timing.

EDPA president **Sue Renner** supported the creation of the EACA (Exhibit Appointed Contractor Association). **Gene Winther** was the first EDPA president to serve on the board of IAEE and helped to create the EDPA Foundation in 2002. EDPA president **Gwen Parsons** created greater awareness for portable exhibits in the mix and energized the female component of EDPA leadership. **Mark Johnson** championed education in the industry and led EDPA to participate in its first exhibit at Euroshop in Düsseldorf. He now owns the Exhibitor Group. **Gwen Hill** supported the greater awareness of the "experiential" component of trade show participation. EDPA then changed its name to address this.

Rob Cohen supported dialog among general contractors and show management groups. He and EDPA president, **Chris Griffin**, also continue to lead the charge to create greater awareness about the exhibition industry in Washington, DC. With the industry contributing over $100 billion to the US economy, why not greater awareness and support from our government? Way to go, EDPA!

Another EDPA representative who did not serve as president but dedicated his passion to the fallen members within of the exhibit industry family was **Rich Johnson.** He helped to create the **Randy Smith Annual Golf Outing** to raise money and pay tribute to those who have passed from within the industry. The event continues today as a thank you for their dedication to a job they loved. Through the years, EDPA had selected a management team to represent the association. Prior to 1997, the EDPA presidents served as the face of the association. In 1997, EDPA then selected a management company that now provides an 'EDPA face', a director, to represent the association year after year. Many thanks to Pete Dicks, Jeff Provost, and Dasher Lowe for doing this so well!

EDPA - *Education *Awareness *Training

EDPA has been passionate about college-level education and grooming talent to attract new blood into the exhibit industry. EDPA continues to support two college-level degree programs for exhibit design: **Bemidji State** with an undergraduate degree and **FIT** with a master's degree in exhibit design. Kudos go out to **Bonnie Higgins** at Bemidji State and **Brenda Cowen/Christina Lyons** at FIT for supporting exhibit design education at their college institutions. Many colleges have declined to create trade show marketing classes, let alone a degree program, for exhibit marketing and design. A Big Thank You to Bemidji State and FIT/NYC for supporting exhibit design at a college level!

EDPA recently introduced a new program entitled *'The Future Workforce Committee."* This EDPA team focuses on introducing college students and vocational schools to career opportunities in the trade show industry. "EDPA will serve as an academic partner to initiate learning sessions related to jobs available in the exhibition industry," says **Michael McMahon** from the EDPA team.

Through the years, EDPA members have consistently supported their industry, an industry that has created a passion in each of their hearts and encouraged them to continue giving back as "Game Changers".

Gary Stewart- *Designer Education & No Spec Design*

Gary graduated from Auburn University in 1971. Like most of us in the industry, Gary fumbled into it. Gary started his career working for a company that designed and built reception furniture and signage for resorts in Hilton Head. In 1974, he left the company to start up **Design South** in Atlanta, doing similar work for information centers and real estate sales centers. They also build architectural scale models. Design South built a scale model of the Georgia World Congress for the architect, who then used it at the grand opening with Jimmy Carter. One day Gary got a call from a Yellow Page ad asking if he could build a trade show exhibit. He had never built a trade show exhibit before but said, "Yes, we can do it." That was the start of Design South doing exhibits. One day Gary got a call from CJ Lynch, the owner of **Shepard Convention Services**, asking if they could fabricate reception and registration counters for the shows, they managed at the GWCC. He won the contract. In 1977, Mr. Lynch invited Gary to his home in Atlanta for a reception to meet members of EDPA. That started his career with EDPA to go on to be president and winner of the Hazel Hays Award. That same year, the largest exhibit house in Atlanta, Custom Creations, went bankrupt. They managed a small group of shows for IBM. The logistics manager from Custom Creations saw a Design South ad in the Yellow Pages and contacted Gary for a job. He was hired and inherited 12 cases of IBM exhibits. From there, they did IBM exhibits for the next 23 years to bring them to be major players in the exhibit business.

Gary was a strong proponent of **No Spec Design.** He had no commissioned AE's and refused to do RFP on spec. Many exhibitors looking for new exhibits would ask 3-5 exhibit design builders for a proposal. Many exhibit companies would spend hours preparing a design rendering or a model and then travel to the client location to present their idea, all on speculation. The cost of doing this if you lost had to be built into the overhead of doing business. A pretty expensive

cost for the exhibit houses in the industry. But if you won the job, the investment was worth it!

Gary joined the board at EDPA and created a college-level course in exhibit design at Auburn University with a professor he went to school there with.

This marketing and design course required the students to design an exhibit for a generic company. EDPA and Gary helped to fund and create a step-by-step "How to Design an Exhibit" workbook for students to follow. This was the start of EDPA support for college-level courses to introduce trade show exhibits within the marketing mix. EDPA has since gone on to get involved with college-level training at Bemidji State (undergraduate degree) and FIT/NYC, which offers a master's degree in exhibit design.

When Gary was president of EDPA, he proposed the concept of **no-spec design** for all EDPA members to follow. They each overwhelmingly agreed. This lasted less than a year when exhibit companies were more desperate for business and broke the truce and went back to NoSpec Design. Gary came from a world dealing with architects and builders who did nothing on spec. This formula just did not apply to the new industry of exhibit builders who hired AEs on commission and agreed to do proposals on speculations. The cost to design and propose a new exhibit was much less than for an architect or contractor to propose the fabrication of a building. Nevertheless, still an added expense. To this day, the industry exhibit companies (not independent designers) will accept doing a proposal on spec.

As a result of following this noble path of not agreeing to No Spec Design and no commissions, Gary lost a few existing good customers and refused to play the No Spec Design game. This forced him to sell off his assets for DesignSouth in 1999. He then started an events management company called StewartMDM.

Gary presented his new business model to EDPA, who hired StewartMDM to coordinate and create a series of EDPA Designer Symposium Meetings for a three-year, three-city tour. The symposiums were designed specifically for trade show exhibit designers to expand their creative reach. The symposiums involved guest speakers, workshops, and seminars. StewartMDM arranged the site, the stage needs, the presenters, the hotel accommodations, and breakfast/lunches. The symposiums were held in Chicago, Washington, DC, and Atlanta during the Olympics.

This series of events was a first and a last for EDPA. A great step in sharing exhibit design knowledge with national exhibit designers. The unfortunate part was that some exhibit company owners used this symposium as a recruiting platform. Lee Knight at Exhibitor Magazine picked up the idea a few years later and created a new Designer Symposium, so all was lost.

Gary Stewart had the foresight about exhibit design education early on. He influenced the growth of exhibit design education in so many ways and was awarded the prestigious Hazel Hays Award in 2003.

Ingrid Boyd - *International Thinking for US Exhibit Companies*

Ingrid Boyd was a native of Germany and owned an exhibit company in New Jersey.

Her company joined EDPA in 1986 and became involved with a new association in Europe called **IFES** (International Federation of Exposition Services). The Federation was made up of six European country associations from France, England, Germany, Belgium, Switzerland, and the and the Netherlands. Their mission was to share knowledge between countries when exhibiting outside of their region of origin. As EDPA president in 1990, Ingrid Boyd met with the board at IFES and convinced EDPA to join IFES as the first non-European Association to be a member. Over the next several years, EDPA remained involved, and Ingrid introduced EDPA board members **Dalton Jenkins** and Larry Kulchawik to replace her after her retirement.

Larry Kulchawik went on to be elected as IFES president from 2004-2006. Exhibiting globally was not so popular in the USA until 2012. Ingrid Boyd can be credited with encouraging international trade show exhibiting services to EDPA members. She was also the first female to serve as president of EDPA, and she was awarded the prestigious Hazel Hays Award in 1998.

HCEA- *An industry specific association dedicated to Healthcare Exhibitors-*

The Healthcare Convention & Exhibitors Association (HCEA) is a trade association representing organizations united by their common desire to increase the effectiveness and quality of healthcare

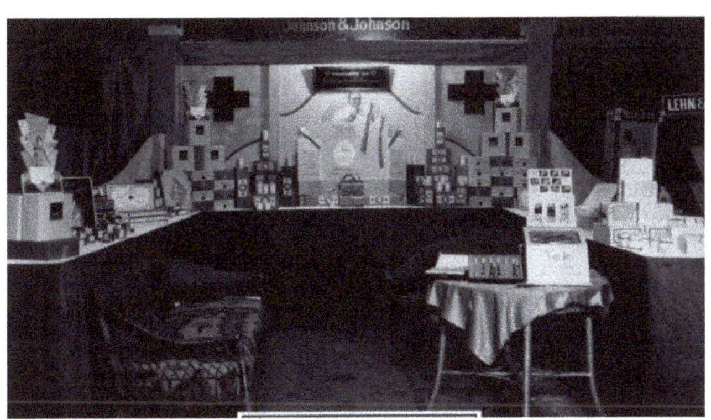

conventions as an educational and marketing medium. HCEA began as the Medical Exhibitors Association (MEA) in 1930. According to historical archives, 12 charter members established a treasury with personal donations of $100 each to fund the new organization. There are only a few industry associations dedicated specifically to the value of trade show marketing for their specific industry. The healthcare industry is pretty unique in that there are over 1000 healthcare-related trade shows each year in the USA. Healthcare trade shows are different in many ways from the average industry trade show. The majority of attendees to a medical conference do not elect to attend to see the exhibits; they attend for the educational sessions that are conducted during the conference. For many, it is a requirement to keep up their medical license and must obtain CIU credits (continued education units) for their specific area of medical training. Their second reason for attending a medical meeting is for networking and general lectures to keep current. Their last reason to attend a medical conference is to visit the trade show. In most cases, a visitor experience at a healthcare trade show discovered an 'Eureka Moment' as a visitor. "I learned something new that I never knew before" was a common response of many. The skills needed to staff a trade show rep at an exhibit require technical knowledge about the product or service beyond engagement skills. All medical visitors know their stuff at medical shows, so staff skills are more critical than at other trade shows. HCEA has worked hard over the years to mold their medical show formats to best benefit the attending healthcare professionals. The greatest contribution HCEA has brought to the industry over their 90+ years is that they continue to be the one and only avenue for their three distinct membership types— corporate, association, and industry suppliers—to meet, network, and share opportunities for solutions and topics that impact the highly regulated health care convention industry. The healthcare convention and exhibits industry is a niche group of highly passionate people that are inspired to utilize the convention platform as a way to share important information for patients and their health care professionals in a compliant way to ensure that these audiences have the most up-to-date information for their specialties and practices.

Over the years, other non-healthcare industry shows have borrowed a page from their playbook and applied it to their industry shows.

The Exhibitor Advocate Association- Jessica Sibila- *A new Approach to Driving Change*

One new association is The **Exhibitor Advocate,** which is focused on enhancing the exhibitor experience through cost reductions and added value at trade shows. They are dedicated to providing expert advice, research, and tools to enhance the value of trade show marketing for exhibitors. They educate industry stakeholders on the needs of the exhibitor. As an exhibitor, if you ever wanted to express something but felt that you couldn't or didn't have the time, The Exhibitor Advocate speaks on their behalf. This valuable new channel raises the voice of the exhibitors and allows exhibit suppliers to identify and address exhibitor pain points.

Jessica Sibila has taken the lead as the Executive Director of The Exhibitor Advocate and has assembled a team of experienced exhibit professionals to collect and act upon the various issues and pain points of exhibitors. Exhibitor challenges are raised with show management companies, associations, show contractors, and exhibit suppliers who collaboratively address regulations and procedures at trade shows in the USA. Many exhibitors are willing to make the required investments in trade shows but wish to be reassured that costs and methods are fair and reasonable. Exhibitors want to be able to predict and budget accordingly for the events they manage. They don't want to be surprised by costs, rules, and regulations.

Jessica Sibila and her team at the Exhibitor Advocate should be commended for the data they collect and the industry relationships they have established with trade show organizers and suppliers to unite and keep the value for trade show marketing a reliable marketing investment for exhibitors into the future.

EAC (Exhibit Appointed Contractors)- The I&D Companies in America

This industry association has taken bold steps to improve the exhibitor experience and the cost of setting up an exhibit at any given show. An exhibitor-appointed contractor **(EAC)** is any individual or company that is not an employee of an exhibitor's company or an employee of the Official Show Contractor. EAC's are hired to install/dismantle an exhibit or provide other non-exclusive services for an exhibitor outside of the official show contractor service offering. (i.e., installation/dismantling, booth designers/builders, florists, furniture suppliers, AV Services, laborers, etc.).

These service providers must get approval from the official show contractor to work on the show floor. The practice of hiring a service provider outside of the official show contractor is a unique practice followed by exhibitors and exhibit design companies for convention center trade shows in the USA. Many shows held in hotels or private halls do not require this. As most convention center cities do not allow the exhibit to set up themselves, they hire an outside I&D service to do so. Independent exhibit installation companies started to get popular in the 70's and now are the most common practice for installing an exhibit outside of using the official show contractor. The EAC Association acts to protect the rights of I&D companies as well as the right for an exhibitor to use a labor source they prefer.

Andy Codamo- *The Birth of I&D as an Exclusive Show Service*

In the early days, an exhibitor would send a set-up supervisor to instruct and manage a crew with labor from the show contractor. With the advent of the mega convention centers in the 70's came the opportunity to refine the I&D profession. Industry pioneers like **Karl Birsa** (CB Display Services), Brad Knox (KIDS), **Andy Codamo** (Sho-Aids), and others made I&D a respectable profession and a valued added service for exhibit builders and the exhibitors.

Andy Codamo owned one of the first I&D companies named **Sho-Aids** on the east coast. They were the exclusive I&D service for a NY exhibit house called Noble Displays. In time, Andy bought Noble in 1972 and provided both exhibit fabrication and a personalized I&D service. This was the start of many other exhibit houses like Exhibit Group and Giltspur to offer a similar service for their clients with complex exhibits. The show contractor labor was not dependable enough to provide a crew of skilled carpenters for a single installation. Andy can be credited for starting a trend and creating an alternative method for installing an exhibit. It saved time and offered the exhibitor peace of mind with a hassle-free experience.

Jim Wurm- *Exhibit Appointed Contractors*

Jim Wurm was very instrumental in leading a new industry association called EACA. The EAC group from Illinois (founded by **Tom Cassell** and **Joe Mondelli)** approached Jim to form the new national EACA association. Their first board meeting was held in San Francisco during the TS2 Show. This association was dedicated to assisting independent I&D companies to be permitted to work along- side the official show contractors carpenter labor pool. As the economy recovered after 9/11, competition in the trade show industry increased. This raised the bar on the need for quality labor throughout the country. The show contractors would not allow labor to install exhibits on the show floor unless they paid a fee and provided a certificate of authorization from the exhibitor 60 days in advance. They also needed to provide a certificate of insurance.

This caused much hardship for exhibitors who preferred to hire carpenters who were most familiar with their exhibit installation. Show management leaders of several industry associations became increasingly concerned that their exhibitors were not allowed to hire their own union carpenters who were more familiar to install their exhibits and would work more efficiently to reduce the time required to install. A group of show managers called a meeting in 1985 with NAEM (Assoc for Environmental Health & Safety) in Dallas with the leading show contractor companies, Jim Wurm of I&D and **Don Stacey** of Stacey Exhibits. The group was tasked with working out a solution for this issue. They succeeded in doing so, and **EACA** was formed to assist the show associations in vetting approvals for I&D companies to assist their exhibitors and allow them to work on the show floor. EACA was formed in the late 1990s by executive director Jim Wurm. EACA now works directly with exhibitor-appointed contractors to improve the client experience, establish best practices, and improve communication between contractors, associations, customers, and organized labor. After 25 years, the actions taken by EACA brought a new level of professionalism to the I&D portion of the trade show industry. Jim Wurm contributed greatly to paving the way for exhibitors to have a choice to select the highest level of labor to install their exhibits at any show in the USA.

Jack McEntee- *I&D Attitude Adjustments*

As owners of the national exhibit installation company, I&D (later to become Nth Degree), Jack McEntee and Pat Alacqua influenced change in the attitude and behavior of show site carpenters when servicing exhibitors and exhibit companies on the show floor.

The attitude of union carpenters on the show floor was such that they displayed a defensiveness and a distain for being told what to do. Listen to your supervisor, and not the exhibitor. After all, they were union carpenters. It started with the show contractor union labor pools of carpenters in each city and permeated into the newly formed independent exhibitor-appointed carpenter crews.

Jack had superior sales skills, but having said that, he prevailed against all competition because, at heart, he was a teacher. Jack was the first EAC to understand that while you can sell something once, you won't keep the account unless you exceed expectations with superior service. To ensure that he did the following:

- Routinely recruited hires from places that delivered great service—restaurants, hotels, and venues.
- Trained all personnel on the value of world-class customer service on a routine basis.
- He went beyond the normal training for an EAC by teaching all personnel about the roles and contributions of the other industry.
- He wanted to be sure that all carpenters facing personnel could be a total resource to the client.

This form of training was a game changer for carpenters on an I&D crew. This change of attitude had a lot to do with exhibitors now preferring to employ their own installation companies in place of the show contractor labor pool. Jack fought to keep his carpenter crews from being denied on the show floor. He stood up for these inequities on the show floor and, as a result, became known as a troublemaker. Over time, many employees of I&D left to form their own companies and took with them the Jack McEntee philosophy of customer service. Today, all I&D service companies in the USA follow this motto—the exhibitor comes first!

Tom Cassell- *Show Site Cooperation & Harmony*

Tom Cassell was a leader in the exhibit-appointed contractor movement and was the first person hired by a convention center (McCormick Place) to act as a show site floor manager to resolve issues between exhibitors and union labor workers during set up. Many regulations during installation and dismantling were often misunderstood. Tom's job was to monitor the show floor during installation and to step in as a representative of McCormick Place to sort out conflicts or violations. This change in show floor management during a set-up took the heat off of the association management when complaints were submitted. His first assignment was for the 2003 Auto Show at McCormick and then remained a full-time agent for McCormick for the next 20 years. Cooperation between exhibitors and labor crews is a wish that all association managers want. Deliver a hassle-free experience for exhibitors. This trend in management thinking helped to establish harmony and keep union regulations understood without arguments

Voices from the Peanut Gallery- Exhibitors & Investors

Glenda Brungardt- *The Voice of the Exhibitor*

Of the many corporate exhibit managers who became active in the trade show industry community, **Glenda Brungardt** from **HP Inc.** became very involved with industry associations and contributed greatly to pushing for shifts in thinking about business as usual as an exhibitor. Her voice, as an exhibitor, was heard loudly. After 46 years as the HP exhibits manager, every year was a learning opportunity for Glenda, and the goal was to make the HP exhibiting program better than the next. HP management trusted and empowered Glenda to make marketing decisions for HP, as well as to participate within the trade show community of suppliers to make exhibiting investments as effective as possible. Glenda was passionate about her job to benefit HP marketing initiatives, but also to benefit the industry her company depended on to do so.

Glenda earned a CTSM (Certified Trade Show Manager) and a CTSM Diamond certification. She is now retired but continues to serve on the board of the Exhibitor Advocate group, contributing her knowledge as a veteran exhibits manager.

Glenda Brungardt had led two initiatives with HP that served to pave the way for other exhibiting companies, as well as the industry, to follow. The first initiative **(Sustainability)** was created during the period in the late 90's when exhibiting costs and methods were being challenged. HP attended 200 trade shows a year. In the past, that meant trucking thousands of pounds of exhibit equipment—counters, display panels, carpet, and more—across the country. Often, booth components and graphics were created especially for a particular event and then disposed of afterwards. Today, that picture has changed—thanks to HP's focus on designing for the environment throughout every aspect of its business and operations. HP's innovative thinking—combined with environmentally responsible materials—has resulted in a modular, reusable exhibit design space that is 30 percent lighter. The weight to reduce drayage costs and the materials used to address sustainability issues was an HP initiative that Glenda led with exhibit supplier HB Stubbs. Together, they examined new exhibit fabrication methods to reduce the company's overall carbon footprint by introducing lightweight, modular systems and incorporating materials that have less environmental impact than those used for their previous exhibits. This program helped to pave the way for other exhibitors to follow and to also establish exhibiting solutions that were more friendly to the environment.

Her second contribution was to establish a **Global Standardized Measurement Program** for HP's exhibiting investments. She partnered with **Skip Cox** at Exhibit Surveys, Inc. to create a method for HP to manage their costs and maximize their return from exhibiting. The program went public when exhibit surveys were acquired by Freeman. As a top corporation and exhibitor, HP and Glenda Brungardt contributed greatly to improving the value of trade show marketing investments.

It should be noted that over the years, many corporate exhibit managers have gotten very involved to support the concerns of fellow exhibitors. The voice of exhibitors and their industry associations surely has the loudest voice to drive positive changes that serve to improve results for trade show marketing.

Sheldon Adelson - *A Big Time Investor*

The Venetian Convention Expo (previously known as the Sands)

Sheldon Adelson was a Las Vegas trade show industry super star. He became one of the richest men in the world. In the late 1970s, Adelson developed the COMDEX trade shows for the computer industry that began in 1979. It was one of the largest computer trade shows in the world through much of the 1980s and 1990s. In 1995, Adelson sold the Interface Group Show Division, including the   COMDEX shows, to SoeBank Group of Japan. In 1988, Adelson purchased the Sands Hotel and Casino in Las Vegas. The next year, he built the **Sands Expo and Convention Center,** then the only privately owned and operated convention center in the U.S. In 1991, while honeymooning in Venice with his second wife, Miriam, Adelson came up with the idea for a megaresort hotel. He razed the Sands and spent $1.5 billion to construct The Venitian, a Venice-themed resort hotel and casino in 1999. Sheldon Adelson went on to invest in many other hotels and centers throughout the world. One of the most famous was the Marina Bay Sands in Singapore, which included a convention center attached. It is said to be the most expensive building in the world! As well as the Condex Show, Adelson brought an added popularity for trade shows held in Las Vegas and around the world. His major investments and belief in the trade show industry contributed greatly to the success of trade shows in the USA and around the world.

Unsung Industry Supporters

Through the years, most of the **Change makers** have been owners exhibit companies or associations with influential people. A fire of passion and dedication for the trade show/event industry also burned brightly in many individuals who did not own their companies but acted like they did to serve within an industry they loved. Here are but a few to mention.

Rich Johnson-

30 years ago, Ted Peterson and Rich Johnson from IDEAS, Inc. in Atlanta stepped up to create a golf outing to raise money for the family of a coworker who died on his way home after long hours setting up an exhibit. His name was Randy Smith, a project manager at the company. The Randy Smith Memorial Golf Classic was started in August of 1995 in hopes of helping the emotional and financial burden that Randy's death caused his family. This expression of compassion for the families of trade show team workers has now taken place for 30 years in Atlanta and at several other cities each year. The Randy Smith Memorial Golf Classic is to help families in the exhibition industry who have suffered severe tragedies or face insurmountable medical expenses. "Our commitment as an industry is to provide financial and emotional support to all past and present recipients and their families," says Rich Johnson. The dedication so many give to make sure that *the show must go on* is a job passion that is never to be forgotten in the trade show industry. Rich Johnson has led this event each year and should be commended for his continued compassion for the people of the invisible industry.

Paul Willett-

Paul started his career in Cincinnati at a company called Product Presentation, later to become Exhibit Group Cincinnati. He became involved in the I&D side of the business in Chicago and moved to Las Vegas with Dennis Bursa to open CB Display. From here, he worked for GES in Las Vegas to become 'Uncle Paul 'on the trade show floor. He then joined Czarnowski, where he retired. Paul was very well respected on the show floor and became very involved with EDPA, where he was honored with the Hazel Hays Award for his ability to provide harmony on the show floor and connect people as industry associates.

Michael Seymour-

Michael worked for some of the top exhibit companies in Chicago in a sales capacity. Michael believed in the power of trade shows and became very involved with the Healthcare Convention Exhibitors Association. As an exhibit supplier, Michael was voted on the HCEA board and gave much of his time to assisting exhibitors in the healthcare industry to discover shortcuts and understand the work rules when exhibiting at a medical trade show. You won't find a more committed or knowledgeable person in the trade show industry. Aside from providing top-notch service for his clients, Michael constantly gives back to the industry with his involvement as the Chapter President at TSEA and a member of the HCEA board. "I work for the good of others. I help exhibitors realize their goals and the means to measure their results, which = success," says Michael Seymour.

Pat Friedlander-

Pat started her career as a marketing manager for a book company. She joined Giltspur, who later became Exhibit group Giltspur, as Director of Marketing. She later started her own company called Word-Up! Pat provided trade show marketing consulting for Fortune 500 companies, particularly in the healthcare industry. Pat has said "that linear thinking is overrated." Creativity doesn't flow from following an agenda. Responding to the here and now is what makes life new every day. Marketing is art; it's fun; it's what I do." Through her career, Pat Friedlander became very involved with industry associations like EDPA and HCEA and with supporting exhibit design education at FIT in

NYC. Some of Pat's greatest contributions to the industry were supporting women in the workplace, internal industry education, serving on the board of HCEA with healthcare exhibiting issues, and sustainability within the exposition industry. She wrote an excellent article for Exhibit City News titled 'The Sustainability Mandate' which tackled the issue head regarding the disposal of waste produced as a result of trade shows in the USA. Her leadership on issues such as this has served to push for the needed changes within the industry. She has been recognized for her industry contributions with the EDPA Hazel Hays Award and the HCEA Distinguished Service Award. Pat has served the industry as a whole for over 50 years!

Jim Obermeyer-

Jim started his career as an exhibits manager for an electronics company and moved to Indianapolis to work for a top exhibit house, Hamilton Exhibits. He started his own exhibit company named Reveal Exhibits in St. Louis and returned to Hamilton as Vice President of the Chicago division. He then joined Bray Leno Events as Regional Vice President of North America. Throughout his career, Jim has used his writing skills to promote the people within the industry and the value of trade show marketing. Jim has served on the EDPA board of directors and the Randy Smith Memorial board. Jim writes a regular column for Exhibit City News entitled 'As the Saws Turn', dedicated to the workforce of people behind the scenes getting exhibits ready for any given show. Jim spends a lot of time on the show floor serving clients and getting their exhibits ready for a show. This hands-on experience has been shared over the years in his monthly column for ECN. Jim's dedication to the invisible industry has been most appreciated.

Mike Boone-

Mike started his career as a GM at The Ski Mogul, a ski vacation company. Funny how the word 'mogul' means the bumps that are found on ski slopes, and today Mike helps exhibitors avoid the bumps experienced on the trade show floor during the installation. After attending many trade shows as a buyer for Ski Mogul, Mike was attracted to the trade show industry and started his own company called Paramount Tradeshow Group. They were later purchased by Coastal International Exhibit Service. Mike took the bull by the horns and became widely known in the exhibit I&D business. He served on the board of EDPA for years and became very involved with IFES (International Federation of Exhibition Services), a world association for exhibit suppliers. This was at a time when international exhibiting was not so popular in the USA. "Mike is a person committed to improving anything that he is involved in and is willing to pass along good information to those whom he is connected with. He gives back to the industry that he has been successful working in. You can always count on Boone," says David Mihalik, CEO/ELITxPO Trade Show Services.

Mike has invested 20 years traveling yearly to meet exhibit company owners from around the world at industry events to offer assistance to them when exhibiting in the USA. As a member of IFES, he has represented the USA well as a trusted partner. Mike also became very involved with the Randy Smith Memorial Outings each year. He serves on their board to encourage fellow industry associates that trade shows are important, but so are the people that make them happen. As Mike has said, Trade shows are important...sort of, but don't be shy to donate to help your fellow peeps in their times of need."

There are many in the exhibit business like Mike, who goes unnoticed as a cheerleader, bringing the industry together as one to serve the needs of exhibitors.

It goes without saying that there are many other unsung contributors in the exhibit industry who were not owners, just dedicated worker bees, and are not recognized here. Most are not looking for recognition and are driven by their passion for the industry they serve. Thus, the invisible industry!

Exhibit Design Ideas and Designers that Influenced Change

Influential Exhibit Designers-

In the early days of exhibit design houses, there were many owners who had designs or decorating backgrounds. In time, they hired others to do the design and production and now put their focus on running their companies. Since there was never an exhibit design school for trade show exhibit designers to be trained, most successful designers came from an industrial, interior, or architectural design background. Some were talented sign painters.

They went to work full time for an exhibit house and applied their artistic skills to designing a trade show exhibit. The early days of exhibit design relied on artistic skills to prepare a hand drawing using water colors or magic markers. A real work of art! The drawing and a floor plan were mounted on a board and presented to potential customers in person. Designer presentation skills were also required. The turnaround time to produce an exhibit rendering is expected to be done quickly. Unlike architects, who have months to produce an idea, exhibit designers have less than a week to produce a drawing. Most exhibit designers work for a company, for a salary. The company gets the credit for the design. Today, CAD designs make it much easier to prepare a design idea quickly. They then present most design ideas via a Zoom presentation. Today, a talented designer needs to have presentation skills as well as design skills for large project presentations conducted in person.

There are few Frank Lloyd Wright's or Helmut Jahn's in the world of exhibit designers. A building can be seen forever in view. A trade show exhibit lasts for four days at a show that is not open to the public. Exhibit designers have never reached the same level of noticeability as the great architects in the world have. Each top exhibit design and fabrication company in the US employs creative designers on their staff, paid a salary. The designers are unknown to the public since most work exclusively for a single company. Those who choose to be a free- lancer designer sell exhibit design directly to exhibitors. If sold, they are built elsewhere. Free-lance designers gained a bit more notoriety for their ideas, but nowhere near that of famous architects. To name a couple of known exhibit designers: **Mitchel Mauck and Harry McMillan.** There have been many damn good exhibit designers, like Rick Lewis, Russ Fowler, Pat Mason, Stan Muklewicz, Jeff Bartle, Will Burtin, and many other creative exhibit house designers who go unnoticed. Exhibit designers will always go on as unsung heroes for the exhibit houses who will get the credit when the exhibit is published in Exhibitor Magazine.

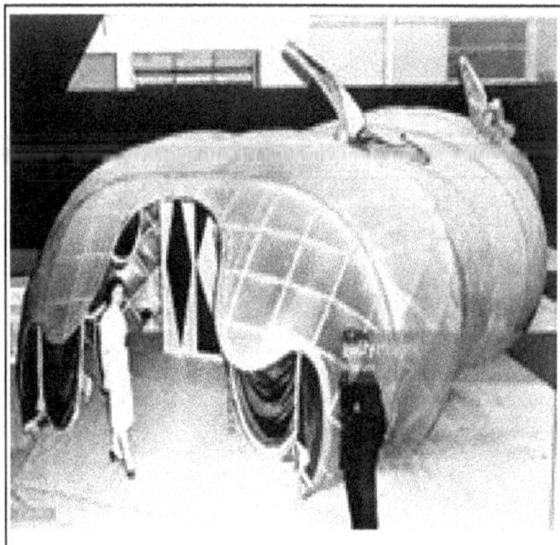

Talk about famous exhibit designers, Salvador Dali designed an exhibit for Wallace Laboratories at the AMA show in San Francisco in 1958. The exhibit included a 60' moving caterpillar that visitors walked through and interacted with. A great example of the experiential exhibit design concepts that are so popular today.

Sidebar on Architecture and Exhibits......

By Larry Kulchawik

I attended a vocational high school and majored in architecture. I earned a degree in design at SIU and had Buckminster Fuller as an instructor. Architecture was my dream job, but I settled to be an exhibit designer. After 25 years in the industry, I became involved with EDPA and had the wonderful experience to meet Helmut Jahn at the grand opening of the Munich Trade Fair in Chicago. Now Helmut Jahn was right up there with Frank Lloyd Wright and Louis Sullivan when it came to famous Chicago architects. Jahn designed the new McCormick Place, the United Airlines Terminal, the Thompson Center, and many other buildings throughout the world.

I was never so nervous as to meet Helmut Jahn. At the time, I was the AE for the Chicago Convention Bureau, which was planning a new exhibit. Who better than Helmut Jahn to design, so I kiddingly mentioned it to him. After our second glass of wine, he leaned over to me and said, Larry, I would like to design an exhibit." I responded with; you are one of the top architects in the world; why would you want to design an exhibit? He slowly responded, "These buildings, they take too long. It is often years later that I see my work completed, and my attention is now on a new project," replied Jahn.

With an exhibit, you can design in January and see your work completed in May. Now this is satisfying as a designer! Exhibit designers today can whip through two designs in a week. Those that sell can be seen completed (sometimes modified a bit) several months later with the focus of your design still fresh in your head. Seeing your ideas come to life is a gratifying experience! The only difference between building designs and exhibit designs is that many of Jahn's buildings may be seen forever, whereas an exhibit design is seen for three days on a show floor, then gone. On to the next show!

Jahn's words have stuck with me 30 years later. What a blessing to have fumbled into the exhibit industry! It continues to evolve. I am so proud that our industry leaders at EDPA have supported formal exhibit training programs at Bemidji State (undergrad degree) and FIT (master's degree) to prepare exhibit designers, rather than learn as you go as in the past. In defense of exhibit designers of the past, education alone does not make for a creative designer, but the added training and exposure will surely help.

Exhibit Materials that Drove Creative Changes

Exhibit designers were challenged to experiment with new **materials and methods** for designing exhibits. Some of the new materials created new solutions for old problems when exhibiting. One problem that surfaced in the late 80's was the cost to build an exhibit and the cost for labor to install. Another problem was the *'drayage fees'*, the cost to unload and handle exhibit freight to and from the show site. This cost was based on weight. How could we build exhibits lighter to save money? The design of the portable exhibit and the use of aluminum systems and fabric were developed long before the drayage problem and now proved to be a solution.

Outlined below are how the inventors and exhibit designers incorporated these new materials into exhibit design and fabrication. The application of lightweight materials created heavyweight solutions in exhibit design.

Let's start with a round of applause for duct tape, double-sided foam tape, and velcro for holding things together. Foam core and sintra gave us new substrates to stick with as well.

Portable Exhibits

Three Exhibit Designers need to be greatly commended for their ideas to create the Portable Exhibit.

In the early 1960s, **Jack Downing** created a portable exhibit system. Like many ideas in the 60's, the idea was not readily accepted and was considered radial for exhibit design.

Three different kinds of portable exhibits were introduced in the 70's.

Jack Downing of Downing Display perfected and introduced his **'folding panel'** portable.

Erik Ahelberg from Outline Display introduced a **'folding frame'** portable.

Theadore Zeigler from Nomadic Instand introduced the **'pop-up exhibit'** (like an umbrella!).

Each portable offered ease of set up, light weight, shipping in a fiberglass container, and graphic-friendly velcro back panels. Today, there are many exhibit companies that exclusively build portables and follow one of these three design types in doing so. Many now incorporate a fabric graphic stretched around a frame. Many portables companies have created a distributor network of selling agents for direct purchases nationwide. They sold to end users and to exhibit design companies. One of the largest portables companies today is Skyline Exhibits, which now does much more than portable exhibits.

Portable exhibits offered exhibitors a lightweight solution to ship and install at an event themselves. Portable exhibits have revolutionized the exhibit industry, giving exhibitors cost-effective alternatives to an expensive custom exhibit. Alternatives also include the use of a tabletop exhibit. Exhibitors now elected to participate in a number of trade show events using a portable at a smaller show and a more dynamic custom exhibit at a major trade show. The power of trade show marketing does not depend on the size of your exhibit, but in some cases a portable does not provide the branding punch desired for the audience at a larger trade show.

Fabric Exhibits

Exhibiting with fabric began with tents and canopies that were used at fairs and outdoor events in the early days. Other than for draped exhibit back walls and table draping that was used by show contractor companies to cover a table, the use of fabric as an exhibit display material was hardly considered. Han Brede, founder of Brede Expo, started the concept pipe and drape for show contractors in the USA, but this was a far cry from what creative exhibiting applications would follow. The concept to use fabric with an aluminum frame to create a wall panel, or any kind of shape, was not considered until the 1970s, when **Bill Moss** and his business partner **Marilyn Moss** started Moss Tent Works in 1975. Over the years, they changed the name to Moss, Inc., and Moss Design International. Moss started with camping tents and canopies and later expanded into trade show exhibiting. Marilyn Moss became CEO in 1983 and now promotes tension fabric applications for exhibit design. Fabric stretched around an aluminum frame began a trend that now caught fire in the exhibit industry. Over time, several other exhibiting fabric specialty companies were formed. They now offer a similar service for exhibit designers to begin incorporating into their exhibit designs. **Bill and Marilyn Moss** can be acknowledged for developing fabric applications for trade show exhibits. Note that exhibit houses did not attempt to do fabric in house as it involved seamstress and metal-forming skills that carpenters could not do. Most fabric design companies were nonunion that also invested in large inkjet printing tools. Exhibit houses now purchase fabric exhibits and graphics on the outside rather than producing them in house as nonunion. A new business niche was born. **Mary Carey** worked for Marilyn Moss and can be credited for talking up the benefits of using fabric for trade show exhibit design with exhibit houses. She visited exhibit houses one by one to promote design possibilities using fabric. Mary Carey also was awarded the Hazel Hays Award in 2004 for her success here. CEO **Jason Popp** is now leading Moss forward with international partners and a strong commitment to sustainability issues regarding fabric design.

Design possibilities really increased when ink jet printing technology enabled images to be printed on large fabric shapes with color images. The trend of using a hanging sign from the hall ceilings started to be popular in the late 80's and is a standard design element today. Fabric signs offered a light-weight solution suspended from above. In the 2000's, most island exhibits included a hanging fabric sign to display a company's name.

The introduction of fabric exhibits and signage pushed exhibit design thinking throughout the world into a new direction. Being light in weight helped reduce the issues about weight when it came to drayage fees. Suspended shapes from the hall ceiling started a new trend for all exhibit designers. Note that fabric design companies are now offering secondary elements like lighting and audiovisuals to their fabric design offerings. Design ideas are unlimited with fabric!

Aluminum Exhibit Systems

In the early years of exhibit design, the aluminum exhibit systems that were so very popular in Europe were not very well embraced by exhibit designers in the USA. The early exhibit systems in Europe were Syma, AGAM, Sodem, MERO, and Octanorm.

A critical difference between the high-end production of exhibits in Europe and the US was the fact that most exhibit designers in Europe were trained as architects rather than as many industrial designers who found their way into exhibit design in the US. The use of systems was a natural feature of European exhibit design tradition. These exhibits were said to be "architect," while US exhibits tended to be more attuned to design features linked to advertising, graphics, and the products themselves. Some resembled a corporate lobby or boardroom. Many of the expo centers in Europe were old and did not have level floors. Exhibit systems required a level floor, so the use of raised floors became ever more popular. (This is another design component that US exhibit designers did not embrace).

The Syma System from Europe was one of the first exhibit systems to be introduced in the US. In Canada, Saul Tolkin from ExpoService Standard developed a modular construction wall system that Freeman took an interest in and bought the rights to produce the MIS Exhibit System. Then Saul Tolkien's daughter married Xavier Decludt, and AGAM opened in Maryland, making MIS, GEM, and AGAM all kissing cousins.

Meanwhile **Hans Bruder** (a Hazel Hays winner) from Octanorm GmbH came to set up a manufacturing facility in Toronto and established several companies as distributors across North America.

Octanorm then set up manufacturing and distribution in America with **Norm Friedrich** taking charge. He and his team grew it to great success, introducing new components each year to expand design possibilities.

Even with the new glut of construction systems, exhibit builders did not like seeing the aluminum uprights and cross beams in exhibit design. The majority thought if it was not Wood, it was not "custom". Promoting and selling for many modular construction system suppliers was akin to running up the down escalator. Exhibit systems began to infiltrate the exhibit industry in the 80's and became ever-growing and popular with the added varieties of aluminum extrusion possibilities to build from.

Aluminum frame applications were applied to everything from pop-ups, portables, and light-weight truss systems to double deck systems. Over the next decade or so, the reluctance to use systems by custom exhibit builders slowly changed due to several contributing factors.

- Portables and pop-ups were replacing many 10- and 20-foot exhibits; major exhibiting companies did not want the added expense of shipping a custom exhibit to a smaller show.
- Modular construction systems gained legitimacy as designers and builders profited from successfully integrating these systems into design.
- Integrate that with large format dye sub graphics, modular two-story decks, inexpensive audio-visual equipment, and LED back lighting; designing and producing custom exhibits went in an exciting new direction.

A New Look at Exhibit Systems-

In 1993, **Edwin Huber,** a Swiss exhibition contractor and stand builder, while at EuroShop, was looking for an alternative construction system and came across Delta Light, a Belgium lighting company. Delta Light used a steel perforated beam for lighting. Edwin teamed up with Delta Light and invested in converting the perforated beam into a modular frame exhibit system. They eventually changed it to aluminum, and Matrix Architecture was born. Edwin did not care who used it, so Delta Light established Delta Matrix to distribute this modular construction system.

Now Edwin's Matrix Architecture in Switzerland, Laarhoven Design International and Laarhoven Design USA, as well as Creaplan GmbH, were using and reselling this new perforated frame system in the USA. A decade later and after a year's absence from buying any Delta Matrix, Creaplan GmbH became Aluvision in 2003. With Edwin Huber moving Matrix System GmbH production to Switzerland and Creaplan GmbH departure, Delta Matrix was reduced to a 1-million-dollar division and eleven years later sold.

In 2004, the word Delta is replaced by "be," representing Belgium, and becomes **beMatrix.** In 2012, Laarhoven Design USA becomes beMatrix USA. They introduce the 62mm frame to the US market, and things begin to change.

The Brush Fire Begins! It is amazing to compare today's trade show environment with the industry's resistance to using exhibit systems "back in the day." We need to applaud the efforts of **Robert Laarhoven** that have made so many in the industry aware of the advantages in designing with the modular frame system. Due to Robert, there is an overwhelming acceptance by exhibit builders who now profit with the use of this system for custom design exhibits, especially for custom rental exhibits.

An exhibit design and construction evolution moved from wood box-framed fabrication to an aluminum system. Systems applications now provide a unique capability to incorporate a variety of in-fill panels, color graphics, and multimedia components to cover the structure completely. Robert then sold his beMatrix shares to his Belgium partners, Edwin Van der Vennet and Stefaan Decroos, who continue to promote beMatrix in the USA and around the world.

Robert Laarhoven- *International Influences*

After graduating from Memphis State, Robert visited his uncle, who owned an exhibit systems company in the Netherlands called Laarhoven Design. His uncle created his own exhibit system called Lacet and introduced it at Euroshop 1984. He then asked Robert to be the Lacet distributor in the USA. Laarhoven Design USA started in 1984 with a small facility in Belle Mead, NJ. From there, he hired Lacet distributors to sell in other US cities. One of his top customers was Geoffrey Winslow, who owned a company in Atlanta called Design Productions, who then sold his company and started another company called Ideas, Inc. At Robert's first EDPA meeting in 1985, Geoffrey suggested that Robert move his company to Atlanta and become his partner at Ideas, Inc. Working for two separate companies and continuing to expand his Lacet dealerships, Ideas then sold and became Folio exhibits. In the early 90's, systems and portable/modular dealerships combined their product offerings and set up sales offices throughout the USA. This was the beginning of exhibits as a commodity vs. custom-built. Laarhoven Design now marketed portable/modulars, as well as the Lacet system in showrooms, in six cities. In 1999, Robert attended Euroshop, where his uncle Fritz Laarhoven introduced him to a new Belgium system with holes called DeltaMatrix. Robert and his business partner Lance Wachholz then became the North American distributor of DeltaMatrix and debuted it at Exhibitor Live 2000. After 9/11, the industry was shattered, and Robert was forced to shut down all his showrooms as well as Laarhoven Design. He then started a new company called e4 Design in Atlanta, which focused on promoting DeltaMatrix. In 2012, the owner of DeltaMatrix in Belgium sold to Robert and Lance in the US to form beMatrix USA. This now was a joint venture with Edwin Van der Vennet and Stefaan Decroos, owners of beMatrix Belgium. They then joined to become partners to create beMatrix, Inc. Robert and Lance then sold e4Design to Freeman, where Lance joined Freeman to promote it further. Robert then sold his beMatrix shares to the Belgium partners and stayed on as a leader with beMatrix Atlanta, but is no longer an owner. beMatrix is today one of the leading aluminum frame components that is used by a majority of exhibit design producer exhibit companies as the inner frame of their exhibits. This change was not readily accepted by exhibit designers and builders in the US at the start, but now it is a standard. Now this was a meaningful change for exhibit fabrication! It saved time, labor, and cost, and reduced the weight to save on drayage. Robert served as president of EDPA in 1998 and won the Hazel Hays Award in 2019.

Exhibit System Applications and the General Contractors

Before exhibit systems were fully embraced by exhibit design companies, general contractors like Freeman, GES, United Expo, Shepard, George Fern, and others became very interested in the use of these systems for general decorations for their contracted events. Typically, systems were used as an "Entrance Unit" archway sign to welcome visitors to the show floor. They were also used extensively for service counters where exhibitors could order various on-site services. With system inventory growing in most cities, the show contractors now developed generic rental exhibits using the system. Not very creative, but reasonably priced.

> Note that this was why show contractors in the early days lost added exhibitor business because the exhibitors wanted a classier exhibit as a rental. Price was not their issue; it was creative design!

At machinery-type shows or for pavilion-style exhibit spaces, many exhibitors were international. The global exhibitors preferred the 'systems look' for exhibit design, as they used at European shows. The show contractors benefited most from this preference, as the US contractors provided exhibit systems as a part of their offerings. The use and integration of systems in exhibit design was finally being embraced in the USA as a building alternative by all.

Philippe Michel- *Ideas from Europe to the USA*

Philippe Michel started his career in trade shows, working for the Brussels Exposition Center from 1971-1981. Philippe worked to promote shows held at the Brussels Expo. In 1981, the director of the RSNA show in the USA (George Schuyler) visited the World Congress of Radiology meeting held at the Brussels Expo. Philippe escorted him around the show and pointed out how many of the exhibits were made from aluminum systems. Mr. Schuyler then invited Philippe to attend the RSNA show in Chicago. Schuyler was fascinated with the use of aluminum systems to create exhibit frames and introduced Philippe to United Expositions in Chicago. He asked that United consider offering exhibit systems as a rental for their exhibitors at RSNA. United Expo agreed and started a new division of United Expo called United Longchamp. Philippe Michel's friend, Philippe Pinckaers, owned an exhibit company in Brussels specializing in exhibit system design named Longchamp. Harry Katz and Bob Lozier of United Expo then proposed to create a partnership with Longchamp and asked Philippe Michel to manage this new division for United Expo in Chicago. Philippe moved to Chicago and developed brochures with exhibit system designs offered as a rental for the exhibitors at shows United managed. These were placed in the exhibitors show kits. Other than exhibit rentals, United Expo liked the fact that the exhibit system could also create show entry archways as welcome signage frames on the show floor. They began by using various European aluminum systems (Syma and Mero) but decided on Octanorm as the system they would use. At this time, Octanorm did not have a distributor in the USA, so inventory was shipped in direct from Germany. In time, Philippe and United Longchamp expanded to Atlanta, Los Angeles, and Las Vegas to provide the same for events held in these cities without shipping in. United Lonchamp was one of the first companies to use CAD for the design of exhibits. In time, both GES and Freeman introduced an aluminum system called GEM to offer rental exhibits to exhibitors and to create entry archways for their shows.

Although aluminum systems were used extensively in Europe, they were never readily embraced by exhibit builders in the US until the 90's. Philippe Michel can be credited for being an early promoter of European exhibit systems as a viable alternative to wood or draped back walls in the US, especially for show contractor applications.

Hans Bruder- *An Exhibit System that United the World*

In 1969, **Hans Staeger** founded Octanorm, and it went on to become one of the leading aluminum systems for trade fair exhibits in the world. Octanorm is headquartered near Stuttgart, home of Porsche and Mercedes. The philosophy of this region was to think and act in quality. Octanorm grew rapidly in Europe. It first came to Toronto in 1985, granting **George Kadoke** a license agreement to produce and distribute Octanorm. A few US exhibit houses and show contractors began to use in the US, obtaining through Kadoke Display. Octanorm was the first eight-sided upright to allow for structures to be built with 45-degree angles in addition to the traditional 90-degree angle. Other manufacturers of systems followed this thereafter. In time, Octanorm recognized the potential of the US market and assigned **Hans Bruder**, from the Octanorm team in Germany, to open a facility in Toronto and buy back the license agreement from George Kadoke to expand their reach to all of North America.

In 1987, Hans Bruder hired **Norm Friedrich** to open Octanorm North America in Atlanta, GA. Norm and Hans worked hard to promote Octanorm to exhibit designers as a worthy alternative to wood construction and to be an Octanorm distributor in the USA. Many companies started to use Octanorm as a rental offering. The creative use of systems was now becoming well accepted. Octanorm then introduced DoubleForm, a double deck solution, and Maxima, a new and sturdy-looking extrusion that was quickly embraced for custom exhibit solutions in America. Norm Friedrich took the reins in the USA and has taken Octanorm to be one of the leading exhibit supplier companies in America. Beyond North America, Hans Bruder's vision was to create a world network of exhibit companies who shared a common exhibit building system. He created the motto, *Design here, built there*, where Octanorm world partners would help each other as partners and not as competitors. Hans Bruder created the **OSPI (Octanorm Service Partners International)** in 1984, which today is composed of 120 OSPI partners from 43 countries. OSPI was the first network of exhibit companies to work together as partners, with Octanorm as the exhibit system of choice. Since 1984, OSPI partners have met every other year in a different country to meet each other and to share the ways of their local cultures. The OSPI network proved to be a major unifier for the world of trade show marketing.

Hans Bruder's contribution to the exhibit industry is that of an international connector for global exhibit builders. Each OSPI partner feels a passion to provide the partner customer with a successful experience exhibiting outside of their country of origin.

The concept of a world network of exhibit companies is now copied by many but started with OSPI.

Tim Searle- Safety in a Double Deck Exhibit

Tim Searle was not an exhibit designer but was a mechanical engineer. He was awarded a Rolls Royce sponsorship from the University of Manchester in the UK and came to work in the USA for icon exhibits and developed a solution for a lighter-weight double deck exhibit.

In the early days, most double deck exhibits were made with steel supports and wooden floor panels. Extremely heavy and often required a show rigger and teamster crew to assist in the installation. The size of the double deckers was always somewhat restricted due to handling and the time to install. All decks required a sturdy stair case and upper-level rails for safety.

In 1990, Icon was tasked with providing a double decker for Phillips Magnavox for the CES show.

Tim Searle and Icon Exhibits designed a light-weight double deck exhibit made from aluminum.

This was an innovative first and went on to become a standard method of double deck construction for the exhibit industry. Most exhibit designers did not want a bunch of posts on the lower level. Double deckers were limited in the beam span between the posts. Tim Searle developed a new aluminum beam with tee-slot grooves in the top that had patented T-bolts that locked the deck to the beam. The resulting 11'-4" aluminum extrusion had a strength-to-weight ratio significantly better than a standard I beam. Icon Exhibitions named it ExpoDeck.

Tim Searle is now self-employed and has gone on to design other varieties of double deckers to make the use of a double deck exhibit safer and easier to set up than ever in the past.

Side note: In 2004, when EDPA was working with Underwriters Laboratory to develop Standards for Safety in exhibit design, Tim Searle wrote the safety standard for double deck fabrication that remains the standard today. The Underwriters Laboratory standard for Exhibition Safety is listed as UL2305 is still available today.

Ray Rogowicz- *Sustainability, the Environment and Internet Exhibit Sales*

During the boom years of the 60's and 70's in Dallas, **Geno Rogowicz** (a carpenter from Chicago) and businessman **Dutch Antonisse** started I&M Displays (Industrial Merchandising & Display) in Dallas. Geno's son Ray Rogowicz started with the firm at 15 years old, doing everything from building crates to driving a forklift to supervising labor at the convention centers for the next 8 years. Ray joined Exhibit group, then joined Bob Powell Display Art as president and created a new company named **Exhibit Dynamics, Inc.,** attracting many customers in the telecom, computer, aerospace, and home building markets for trade show marketing. The company grew to have 250 employees in a 500,000-square-foot facility. Ray retired in 2001 and in 2003 started a new company with his son Chad called **ExhibitTrader.com.**

This new company introduced a new concept of using the internet to buy and sell **pre-owned exhibits.** It came at a time when 'green thinking' was growing. A green alternative to reuse exhibits, reduce cost, and recycle properties sitting in storage. Along with promoting pre-owned exhibits via the internet, Exhibit Trader also offered rental systems and modular displays. A break away from brick-and-mortar fabrication, this approach was an innovative move at a time when internet marketing was beginning to be embraced.

Through the decades, the open-minded thinking from the owners of exhibit companies nationwide was willing to take a chance and see things differently. Their visions beyond business as usual served to change the landscape of trade show marketing for others to follow.

Change Makers- Pushed the Industry Forward each Decade

So many of the pioneers in the early days really had the guts to start a new company or to run with a new idea. Many copied and then improved their ideas to gain greater success. Like the self-contained exhibit, not all new exhibiting ideas go on to have greater success. But many did! The innovative thinking of people and associations in the early days served to change many of our methods today.

The exhibit industry in the late 60's was similar to the TV series called Mad Men. People dressed in suits for work, few female managers, everyone smoked, Martini lunches, client gifts, and womanizing—all no-no's today. My, how the industry has evolved!

The trade show industry quickly changed from a 'Convention Party' to 'Trade Shows Mean Business', and I mean big business! The many individuals and associations noted above, as well as many others not mentioned, must be highly recognized for pushing the industry forward. It did not grow totally on its own. They each acted out of a passion to support the power of face-to-face marketing—a $1 trillion impact for the US economy. The Invisible Industry!

"Progress is impossible without change, and those who cannot change their minds cannot change anything." ….. George Bernard Shaw

"The first step toward change is awareness. The second step is acceptance." ….. Nathaniel Branden

CHAPTER TEN

Trade Shows Today

The pandemic devastated the convention industry in the USA. Venues shuttered. Businesses closed. Millions of people lost their jobs. But the industry rebounded and continues to do so.

By the start of 2023, trade shows on multiple continents were entertaining large crowds. The adjacent photo is GSSSA in Orlando; the two photos below are from CES in Las Vegas and NPEW in Anaheim. Tyre Expo in Singapore, Mobile World Congress in Barcelona, and EuroShop in Düsseldorf are additional examples. The largest trade show in the US in 2023 was Conexpo/ConAgg, with 139,000 attendees and 2400 exhibitors covering almost 3 million square feet of exhibit space.

People and businesses returned in large numbers because face-to-face is better than virtual. To put it quite simply, trade shows work.

In 2023, many companies servicing trade shows—display houses, general contractors, and EACs, for example—not only rebounded from the COVID depression but rebounded with record-setting years. In 2024, industry metrics (numbers for total attendance, net square footage, and exhibiting companies) are expected to exceed the record numbers of 2019.

A recent Barameter Report conducted by UFI (the world umbrella association that includes all segments of the convention industry) conducted a survey from 68 countries to ask about their plans in the next six months for business in the convention industry. The report showed 2024 to be a record year for global industry revenue, according to Kai Hattendorf, UFI managing director and CEO. Globally, 48% of world companies declared that they plan to increase their staff numbers, while another 48% declared that they will keep current staff numbers stable. The US exposition industry results coincide with these positive world industry results.

The Size of the Industry.

Trade shows are arguably the most cost-effective form of marketing that exists today—that is why the numbers and sizes of shows have increased significantly in the past seventy-five years.

Globally, business events contributed **$1.62 trillion** to the GDP in 2019 and accounted for $2.8 trillion in business sales, according to the Events Industry Council/Oxford Economics report. Detailed in the release of the "2023 Global Economic Significance of Business Events Study," the numbers are from 180 countries and include direct, indirect, and induced impacts of business events throughout the world.

A "trillion" is sometimes heard on the news in terms of government spending or in the valuation of a few, a very few, international corporations. But what does that number mean? How large is a trillion, really? A "trillion" is a million times a million. Think about that: one million dollars multiplied one million times. To further put it into perspective, a trillion one-dollar bills, laid end-to-end, would stretch 96,906,656 miles into space (greater than the distance from the earth to the sun). To transport a trillion in one hundred-dollar bills would require 478 trailers, full of double skids, each skid four feet by four feet by forty inches high and once unloaded, the skids would cover an entire football field. A trillion seconds is more than 31,688 years. To understate the obvious: a trillion dollars is a lot of money.

Global numbers are great, but what about the impact in the United States?

Business-to-business trade shows in the United States have a huge impact on the economy, employing millions of people and generating **$161 billion** in total business sales. Prior to the pandemic, 1.7 million companies exhibited at US trade shows, and 81.3 million people attended 11,400 events.

As mentioned above, the industry has been rebounding since the pandemic and continues to do so, as is evidenced by recent CEIR reports.

Since 1978, CEIR, the Center for Exhibition Industry Research, has been the premier US industry resource for data, insight, and analysis of current and future trends. As defined by Cathy Bredan, CMP, CAE, CEM, and former CEO of CEIR, the organization is "a non-profit foundation that provides business insight and intelligence for the trade show industry. Our single focus is to conduct research. Nothing more, nothing less." CEIR reviews business-to-business trade shows in the United States; their data allows industry businesses to develop better decisions and create solutions for better events. Nancy Drapeau, CEIR's Vice President of Research, has stated: "2024 is the year when the industry is expected to surpass the 2019 results. The industry outlook is strong, as is the anticipated contribution to the US economy by supporting jobs, driving commerce, and providing tax revenues at the local, state, and federal levels."

The 2023 CEIR Index report, released in 2024, summarizes the national economic impact of B2B trade shows:

Trade shows also impact local economies. A trade show attracts crowds to a city and crowds spend money. They spend money on the event itself; and they also spend money on transportation, lodging, food and entertainment. It is similar to the economic effect of a concert or a sporting event held in a city, but trade show attendees contribute much greater in their spending.

Conventions have a greater economic impact than other types of live events. Consider these two examples: Ticket sales for live music events in the US in 2023 totaled $25 billion (according to a 2024 report by the Music Business Association). Total attendance at NFL and MLB games was less than B2B tradeshows in 2019.

An explanation of the data sources.

The EIC/Oxford Economics study defines "a business event" as:

"A gathering of ten or more participants for a minimum of four hours in a contracted venue. This includes business events but excludes social, educational, and recreational activities. Consumer exhibitions are included."

The EIC survey included participants who attended a trade show and public business events from 175 different countries. Each meeting has an economic impact on the world cities in which they are held. Of all of these meetings, trade show events deliver the highest level of economic impact to any country in the GPD. The Exhibit Industry Council (EIC) measured business events, B-B trade shows, and B-C events globally. This study included a much larger audience than B-B trade shows alone.

Here in the USA, CEIR (Center for Exhibition Industry Research) measures the size and impact of US B-B trade shows only. Their study does not include B-C public events like auto shows, boat shows, travel shows, etc. But it doesn't matter which study one reviews; the bottom line is, the size of the convention industry is bigger than anyone could ever imagine.

Business Sectors and Products.

Business sectors hosting trade shows include: technology; healthcare; food; manufacturing; government; defense; construction; transportation; sporting goods; financial services; and others. Whatever industry or niche you can think of, there is a trade show for it.

Trade shows have been a proven and powerful way to display an invention or product first to individuals and then to the world.

A great idea or a new technology is meaningless if no one knows about it or if no one buys it.

"As illustrated in the chart below, Trade shows display staying power. Many have been in existence for a long time; some have merged to create a new show. And others have ceased to exist. The chart below lists some of the largest shows from 2019 (based on the square footage of exhibit space). It lists shows from every decade up to 2010 and includes details on size, the number of attendees, and the number of exhibiting companies.

Show Name	First Year	2019 Rank	# Attendees	# Exhibiting Companies	# Sq. Feet
IACP	1893	98	12,980	618	185,000
Music Merchants	1901	19	115,303	1,917	616,065
Toy Fair	1903	33	12,820	1,039	447,458
PPAI	1904	59	12,922	1,236	309,200
IAAPA	1918	23	27,900	1,144	589,600
Natl Restaurant	1919	16	42,544	2,364	725,869
NAB	1922	8	40,111	1,632	924,876
MAGIC (August)	1933	13	76,819	4,697	777,555
Housewares	1939	11	34,500	2,203	812,135
NAHB	1942	20	63,816	1,484	609,261
Natl Hardware	1946	26	11,125	2,654	556,000
NBAA	1947	6	24,823	970	965,700
Cardiology	1949	140	12,387	262	110,500
IPPE	1949	22	32,655	1,426	594,052
AORN	1953	135	6,007	467	118,500
Pack Expo	1960	9	31,007	2,015	889,599
HIMSS	1961	21	17,655	1,328	606,750
SEMA	1963	4	161,829	2,400	1,181,000
Utility Expo/ICUEE	1966	2	11,458	1,107	1,340,749
CES	1967	1	107,148	4,550	2,930,421
OTC	1969	25	35,968	2,325	564,840
ICSC/RECon	1972	12	31,337	1,088	806,000
Concrete	1975	14	40,402	1,504	773,728
SHOT	1979	17	20,025	2,513	689,010
Licensing	1980	78	9,176	400	240,000
Fabtech	1981	10	48,828	1,696	815,455
GIE+Expo	1984	7	18,231	865	953,698
Surfaces	1989	40	25,500	745	403,004
BIO	1993	106	13,241	1,800	160,000
Solar Power	2004	76	18,323	701	250,600

The inventors and their world-changing ideas would not have achieved their goal of launching their idea without a worthy event, an effective 'stage setting', with a crew behind the scenes to make it all happen. Selecting the right event and the best use of props in the right exhibit space enables an exhibitor to communicate an idea worth hearing about. Achieving results from a trade show is a team effort. "Invisible" people set the stage, but visible ones do the selling.

Two Types of Trade Shows

When we speak about the invisible industry, it is important to clarify the different types of events that are included to define the entire industry. Trade shows account for the majority of events that make up the whole. There are basically two types of trade shows: B2C (business to consumer) and B2B (business to business). While both may charge for admission, the first one is open to the public, and the second one is not. Most people are familiar with B2C shows; examples include boat shows, travel shows, RVs, and auto shows. Both B2C and B2B shows attract crowds and impact the economy; one is directed to the public, and the other is directed to a specific audience.

Business to Consumer (B2C). Auto shows are the largest example of a B2C event and occur in cities all over the world. Historically, some events have attracted over a million people annually, with displays showcasing more than 1,000 vehicles.

The first presentation of cars at an event in the US was in New York in 1897, with "over a half dozen cars" at a bicycle exposition; the second was in Detroit in 1898, with "a few cars" at a sporting goods event. The first stand-alone auto show in the US was in New York City with 160 vehicles displayed in Madison Square Garden. It attracted a crowd of 48,000 people over seven days. Chicago's first show was in 1901, with a display of ten cars; the number increased tenfold the next year to 100 vehicles in 1902. Detroit and LA hosted their first stand-alone auto shows in 1907. Throughout the century, Detroit, Chicago, and New

York would vie for the title of largest auto show in the country.

In 1900, there was one horse for every four people in the United States and one car for every 10,000 people. At the end of 1940, after decades of auto shows, there was approximately one car on the road for every four people living in the country. In 2022, there were 283,400,986 registered vehicles on the road in the US.

Business to Business (B2B). B2B trade shows are more numerous and more impactful than B2C events. One example of a B2B event is the Consumer Electronics Show. It is a cutting-edge technology event that brings next-generation ideas and products to the exhibit floor. It displays breath-taking, museum-quality brand architecture. It allows industry professionals to see, touch, compare, and sometimes even use the newest and coolest gadgets. It allows retailers and vendors to make deals and order items six-to-nine months in advance of the holiday buying season.

In January of 2024, CES displayed products in over 2.5 million square feet of exhibit space. It hosted more than 4,300 exhibiting companies. It attracted over 135,000 attendees, including the most international attendees

at this show in its fifty-seven-year history. With a record 1400 new start-ups and over 300 of the Fortune 500 companies represented, it was the place to see, be seen, and to do business.

CES attracts massive crowds and showcases future-looking technology. But that was not always the case.

The Shows History: The CES show started in 1967 as a spin-off from the Chicago Music Show. Located in two separate NYC hotels, the first show hosted approximately 100 exhibitors and attracted 17,500 attendees. It expanded to three hotels in New York before moving to Chicago in 1971. For the first decade, the show was dominated by the music industry and was unique for the number of international exhibitors and their "booth babes." Some of the early exhibitors included LG, Motorola, and Phillips. Sony joined the show floor in 1971, when the show relocated to Chicago. The show attracted 40,000 attendees in 1972; in 1977, the show attracted 50,000 attendees and had seven hundred exhibitors. A second event, called "The Winter Show," opened in Las Vegas in 1978 with a half million net square feet of exhibit space. In 1984, CES attracted over 100,000 attendees at each of their shows, both the summer and winter events. Between 1994 and 1997, CES experimented with shows in six different cities—Chicago, Las Vegas, Mexico City, Philadelphia, Atlanta, and Dallas—before settling on one show a year, and that show was in Las Vegas. In 1997, the show broke the million-square-foot barrier and has never looked back.

Some products debuting at those shows in the early years were: VCRs in 1970; Pong in 1975; Atari in 1979; CDs in 1981; Commodore 64 in 1982; Amiga (the first "home computer") in 1984; and Nintendo in 1985. The John Madden video game appeared in the early '90s. DVDs premiered in 1996, HDTV in 1998, Xbox in 2001, and Blu-ray discs in 2004. Other items showcased on the exhibit floor over the years included satellite radio, computer tablets, and notebooks. A few automobile brands were present off the show floor as early as the late 1990s, but car technology did not take off at CES until the 21st century.

Self-driving cars were present in 2014, with electric vehicles appearing in 2016.

Some of the attractions on the show floor in 2024 were:

- A 4K wireless, transparent TV from LG
- A prototype flying car from Xpeng Aeroht
- A 22-ton autonomous tractor from John Deere
- Robots, hydrogen cars, electric vehicles, healthcare tech wearables
- A super dehumidifier producing 120 gallons of water a day
- Compact solar-powered emergency generators
- A pedal desk capable of charging cell phones and other devices
- Designer glasses that aid the hearing impaired from myriad display houses.

Each January, CES showcases present-day technology, demonstrating future possibilities. This show is one more example of how and why trade shows work—they work very well.

The American Trade Show Model vs the World Model

Different Methods to Achieve a Similar Goal

The success and popularity of trade shows really started in Europe and made its way into the USA in the 1900's.

When countries first started to conduct trade fairs in their cities, they borrowed a page from the European model of organizing. They followed their methods of organizing a trade show. US trade show organizers did the same, but soon developed their own methods for organizing and managing their trade shows in the USA. The number and importance of American trade show events represent a significant portion of the overall number of trade shows conducted in the world. The American objectives at trade fairs are similar to those of Europe, but the American methods of doing so are quite different.

The **American Model** of trade show organization is much different than any other country in the world. For American companies just beginning to exhibit abroad or for international companies planning to exhibit in the USA, it is critical that these differences, regarding rules and methods, are understood and respected.

The biggest difference is that industry associations seeking to organize a conference in the US with a trade show component will select a 'show contractor' company to organize and manage the exhibit floor area. Other countries do not. The US industry association will then directly select a city venue location and will rent a floor space to conduct meetings and a trade show. They then authorize a show contractor to organize the show floor area and manage the exhibiting services needed for exhibitors to set up their displays.

The show contractor will prepare a trade show floor layout with booth spaces that are sold to exhibitors on a per-square-foot basis. The show contractor then sends out an 'exhibitor show kit' with order forms for exhibit services, which include the exhibit space show rules. All freight, services, and labor authorization must go through the show contractor. The show contractor, the show organizer, and the venue facility rule the show floor. The show contractor provides their association clients with registration stands, show entry archways, aisle signs, booth space assignments, aisle carpet, rental exhibits, and components, set up labor, and forklift services, all part of their contract agreement. All exhibitor freight shipped to the show must be unloaded and handled by show contractor teamsters. Note that most exhibit parts are packed in a crate vs. skid-wrapped. The exhibitor is charged for each one hundred pounds of freight delivered. Exhibitors preorder this service and pay the show contractor directly upon weighing the truck at the show site. Exhibitors are allowed to contract installation labor outside of the official contractor labor but must submit an EAC (Exhibit Appointed Contractor) form with a certificate of insurance. Exhibitors are not allowed to set up their own displays, unless a portable where no tools are required. All electric, water, air, and catering must be ordered through the show contractor. Exhibitors are not allowed to make electric or air connections; this must be done by officials. Vacuuming of exhibitors carpet must be done by the show contractor. These rules can change slightly from city to city.

The American model of organizing a trade show is only done this way in America. The organization and show rules that are followed in other countries offer less restrictions and at less expense. You are in for a big surprise if you are not aware of these differences when exhibiting internationally.

We are not here to say that one of the methods for organization is better than the other. We are simply saying the methods are very different. Arguing about this with the organizer or the show contractor will not change a thing, at least for now. When in Rome, do as the Romans!

Trade shows are held worldwide but managed and organized differently in the USA compared to Europe and the rest of the world. Here are the major differences.

American Model **USA**	**European Model** **World**
Exhibit space sold in sq ft	Exhibit space sold in sq meters
Exhibit spaces arranged in 10' increments	Exhibit spaces arranged in any shape in meters
Exhibit walls and height restricted per space	Exhibit walls can be positioned cubic content
Floor area is carpeted with a pad	Floor area covered with a raised floor
Strong exhibit identity with graphics	Subtle exhibit identity with minimal graphics
Entry Badges for preregistered attendees	Entry fee charged at entry, no badges
Open exhibit design space	Enclosed exhibit design space with offices
More unscheduled exhibit meetings	Most meetings are scheduled
Minimal catering	Most exhibits have a bar and formal catering
Associations hire a show organizer and a show contractor	Associations work with the venue and with an organizer to arrange the show floor

The **Invisible Industry** *was written to share how trade shows began in the world, and how they evolved in the United States as an industry. The American trade show industry follows a different method for managing and organizing their trade show events. This American method of management and organization is embraced by nearly every major US city that hosts a trade show event. The history of the development of the trade show models for management and organization in other countries is topic for another book.*

The history, the methods, the people, and the impact of trade shows in the USA is the major focus of this book.

Note that the objectives of both the American and the European exhibit management models are the same, but their methods for getting there are different.

"Understand and respect the differences, and you are on your way to success when exhibiting internationally," says Larry Kulchawik from his book, Trade Show from One Country to the Next.

Trade Shows Mean Business in Any Country!

CHAPTER ELEVEN

THE FUTURE

Where is the Industry Heading?

The past shows what we have done — the future of our industry will show what we have learned about face-to-face marketing.

We can change the future by what we do today. The best thing about the past is learning what not to take into the future. The landscape of the trade show playing field changes each year due in part to technology, or to a crisis. How we adapt is key. The Future — that's when you'll be sorry for everything you could have done today but didn't.

Here are some different views on the future of trade show marketing from trade show industry veterans and some crystal ball gazers who believe in the value of face-to-face marketing and its path going forward.

The methods and ways of trade show marketing have evolved many times in the USA over the past 100 years. Adjustments made each decade brought improvements to face-to-face engagements at a trade show. Improvements came from either new technology, innovative thinking, or the addition of secondary benefits to the trade show event. In the end, it's all about results. No one really knows the exact answer here, but speculation from those in the trenches of the industry would be a good place to start.

The industry has recovered nicely and is moving strongly forward, after a two-year setback due to COVID mania. But how does the future of the industry look for the next ten years? We asked a few industry veterans and an AI fortune teller just how they see the near future.

The question **"What is the Future of Trade Show Marketing in the Next Ten Years?"** was first asked to an AI (Artificial Intelligence) source. Depending on the day you ask the question, the answer can be different from AI intelligence.

Here was the most recent reply from an artificial intelligence source.

What is the future of trade show marketing? - *From Artificial Intelligence*

After all, AI surely knows everything. So how right are they? Time will really tell.

The future of trade show marketing is likely to evolve in several ways:

1. **Hybrid Events:** With the rise of digital connectivity, trade shows are likely to incorporate more hybrid elements, allowing both physical and virtual attendance. This can increase reach and accessibility for participants worldwide.

2. **Technology Integration:** Expect to see more advanced technology integrated into trade show experiences, such as augmented reality (AR), virtual reality (VR), and interactive displays. These technologies can enhance engagement and provide immersive experiences.

3. **Data Analytics:** Data analytics will play a significant role in trade show marketing, helping businesses understand attendee behavior, preferences, and engagement levels. This data-driven approach can optimize future marketing strategies and personalize interactions.

4. **Sustainability Focus:** As environmental concerns continue to grow, trade shows may prioritize sustainability initiatives. This can include eco-friendly booth designs, digital materials to reduce paper waste, and carbon offset programs for travel.

5. **Content Marketing:** Trade shows will likely emphasize content marketing strategies, offering valuable insights, workshops, and educational sessions alongside product showcases. This can attract a broader audience and position companies as industry leaders.

6. **Networking Opportunities:** Networking will remain a key aspect of trade shows, but with advancements in digital platforms, networking can extend beyond the event days. Expect more year-round networking opportunities through online platforms and communities.

7. **Personalization:** Personalized experiences will become more prevalent, with exhibitors tailoring their presentations, demos, and interactions based on attendee profiles and interests. This can enhance engagement and conversion rates.

8. **Global Reach:** Virtual elements in trade shows can break geographical barriers, allowing companies to reach a global audience without the limitations of physical travel. This can lead to more diverse participation and market expansion opportunities.

Overall, the future of trade show marketing is likely to be a blend of physical and digital innovations, driven by technology, data insights, sustainability efforts, and a focus on delivering valuable content and personalized experiences.

Opinions from real Human Intelligence……

Brett Haney- CEO
Derse Exhibits
Mergers and Acquisitions

While the COVID pandemic was something I wished had never happened, for all the obvious reasons, I believe that it is the milestone event that has forever reinforced the importance of trade shows and face-to-face marketing. At the root of key personal and business relationships is the need to establish trust. We all want to work and do business with people we trust, and the most effective way to create and build trust is through face-to-face interactions. It is the most effective way to move a relationship forward.

We work hard to do this as a company and for the clients to serve and achieve their objectives.

As a national exhibit design company, we are seeing more merger and acquisition activity and an interest from private equity companies who are now interested in the trade show industry, more now than ever before. Key market players are making R&D investments to bring advanced technologies and solutions to the market.

I think they understand a basic fact: to market effectively, you need to establish trust that only in-person interactions can help deliver. This is what we help our clients to do. While technology keeps changing, I do not foresee a future in which the basic need of interacting with people in person will ever go away. Face-to-face marketing will continue to create the strongest business opportunities.

Doug Emslie- Chairman
Cuil Bay Capital, Racoon Media Group
Show Consolidation: Are We in Danger of Losing Our Soul?

In the wake of the pandemic, the trade show industry has entered a phase of accelerated consolidation, marked by significant acquisitions of companies by the large corporations. The large corporations have so far been the key players in this consolidation, and private equity firms are increasingly investing in the sector, driven by confidence in a return to pre-pandemic performance and a notable uptick in acquisition activity compared to the subdued levels of two years ago.

What does this mean for the future of the industry? There is a growing concern that the focus may shift away from the core drivers of our industry—entrepreneurs who launch, innovate, and grow the shows of the future—and toward corporations primarily focused on growth by acquisition. It is imperative that we establish the right ecosystem to support the new wave of entrepreneurs who will shape our industry's future. The technology sector provides an ideal model, with its robust financial support systems and extensive networks that help entrepreneurs in their growth journeys.

Over the past decade, the process of launching new shows has evolved significantly. Where previously it was possible to finance launches through advanced exhibitor payments, this is no longer viable. Costs have risen dramatically, venue deposit requirements have 9ghtened, and there is a greater need for investment in the visitor experience. Consequently, we are witnessing a shift in behavior. Corporations, constrained by less flexible structures, are increasingly focusing on acquisitions rather than launches. Entrepreneurs, on the other hand, must now seek capital to navigate the early stages of their ventures, a process that is neither easy nor straight forward.

This issue is beginning to be addressed with initiatives such as the launch of the Event Venture Group (EVG), which aims to provide both financial and practical support to the entrepreneurial community. Additionally, the US trade association SISO is working diligently to offer practical assistance through its small business group, where entrepreneurs can collaborate to overcome growth challenges.

Looking ahead, the future of our industry will hinge on creating a supportive environment for entrepreneurs and drawing lessons from other industries, particularly technology. As consolidations and private equity involvement grow, gaps will inevitably emerge. It is crucial for the future of our industry that we empower entrepreneurs to seize these opportunities and continue driving innovation in the trade show sector, or we are in danger of losing our soul!

Sue Hatch- MeetingsNet Magazine
The Attendee Experience

"For trade shows and other parts of the business-events industry, the future will be shaped by the adoption of artificial intelligence tools," noted Sue Hatch, content director for MeetingsNet. "Over the past decade, organizers have worked to create more personalization and richer engagement for trade show attendees. With AI, those goals are now within reach. For example, AI can analyze attendees' interests, demographics, and past event attendance to personalize their experience by suggesting relevant sessions and exhibitors. AI chatbots can remove some customer-service friction by providing on-demand answers to attendees' frequently asked questions. Similarly, exhibitors' interactive touch screens are using AI to deliver and adapt content based on attendee interactions. AI is also improving the accuracy of translation tools and driving down the cost compared to live translation, helping to break down language barriers and drive a more diverse and international attendee base. We're just beginning to see how AI can help organizers create more immersive, personalized experiences that grab attendees' attention and foster deeper connections with exhibitors."

Kevin Sweeney- Vice President Art Guild, Inc
Understanding Tomorrow's Audience: Catering to Diverse Needs

It's important to acknowledge that tomorrow's audience will have diverse needs and preferences compared to the past. Generation X, Millennials, and Generation Z bring unique perspectives and expectations to trade show engagements. Understanding and catering to these differences will be pivotal for success in the future of trade shows and experiential marketing. Show organizers will need to address these new needs. In traversing the labyrinth of the evolving marketing landscape, one axiom shines bright: the future of trade shows and experiential marketing hinges on innovation, adaptability, and an unwavering commitment to delivering unparalleled value to both attendees and exhibitors alike. The era of trade show experiences that were tailored to the preferences of baby boomers has drawn to a close. The emerging generations, with their distinct values and expectations, are catalyzing a paradigm shift in event and exhibit design. No longer can generic experiences suffice; today's attendees yearn for personalized interactions that resonate deeply with their individual interests and interests.

Measuring Success in the New Era: Embracing Nuanced Metrics

In the fast-evolving world of trade shows and experiential marketing, measuring success has assumed paramount importance. Businesses face mounting pressure to demonstrate the ROI of their marketing spend, rendering traditional metrics inadequate. Instead, forward-thinking companies pivot towards a nuanced approach to measurement. Success is no longer gauged by mere business cards collected; rather, it hinges on the quality of leads generated, the ability to follow up effectively, measuring the value of the opportunity, relationship building, and the discovery of unmet needs. Measurement can also include other objectives beyond leads—engagement with existing customers, finding reps, company impact on the show floor, introducing a new product, or brand change. All can have a value measurement attached to them.

Leading Trends for the Future: Charging a Course for Innovation

Peering into the horizon, several trends emerge as harbingers of change in the future of trade shows and experiential marketing. Proprietary events, hybrid engagements seamlessly blending in-person and virtual experiences, technology integration, and a steadfast commitment to social responsibility stand at the forefront. These trends are poised to redefine the very essence of trade shows, shaping them into immersive, purpose-driven experiences that resonate deeply with tomorrow's audiences. In the traditional model of trade shows and experiential marketing, the focus predominantly revolved around creating brand experiences that appealed to the masses. However, as the next generation's preferences veer towards personalized interactions, **brands** must pivot towards a one-to-one, more tailored approach. In conclusion, the evolution of trade shows and experiential marketing will be a journey of innovation and adaptation. What once was a modest display of products has blossomed into an intricate tapestry of brand immersion. Today's trade shows transcend mere showcases; they seek to deliver unforgettable experiences that resonate with attendees long after the curtains fall.

Glenda Brungardt- Past Exhibit Manager
HP & CTSM Diamond
Technology and Sustainability

Over my years in the event industry, some things have remained constant. Tradeshows and events have always been a platform/marketplace where companies like HP could showcase their latest innovations, connect with customers (current and future), and network with industry peers. Yet, they've always been more than just being able to have business transactions; they're also social gatherings where ideas are shared, collaborations are made, and innovations are moved forward.

Our industry has seen significant shifts, particularly during times like the pandemic, when technology became vital for being able to gather—even if it was virtual. Looking ahead, technology will continue to enhance attendee experiences, with elements like VR and AI playing key roles in creating a more personalized experience. However, history teaches us that even with technological advancements, nothing quite replaces the power of face-to-face interactions. We learned this lesson following the.com crash, where the concept of virtual trade shows couldn't replace the desire for the face-to-face connections. And while hybrid events offer accessibility, they also won't replace the desire or tradition of face-to-face interaction.

For me, **sustainability** is the next shift our industry must focus on. It's not just about following trends or cutting costs; it's about fundamentally reshaping how we approach event and tradeshow planning. Sustainability must be woven into our practices, from venue selection to waste management and even in fostering diversity and inclusiveness in event and tradeshow execution. It's about acknowledging the impact our industry has on the planet and ensuring our events leave a positive mark on both the environment and the communities they touch. It's time for sustainability to transition from being a mere checkbox on a list to being a core part of a company's planning and commitment to responsible event and trade show practices.

Jim Obermeyer- Vice President
Bray Leino Events

The Art of Survival: In my tenure in this industry, we have survived the Energy Crisis, the recession of 1981-1982, the Gulf War recession of 1990-1991, the Dot-Com/911 recession of 2001, the Great Recession of 2008-2010, and the Covid-19 pandemic. While hard times and swift changes often occur during these periods, the resilience of our industry and the passion of the people that are devoted to this industry seems to always shine through the darkness, and we come out of it fired up and ready to go again. Whatever happens in the future on a global level—and to our local economy I have no doubt this industry and its people will pull through.

Will changes in exhibitions and events happen in the future? Absolutely. Will exhibitions and events adapt to this change? Absolutely. What we experience on the show floor today is quite different than it was just a short time ago—I still remember when the very first 'plasma' TV was used on the show floor at RSNA. It created quite a WOW factor. And now entire walls are lit with LED tiles. What will technology and change bring to trade shows next? Who knows, but I know we will experience it at an exhibition or event.

Here are some points I see regarding the future of trade show marketing.

Generational Differences: You can read all you want about how different all of our generations are—the Baby Boomers, Gen-X, Millennials, and now Gen-Z—and why things must change to suit the needs and desires of how the next generation will perform in the business world. But I will argue that there is one thing that all of these generations have in common: the need—and desire—to meet face-to-face, to actually see each other, and to have conversations in person. Sure, due to advancements in technology, we can do a lot of our work now through the virtual world, but there is still a desire to have conversations—and to see and experience a product—in person. And what better place to do that than at an exhibition or event with all your industry colleagues?

Artificial Intelligence (AI): With the recent onslaught of Artificial Intelligence in our world, there are those that believe it could be the end of our industry as we know it. But there were also those that had that exact same belief with the invention of the internet decades ago. The trade show world was going to end. Maybe not so much. Will AI have an impact on this industry? Absolutely, and in a variety of ways, from exhibition and event design to on-the-floor attendee experiences. But will it mean the end to our world? I don't think so.

Sustainability: Like it or not, the issue of sustainability in the exhibitions and events industry is here to stay. Driven initially by our clients (the exhibitor) who are now asking us about sustainability practices at trade shows, it is an issue that cannot be ignored. The global Net Zero Carbon Events Initiative is an international effort by numerous industry organizations to create standards and processes to address this issue across all aspects of our industry. The recently released EDPA/ESCA Sustainability Guidelines document is aimed specifically at the exhibit house/show contractor/supplier side of the industry. And we're just getting started.

Pre-Show/At-Show/Post-Show Marketing: While the methods and tools to market your presence at an exhibition or event may have changed and evolved over time, the fact that it is still critical to address these areas has not changed and will not change. Reaching your clients and prospects before the show to inform them of your presence and your promotions, establishing the correct messaging and experience for attendees at the event, and following up with your contacts from the show to prove return on investment are all essential to making your presence worthwhile, both now and in the future.

Tradeshows vs. Private Events: The COVID-19 pandemic brought on a variety of changes to this industry, from the full industry shutdown in 2020 to the development (and eventual demise) of virtual shows to a growth in private corporate events as the world came back to life. But will private events mean the end to the exhibition side of the industry? I don't think so. The opportunity for attendees to see and experience a wide variety of product and service options in one setting is best done at an industry-wide exhibition. Private events will remain critical to companies wanting to reach their specific client and prospect base, but exhibitions will work alongside them for the greater industry audience.

Chris Kappes - Strategic Advisor
Exhibit City News
Collecting Data - The Engine that Drives Trade Shows in the Future

For exhibitors, **accountability** for their trade show investments is a key issue for continued participation in trade show marketing going forward. The structured data solutions that attendees, show organizers, and exhibitors enjoy today weren't possible decades ago. Before registration and lead management systems, employees would fill out a form with a golf pencil, get in line, and wait until a typist was free to enter their information. Lead generation in exhibits was done with a handshake followed up with a business card. Regrettably, many cards were left in the exhibit counter drop slot and shipped back to the exhibit house to rest in peace.

The industry evolution for data collection started modestly in 1976 when Compusystems Founder & Chairman, Clark Williams, and "one fantas9c data entry worker," started a typesetting company.

That company is credited today with 23 "firsts" in tradeshow registration, data analysis, and lead retrieval systems.

"The registration and lead industry started from nothing in the 70's," Williams explains. "We were the first. Trade show registration was a real struggle. It wasn't until the Consumer Electronics Show in the early 80's that advanced registration and data collection became a "thing."

That "thing" was powered through a relationship Williams forged with Bill Glasgow, who was hired by the Consumer Electronics Association (CEA) as show manager for the fledgling Winter and Summer Consumer Electronics Show (CES). As a show manager, Glasgow was an early pioneer that recognized that the registration experience and data transparency were key to his show viability.

"Bill Glasgow changed my life and my business," concludes Williams. "The advent of microcomputers and dot-matrix printers allowed us to enter, store, and output registration data, which was the beginning of the on-site printing of badges. CES was one of the first shows to use our product, and it evolved from there with the advent of the internet and new technology."

Evolved it did. The tradeshow industry boomed, and show organizers raced for solutions to manage front and back-office requirements to better service shows and their attendance. Effective data collection and management will be a leading driver in the continued success of trade show marketing.

The noise around AI is deafening. But whispers of new innovations can be heard. Compusystems, Convention Data Services, and others are dreaming up what's next, and it centers around two areas: richer and more predictive data.

"Show organizers want more access to everything," explains Kahle Williams, Compuserve CMO and son of Clark Williams. "AI will help to provide more sophisticated dashboards and streamline customer service operations.

ChatGPT, for example, will help organizers slice and dice registration data. Chatbot use is exploding. Customer queries can be promptly answered and connected to learning databases. Finally, AI will help organizers and exhibitors with lead scoring. Being able to create an attendee profile that aggregates data based upon the show going experience."

If data is power, then absolute power is the predictive analysis of the attendee. The focus in the future requires taking the hard science of data and applying it to behavior science. Post-show surveys are the current data source for event evaluation. But the holy grail is being able to predict conference attendance, workshop preference, exhibit visits, attendee activities, and more. AI is viewed as key to this development, and it's going to be here for greater use before you know it. The whisper says so.

Lee Ali- Managing Director
Expo Stars Interactive
<u>365 Day Engagement</u>

The future of trade show marketing, in my view, will be heavily influenced by the integration of technology and personalization. With advancements in artificial intelligence (AI), virtual reality (VR), and augmented reality (AR), I anticipate a more personalized, immersive experience for attendees. This will allow exhibitors to showcase their products and services in innovative ways that were previously impossible. For example, exhibitors will now be able to segment and measure the experiences for existing clients vs. engaging new prospects much more effectively using these tools.

Another pivotal trend in the future of trade show marketing is the focus on building communities for 365-day engagement. Exhibition organizers are increasingly recognizing the value of sustaining engagement beyond the event itself. This year-round community building transforms trade shows from isolated events into ongoing platforms for networking, learning, and business development.

By leveraging digital tools and social media, organizers can create vibrant communities where exhibitors and attendees continuously interact, share insights, and collaborate. This approach not only enhances the value proposition of trade shows but also helps in building stronger relationships and brand loyalty.
Such communities can offer a mix of content, including webinars, workshops, and networking events, and discussion forums, enabling continuous learning and interaction. This ongoing engagement ensures that the momentum and connections generated at the trade show are maintained throughout the year, leading to deeper relationships and more meaningful business opportunities.
This shift towards building and nurturing communities is particularly significant in an era where digital interaction is becoming increasingly prominent. It allows trade shows to remain relevant and valuable as industry hubs, not just during the event but as continuous sources of innovation, collaboration, and growth.

In conclusion, the future of trade show marketing lies in the balance of technology, community building, personalization, emotional intelligence, and sustainability. By embracing these elements, trade shows can remain a vital platform for businesses to connect, engage, and grow in an increasingly digital world.

Julie Kagy- CEM / ESCA-Executive Director
Exhibition Services and Contractors Association

As we look ahead, the future of trade show marketing will be defined by a blend of cutting-edge technology and a renewed emphasis on human connections and experiences. The core of trade shows remains the in-person experience.

Sustainability will begin to move faster as an issue in the USA. Exhibitors are now more concerned about eco-friendly practices, from reducing waste to creating more sustainable booth designs. Attendees and exhibitors alike are demanding greater accountability in this area, and it's driving innovation across the board.

The next generation of attendees craves immersive experiences that deliver beyond traditional exhibitions. They seek an environment where they can interact, learn, and engage on a deeper level. The show organizers and the show contractors will work closely together to set the stage to make it all happen.

Trade shows will become more than just a place to showcase products – the events will evolve to become dynamic hubs of knowledge exchange, community building and collaboration. The focus will shift towards creating an immersive environment that fosters meaningful connections with a combination of exhibits, learning sessions and activities that encourage connectivity.

Al Mercuro- Strategic Marketing & Client Engagement Advisor
Genesis Exhibits, Apprupo
Sustainability & Advancements in the Visual Experience

Trade shows have been a constant presence throughout history, evolving alongside advancements in technology and societal changes. Bob Dylan aptly reminds us, "*The Times They are a Changin.*" Before Covid, the trade show industry faced similar skepticism during the dot-com era, yet it not only survived but also thrived. Despite the rise of virtual platforms, live face-to-face trade shows remain resilient, with increased participation and innovation. Adapting to new technologies and engaging younger audiences will be pivotal for the continued success of trade shows.

As the trade show industry looks ahead to the future, the focus on sustainability and technology will be paramount. The shift towards sustainability is already evident in the events we produce and the exhibits we build. Exhibits designed with sustainability in mind are becoming more accessible, aligning with the exhibitors desires and their marketing budgets. This positive development, combined with a growing industry enthusiasm about 'green', gives hope that we are progressing towards a more environmentally conscious approach.

We're on the brink of a new era in the events industry, with AI leading the way in revolutionizing event planning and production strategies. LED walls may be in the spotlight now, but AI features are quickly rising to elevate the visual experiences at trade shows to new levels.

Tom Bowman- President
Bowman Change Inc.
The Issue of Sustainability

The American identity has always been about exploring and conquering new frontiers rather than taking care of "home." Europe has a much, much longer history. European society is much more grounded in family, "tribe," and class rather than an individual's freedom. They have taken a stronger position on sustainability issues than then in the USA. This makes us a very innovative society, but it probably puts us at a disadvantage in terms of sustainability. Nobody has defined sustainability goals in attractive ways. It's all about avoidance, and it often seems very abstract rather than emotional. Humans seem to respond much better to emotional and sensory visions.

Even though C-suite folks are taking sustainability seriously now, very few corporations have translated this into an incentive and reward system for middle managers, such as exhibit managers. I must say that HP has taken some big steps in this area. We all know what an exhibit manager's life is like: so many things to get done on schedule while being under constant pressure not to go over budget. Anything that sounds good but doesn't help a manager meet these goals is pretty hard to implement, unless pressed to do so.

Today in the exhibit industry, there is a strong chance that sustainability will become an expectation that brands will be widely rewarded for. If this happens in a big way—and there's no telling whether it will happen—exhibitors will start competing to prove they're on the right side of the 'sustainability' trend. We'll have to see how this goes.

As for the future of trade shows, the emergence and adoption of new technologies will change communication methods. I doubt these will replace the ancient desire for people to gather (I'm not predicting the end of exhibiting by any means), but practices will certainly change in the USA.

Charles Pappas- Senior Writer
Exhibitor Magazine
Author of "Flying Cars, Zombie Dogs, and Robot Overlords."

I'm tempted to say, "AI is the future of exhibitions," look smug, and drop the mic. That prediction, though, would be as vague and "accurate" as anything Nostradamus said. AI will play a role in exhibition planning, logistics, and marketing, but it isn't likely to usurp the designers per se. Designers will likely embrace it to produce more work faster, like a souped-up Photoshop. I don't see it as a clear and present danger to designers because creativity isn't an algorithm. It's a spice blend of experience, serendipitous connections, spacing out, intense focus, shower thoughts, anger, depression, and awe. These mental states rooted in biology become the clay or marble only humans experience and therefore create from.

More important than AI, though not as sizzling hot a topic, is sustainability. Whether it's reusing exhibits, recycling materials, or simply holding on to exhibits longer, this trend won't have the headline-making allure of AI, but it should continue well into a century of encroaching environmental disaster. Events of all kinds will make more efforts to be visibly carbon neutral. My best guess is eco-friendly materials like bamboo, recycled plastic, or FSC-certified wood will be even more mainstream, while minimizing waste and promoting/practicing recycling will be beyond routine. Exhibitors will make an effort to reflect in the most visible ways they can a more concerned attitude about the environment. Not to show it through your exhibit design tomorrow might be as socially unacceptable as littering today.

Nonetheless, technology will play a larger and larger role. Especially kinetic devices that become traffic builders in and of themselves to arrest attention through their movement, e.g., from robotics and 3D maps to reactive mirrors and touchless devices. Even AR and VR will continue to make inroads here and there, but they are only as good as their processing power. (That is, so there's no lag time in imagery, allowing the visual landscape to look more real.) VR's future popularity will hinge on the use of headsets that don't look and feel like deep-sea diving helmets. Mixed reality combining physical and digital elements is likely to increase as well if costs continue to decline in proportion to their capabilities.

As for the metaverse popularized by Mark Zuckerberg and Facebook, remember that the metaverse itself is taken from "Snow Crash," a dystopian novel of an impoverished world run by corporatized mafias after an economic collapse. Zuckerberg may not have gotten the memo or the text about that). And so far, the examples of the metaverse I've seen combine the clunkiest of animation with the most obnoxious of advertisements.

Localization is another trend I see that will spread further and further. The pandemic partially answered why we would physically attend a show even when we can view it online — the ROI on virtual-only events was terrible and the need to connect physically is hardwired. Using screens to experience events is like staring at pages of Bon Appetit magazine when you could be dining at Pujol in Mexico City or French Laundry in California.

Why experience events in real life? In part, it's because they can offer the sounds, smells, and an overall experience grounded in local culture that's not reproducible enough through technology to make remote viewing a preferable option. For example, I think of the way Expo 2020 used textiles in its signage that were woven in a traditional Bedouin style, or the way EXHIBITORLIVE brought in the Kentucky Derby bugler Steve Buttleman to open its Louisville show. Or the way the International Association of Horticultural Producers created a pavilion for the 2023/2024 International Horticultural Expo in Qatar that duplicated the look of a Qatari fisherman's net being cast over the water.

In an upcoming era of AI producing Deep Fakes in almost every conceivable context, the authenticity of live face-to-face events will be the part of the human experience that AI can't reproduce—and which we can't afford to lose.

Laura Palker- Founder/President
Exhibitions and Events Workforce Development Federation
<u>No More an Invisible Industry</u>

From the ashes of invisibility, the trade show and events industry will grasp the opportunity for greater recognition to rise like a Phoenix. The industry associations are determined to bring greater recognition to the many people who work in the convention industry. The workforce will no longer remain in the shadows but will instead become a visible and recognized force within our nation's economic ecosystem. Greater awareness from key institutions such as the Department of Labor (DOL), the Department of Education (DOE), and the Federal Government will evolve to recognize the industry as a driving force in the growth of the US economy. Our cities, which rely heavily on the contributions of the convention and events workforce, must also acknowledge the importance of fiscal responsibility in sustaining growth within the industry. Looking forward, we will inspire and empower the present industry, and the future, workforce to take on the mantle of becoming ambassadors for our cause. As a united industry, we must broaden our horizons to ensure that our industry is no longer invisible. Through collective efforts and determination, we must secure the recognition and respect that our workforce deserves, never again allowing ourselves to be overlooked as invisible. The future holds promise, and together, we will shape and build career opportunities within the convention and events industry. Invisible no more

Sam Lippman, President
Lippman Connects
The Evolution of Trade Shows Through 2023

The trade show industry is not undergoing a revolution. Nevertheless, it is subject to the same rapid pace of change as the rest of the world and will undergo significant transformations over the next five years.

When we look at attendees, exhibitors, speakers, and sponsors, we will notice only a gradual change from 2024 to 2026. Partly, of course, because we will not have the benefit of perspective. By 2030, when the Baby Boom generation has largely retired, the show floor will look very different than it did in 2024. In general, attendees and booth personnel will be younger and more diverse than ever before. The show floor environment will be more intentionally aware of the sensibilities of women, a broad range of minorities, and people with special needs.

This new audience will expect trade shows to be responsible corporate actors. The gap between environmental sustainability and commercial sustainability will narrow and close. Because me and again this medium has proved itself to be remarkably resilient, responsible organizers will rise to the challenges to encourage exhibit designers and show contractors to think greener and leave the venues better than when they arrived.

More importantly, trade shows will continue to be a powerful haven of trust in a world where the line between real and fake becomes harder to find every day. Face-to-face engagement at trade shows creates trust and enhances relationships that professionals are not getting from the virtual universe. By 2030, professionals will be yearning for authenticity. Trade shows will offer additional opportunities for acquiring knowledge and earning professional certifications.

Combined with the post-millennial preference for unique experiences, trade shows will be positioned to become bleisure destinations. Organizers will work more closely with destinations and other suppliers to amplify and extend the trade show experience as long as possible. This will add to the networking experiences. For some professionals, a trade show will become a status brand, like an elite university.

In 2030, trade shows will continue to thrive for the next generation because they will continue to provide all the very same professional benefits they do today. The balance of priorities will shift quickly and significantly with the winds of societal progress. This will create problems for organizers that won't, or can't, adapt and will create opportunities for the innovators. But that's true every year.

Views on the Future- An International Point of View

Kai Hatendorf- CEO- UFI
The Global Association of the Exposition Industry

As Peter Drucker famously said, "The best way to predict the future is to create it." We have been good at that as a meetings and trade show industry. Our service to the global expo industry evolves around the core international marketing services that support the issues of the many segments that are included in the industry. As long as UFI stays focused on serving the needs of our customers, we will be fine. However, these customer expectations are always evolving, and they are changing ever faster. Addressing the changing needs within the industry will be our ongoing "stress test" in the years to come. The megatrends for the next decade focus on digitization and resourcefulness. Digital tools and services will play an even bigger role before, during, and after a trade show.

Smart show organizers will engage their show attendee communities online all year round between the physical trade shows.
At the same time, globally, we are under increasing pressure to show that trade shows are an efficient way to facilitate and grow a business. Therefore, part of the challenge is to also meet the challenges of climate change and sustainability. Europe and Asia are leading on this trend, and the USA must catch up.

Last but not least, the face of our industry will change as we recruit and bring in new talent with new skills. We did not just rehire the staff numbers we had before COVID. UFI data shows that the industry businesses in the US expanded staff numbers in 2024. These new colleagues will bring new ideas and new innovations and will be very visible on and around the trade show floors of 2030.

Koen Bogaert- A founding father of IFES- Brussels, Belgium

So how will the trade show methods of today change for a new tomorrow?

It's been amazing how the science fiction film industry did foresee a future that we many years later discovered to be close to reality. However, the world is continuously changing, and we adjust. We do not need to be apocalyptic and fear the end of trade show marketing as we know it. We can assume that the world will always be a big network of real and emotional personalities. If we follow scientific evolutions, I think we can be optimistic about the future. Progress will always bring us a wide variety of new techniques to communicate worldwide and will help us to be more efficient. However, at the end (no sorry), to begin with, most of it will be based on real contacts with companies, associations, governmental organizations, and individuals and therefore the trade show industry will continue to play an important role!

The Trade Fair Organizer of the Future

In order to share the right insights and industry trends, the trade fair organizer must realize that their role is not only to sell floor space but to study the future of the concerned market and to bring the right people together to create more than a hall with booths. The show organizer and show associations will have to bring a vision about a changing industry domain. Both exhibitors and visitors will exchange thoughts to put this vision in clearer focus. Hence the organizer will need to work with the government, the research institutions, the associations, and the leading companies to arrive at cooperative solutions going forward. Each trade fair should become a window on the future, rather than a catalogue of what we have already. It is necessary to keep the event interesting, or trade shows will lose their relevance. The trade show organizer will have to become the trend watcher of a certain industry and turn the perspective on the future into a virtual "and" a physical event.

Be virtual to get real.

Discussions and thinking about the state of an industry need to be taking place 365 days a year with the purpose to end up addressing key issues at the big event, the physical trade show, where people meet face-to-face. A trade show organizer will need to embrace the virtual world throughout the year. The industry trade show will then be a gateway portal for all concerned industry players to discuss and act further, if in agreement. Organizers can be very successful financially, but success can also be the grave without a long-term strategy.

The Venues and the Visitors of the Future

Venues will be more than huge halls with exhibit hall space and loading docks. They will accommodate visitors and organizers with mee9ng spaces to include the most advanced visual, lighting, and sound technology with internet connectivity. They will serve as an extension of the exhibit floor for added communication. They will feel like a fine theater with the comforts of sitting in a first-class board room. Besides the most advanced technology for communication and real-time streaming, the venues will provide rooms for hospitality and networking. Concerning infrastructure, venues will need to convince the city authorities to allow this business of communication to be professionally complete and user-friendly. They will need to allow the visitor to live all that as one big experience.

The visitor of the future will be spoiled, and he will have an aversion against all that makes his life difficult, whether it is the registration, the hotel, the transport, the parking space, the catering, or whatever aspect while visiting the virtual or physical event. The visitor is and remains the most important stakeholder in our communication efforts because they are who we need to reach, meet, convince, and relate with. Make it comfortable.

Jan Götze- Creative Director & Innovation Manager
Cultural Crossroads: Personal Insights about American Trade Shows- 2034

As a German stepping into the vibrant world of US trade shows, I found myself navigating a landscape rich with cultural nuances that define American society. These bustling arenas of business and hospitality were a revelation, highlighting the contrasts and commonalities that shape our global interactions. These following lines embark on a journey into the future of trade shows, imagining our industry 10 years from now and examining how new practices may traverse borders and blend cultures.

Picture this: It's 2034, and the exhibition industry is almost unrecognizable. We've witnessed the convergence of advanced technologies such as AI, VR, AR, Blockchain, the "Metaverse" (spatial web), and the Internet of Things (IoT), revolutionizing every aspect of trade shows. Attendees now find themselves in fully immersive environments where digital and physical realities intertwine seamlessly. Virtual trade shows complement physical events, breaking down geographical barriers and enabling global participation. Smart glasses and other wearable devices deliver real-time data and analytics, enhancing networking opportunities and engagement. AI-driven personal assistants and intelligent guides help attendees navigate the myriad of exhibits, tailoring recommendations to individual preferences and interests. These technologies not only elevate the visitor experience but also unlock new realms for interactive storytelling, product demonstrations, and global connectivity.

Generative AI has become the bedrock of our industry. Imagine a world where the design process is streamlined by AI, generating multiple architectural ideas and layouts in the blink of an eye. Exhibit designers and builders will explore a broader range of options and refine concepts with unprecedented efficiency. Exhibitors will create highly personalized exhibits that adapt in real-time based on visitor interactions and feedback. Sales and pitching processes are transformed by AI-driven tools providing data-driven insights into a visitor's behavior and engagement preferences. This allows exhibitors to tailor their pitches more effectively, creating personalized experiences that will resonate with multicultural audiences. AI also automates aspects of stand construction, optimizes logistics, and offers real-time language translation to bridge communication gaps at international trade shows.

Trade shows in 2034 will be more international than ever before. Cross-cultural collaboration is the norm, with exhibitors and attendees from diverse backgrounds coming together to share knowledge and forge partnerships. Global trade shows will feature multicultural themes, with each event highlighting the regions' unique contributions to the industry. This is what World Fairs did in the early 1900's. Advanced translation technologies will facilitate cultural exchange, ensuring seamless communication between participants from various linguistic backgrounds. Exhibitors tailor their strategies to resonate with diverse audiences, borrowing the engagement tactics used by different countries to create universally appealing experiences.

The influx of global talent has significantly shaped the future of the trade show industry. As professionals migrate across cultures, they bring unique perspectives, skills, and traditions that enrich the host culture. This constant flow of ideas and practices bridges gaps and fosters a more cross-cultural industry.

Consider the meticulous craftsmanship and precision of German exhibitions integrated with the engaging presentation styles at

American trade shows. Or the technological advancements and efficiency seen in Asian markets inspiring improvements in logistical operations and digital interactions globally. This blending of cultural practices leads to more comprehensive and appealing trade shows, attracting a broader audience and fostering global connections.

Understanding and respecting regional and cultural differences remains essential. In Germany, for example, business interactions are more formal, focused on detailed information and precise demonstrations. This contrasts with the U.S. approach, where business interactions are more casual, and decision-making is often quicker and more flexible. Exhibitors borrow universally appealing engagement tactics but tailor their strategies to resonate with a local audience. In 10 years, we may witness a harmonious blend of these approaches. Formal and precise German methods merging with the casual and dynamic American style, creating a new standard for international trade shows. Exhibitors will design stands that are meticulously crafted, combining all the senses, to create a welcoming atmosphere. At this point, telling and selling can begin.

Risk tolerance continues to shape our exhibition landscape. Americans have a higher tolerance for risk, are accepting of innovation, and have an open mind toward new technologies and trends. In contrast, German businesses favor stability and long-term planning over rapid growth and high-risk ventures. This cautious approach leads to more sustainable and meticulously planned exhibits. In the future, a balanced approach will emerge where the American spirit of innovation blends with the German focus on stability and precision. This creates an environment where cutting-edge technologies can be adopted thoughtfully to create a consensus of opinion with each team member about the business decisions to be made.

Communication styles evolve as cultures blend. Germans are direct and explicit, valuing clarity and precision. In the U.S., communication tends to be more indirect, emphasizing politeness and positivity. By 2034, a hybrid communication style will emerge, combining the German directness and clarity with American friendliness and openness. This trend will also apply to the many other business culture differences now practiced throughout the world. This will foster a more inclusive environment at all trade shows for generations to come.

The future of trade shows in the USA and globally lies in a blend of technological innovation, cultural sensitivity, and the strategic application of generative AI. By leveraging advancements in digital tools and respecting regional engagement methods, the exhibition industry can forge a more meaningful and effective connection between exhibitors and visitors. This approach drives sustainable economic growth and fosters a deeper understanding and appreciation of cultural diversity in the global marketplace. In 10 years, the trade show industry will blend to accommodate the various levels of engagement and communication. The use of technology and cultural blending will create a universal and inclusive environment where global collaborations will thrive. I am looking forward to all of that!

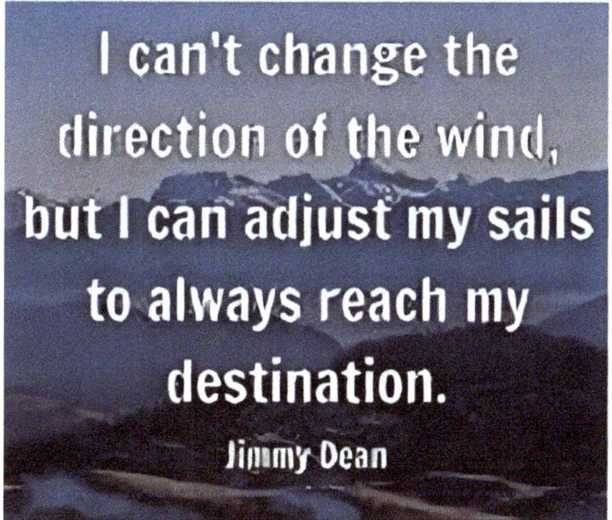

Final Thoughts

The trade show industry may be unnoticed by many, but the financial impact it brings to the USA and countries around the globe, cannot be denied. The collective economic benefits from trade shows and business events represent a $2.8 trillion contribution to the global economy. That is a huge number…and even more impressive when talking about the impact of a so-called "invisible" industry.

So how did trade shows and events become so important? Why do companies continue to invest in face-to-face marketing? The answer is simple: when people gather in person to promote products and services- business happens. The magic first began in old world markets, when people mingled to buy and sell merchandise. It then evolved with displays at World Fairs, and then at industry specific trade shows. These selling and telling events unleashed the element of *emotion* through face-to-face interaction. It is emotion that strongly influences a decision to make a purchase. Today, companies invest in trade show marketing because it generates results. Trade shows and events display products, showcase original ideas, and enable industries to feed themselves with new business.

The American Model- Throughout the history of trade show marketing in the United States, the industry has confronted issues that it deemed important to managing an event. Issues like show contractor management, standard space sizes, union labor and regulations, floor carpeting, material handling (drayage), space costs, exhibiting rules, safety, equality, diversity, sustainability, and health were all important issues. But these issues were not viewed the same as the rest of the world. The use of exhibit systems, floor space sizes, raised floors and sustainability were viewed differently than in the USA.

The evolution of the modern-day industry Trade Fair in the USA has taken many twists and turns to evolve to its present state to create the American Model of event management. This model, exclusive within North America, has often been criticized, but it works. The overall purpose of a trade show is similar in Europe and Asia, but the events are managed and conducted a bit differently in the USA. In all regions of the world, trade shows have evolved to be a powerful marketing tool delivering economic growth for the past 100 years. The belief in the power of face-to-face marketing is universal.

Convention Center Investments- Convention Center growth skyrocketed in the eighties and nineties and the demand for expansion continues today. US cities invested billions in construction and they look for a return on their investment. Trade shows create business for the exhibiting companies; they also create jobs and added business for the cities where they reside. Can this be achieved in any other way?

Will the desire to meet in person continue to be a need that requires a convention facility? So how long will the modern-day trade show continue to grow and deliver the same results? Will our city meeting places be utilized the same? Or will they be viewed like relics like of the once famous Roman Coliseum?

City Attractions- As digital technology expands, will the desire to mingle shrink? Will the concept of traveling to attend a face-to-face trade show remain an attractive investment for corporate America? We believe it will, but digital technology and emotional attractions will play a role in a the decision to attend. The city investments to improve their 'city attractions' (other than the trade show facility itself) provides an added reason to encourage attendees to travel and experience the other sides of life. Las Vegas and Orlando are a case in point. San Diego, New Orleans, and several other cities have similar emotional attractions. Location attractions play a strong role in the decision to attend a trade show. As a trade show attendee, creating business opportunities for one's company is important, but so is enjoying life. Having a trade show event to attend simply becomes a greater excuse to travel. Especially true if the company feels that attending a show is a good investment for learning and building business relationships.

Government Involvement- The US government cannot push this to happen, but it can help specific cities with their investment costs to build or expand their convention centers, as well as to improve their infrastructure costs for transportation, hotels, and attractions within the region. With a growing international market, the government can support the value of trade shows by decreasing the time needed to issue a visa for international visitors to attend, or exhibit at a show. The government can also offer tax benefits for event participation. The trade show alone becomes a worthy excuse for a city to invest in an event center. But the real objective for the city is to gain added economic benefits from the thousands of visitors that events attract.

Creative Organizers- Trade shows will continue to be a powerful marketing tool as long as participants continue to believe in their power to deliver results. It is incumbent upon the organizers to select attractive locations, to be aware of participant needs, and to create engaging experiences for visitors and exhibitors to mingle and to enjoy life. The trade show should be an experience to remember!

A Team Effort- United for a Cause-

The trade show and events industry may be called an Invisible Industry by some, but it takes a gigantic number of people to pull any show together for a 3-4 day event. The industry employs millions of workers throughout the country to make events happen Organizers, carpenters, electricians, fork lift drivers, audio visual technicians, florists, furniture providers, caterers, carpet layers, exhibit builders, show contractor staff, convention center staff, and security staff all work in harmony to prepare a trade show to be ready for opening day. Today's trade shows owe a debt of gratitude to the positive energy from behind the scene labor force, and the exhibit suppliers who make it all happen.

Invisible Workforce- Convention cities, rely heavily on the contributions of an unseen workforce, these cities must acknowledge the importance the part that each worker plays to sustain growth in the trade show/event industry. It is truly amazing how most employees within this industry have discovered their careers by accident. This workforce is not specifically trained for trade show work, but quickly have acquire the skills needed. Most who have discovered this unique career never leave it and have developed a passion for what they do. They complete their tasks in a designated time frame and are ready for the next show opening. This silent and out of sight army of people is the heartbeat that brings each event to life.

Workforce Training- Training and labor recruitment will be required from the industry stakeholders, the government, the associations, and from each trade show city to ensure that the needed skills to put on a trade show are there when needed. United, the industry must broaden its horizons to secure a capable labor force. This will ensure that the industry is no longer invisible.

International Involvement-

Trading worldwide will become more necessary for business survival and international trade shows will gain in prominence. Show organizers will begin to blend elements of the American Model with the World Model of managing a trade show and will set standard practices. The metric measurement may become the standard for trade show. English may be the world language for business communication, but cultural business differences will be strongly embraced. When in Rome do as the Romans. Time will tell here.

In conclusion, this industry didn't just happen. Much thought and effort, with new shareholder blood each decade, pushed it to. become more effective. These stakeholders collectively improved the methods to grow the industry each decade. Trade shows, event, and business meetings brings the total economic impact in business sales for the USA to $1.1 trillion, and to $2.8 trillion in economic impact for the world economy. Wow! This Invisible Industry brings business to life! Hopefully it will be more visible in the future.

"You will never see eye to eye, if you don't meet face to face"

... Warren Buffett

A WORD FROM THE AUTHORS

Each of the two authors served over 50 years in the trade show and events industry. Larry Kulchawik and Bob McGlincy have experienced the industry changes firsthand and have met many people along the journey. It gives us great pleasure to acknowledge the exhibit industry professionals who assisted in contributing their first-hand industry memories to create this book.

The fingerprints we leave behind say a lot about our belief in the power of trade show marketing!

ACKNOWLEDGEMENTS

Collecting facts about the history of the trade show industry in the USA was not an easy task since many of the movers and shakers are gone. Fortunately, many are still with us and graciously shared their thoughts on how they remembered the origins. We express our sincere gratitude and thanks to the following people and associations who shared their memories of a time gone by and their thoughts on the future.

For information we collected regarding each region in the USA, we would like to thank:

New York and East Coast: Doug Zegel, Kevin Sweeney, Vito Bonaventure, Jim Leix, Della Smith, Charlie Corsentino, Don Lyon, Bill Nixon, Tony Vastardis, Jim Kelley, Howard Oshman, Les Bungee, Jim McGrath, and Skip Cox.

Chicago: Tom Cassell, Tom Bacha, Tony Vastardis, Don Svehla, George Furman Jr., Michael Seymour, Phillipe Michael, Bruce Robertson, Jim McGrath and Bruce Fisher.
Detroit: Derek Gentile/EEI Global; **Milwaukee:** Bill Haney; **Minneapolis:** Mark Bendickson. **Indianapolis:** Dan Cantor/Hamilton, J. Frisby/ExhibitHouse, Debbie Parrot, Tim Searle. **Dallas-**Ray Rogowicz, Carrie Freeman, **Atlanta:** Gary Stewart, Carl Mitchell, Robert Laarhoven, Martin Long, Jeff Hannah, and Pat Alaqua. **San Francisco:** Frank Grossman, Dave Hardbarger. **Las Vegas:** Paul Willett, Dennis Bursa, **ECN:** Don Svehla.

Associations:
IAEE: Steven Hacker/Marsa Flanegan, **CEIR:** Nancy Drapeau. **EACA: Jim Wurm - EDPA:** Dasher Lowe/Larry Kulchawik. **HCEA**-Michael Seymour. **Exhibitor Advocate:** Jessica Sibila, **Exhibition Workforce Development Federation:** Laura Palker, **ESCA:** Julie Kagy, and **ECN** (Exhibit City News): Don Svehla.

Book cover design: Sarah Miorelli, FIT/NYC graduate student in exhibit design
Publisher: Books Writer USA

Lastly, Bob and Larry wish to thank their families for their many years of support while working endless hours away from home and then to do so again to write this book. We're certain that being away from home for long hours to set up an exhibit can be said for each and every person who has worked in the trade show exhibition business. This book is dedicated to all the workers in our industry who have sacrificed much, being away from their families, and to have worked in a career that makes you smile. The industry is no longer invisible!